Praise for *The Veganic Grower's Handbook*

"Back in 2014, when Jimmy helped promote Cowspiracy's eastern Canadian tour, I learned of the veganic farm project, La Ferme de l'Aube. It was my hope that an eventual book would transpire. By the grace of their (Mélanie and Jimmy's) efforts, they are spreading the message of veganic growing, and shining the light on the suffering of the old ways of farming and transforming the evolution of small-scale compassionate farming. *The Veganic Grower's Handbook* is a step-by-step guidebook to a multitude of tools anyone can use to shift to a completely 100% plant-based system."

—**Kip Andersen**, co-director of *Cowspiracy* and *What the Health* and founder of AUM Films

"Mindful gardening can save the world and the way we garden affects the healthfulness of our food. Jimmy Videle knows this! His book is a guide to feed ourselves in a gentle way that allows other organisms to simply live. It also helps us to be better humans, delve more deeply, and ask questions about even "natural" and "organic" gardening inputs and practices. He helps us understand that when looked at closely, many of the inputs and practices we take for granted actually have a huge impact on our planet. Jimmy shows us that we can eat well, connect with the natural world, and be kind to all living things. What a relief!"

—**Helen Atthowe**, Woodleaf Farm, and author of *Farming as If Ecological Relationships Mattered*

"Although a great deal of the ink spilled on these pages deals with practices which are "merely organic", Jimmy Videle also makes convincing arguments for "veganic", the radical sub-cult of organic to which I belong and which gives the book its' title. I was particularly interested in following his personal journey of discovery which led him through several tropical and arid environments, eventually landing in Quebec, and en route, documenting his own evolving perspective regarding livestock-based fertility. An especially inspiring (for me) and radical feature of his writing is the veganic approach to pest management. While I embrace the "harmless" ethic, I have not practiced it to the extent he advocates (e.g. exclusionary row covers, etc.), partly due to laziness and lack of labor. Jimmy Videle is not against the idea of species being killed, he simply prefers the natural predators to eat them - after all, for them they are food, all we want is the crop plants and for all beings to thrive. Quite reasonable. I must re-think some things."

—**Will Bonsall**, Khadighar Farm and author of *Essential Guide to Radical, Self-Reliant Gardening*

"Producing, raising, exploiting, and killing sentient animals for our purposes almost always violates their most fundamental interests. Adopting a vegan lifestyle is therefore morally desirable. Except, of course, that "owe implies can". Veganism is a requirement of justice only if it is possible to feed ourselves through veganic agriculture. The thorough and very precise work that Jimmy Videle presents in this book is thus of crucial importance. By showing us how to produce healthy food in sufficient quantity and diversity, even in difficult climates such as those of Canada and the United States, he gives us nothing less than the key to avoid causing untold harm to countless animals."

—**Valéry Giroux**, LLM and PhD of Philosophy, co-publisher of *Le Véganisme* and *L'Antispécisme*

"I wish this book had been available back when I was studying organic farming! With his rich knowledge and experience acquired over 20 years of farming, Jimmy Videle shares everything you need to know about the importance of growing food without animal inputs and how to do it. *The Veganic Grower's Handbook* covers all aspects of growing produce and gives a head start for anyone interested in growing their own food or starting a commercial farm. For us at the Veganic Agriculture Network, this book is particularly valuable, since it's a new reference for gardeners and farmers in cold Northern climates. And proof that veganic growing is not only possible in our region, but more ethical, economical and ecological than other farming approaches. We're grateful to Jimmy for writing this useful and comprehensive resource. His long-time commitment to animals and the planet will have far-reaching benefits for everyone."

—**Stéphane Groleau**, Veganic Agriculture Network

"Jimmy Videle is a visionary—and one who has the practical knowledge, skills, and insights necessary to bring a beautiful vision to fruition!"

—**Shelley Harrison**, Convener, Humane Party

"*The Veganic Grower's Handbook* is a shining example of how we can grow our food while reestablishing biodiversity, treading lightly on the planet, and extending an ethos of kindness to all species. Beyond being a powerful how-to guide for new and experienced growers, it's a reminder that we're active participants in the wider ecosystem upon which we all depend."

—**Meghan Kelly**, Learn Veganic

"*The Veganic Grower's Handbook* is an incredibly comprehensive companion to any aspiring or veteran grower alike. The breadth of information covered in the book is astounding and will be a resource returned to often during the years of planting and growing."

—**Keegan Kuhn**, co-director of *Cowspiracy* and *What the Health*, and former veganic farmer

"The ecological and social crises we are facing today can only be addressed from the ground up: by transforming our food systems, what we grow and how we treat the soil. An ever-larger number of people are becoming aware of this and are working towards a transition to small-scale, ecological farming, but very few include animals in their circle of compassion. In fact, as food system change and soil regeneration became hip topics, the myth that ecological farming required animal exploitation served as a buffer against the changes that the animal liberation movement has been pushing for. In maintaining this fundamental status quo in agriculture–the exploitation of other animals–the food and small farming movements have reproduced some of the problems they have purported to solve. The value of this book goes beyond its practical teachings–it is a testament that we can move on from animal exploitation, that veganic methods can yield healthy and abundant food while allowing us to liberate land for rewilding, and that ultimately this world can be one of abundance. Jimmy Videle has written not only a clear and accessible guide for veganic growing, but for a revolution."

—**Nassim Nobari**, co-founder of Seed the Commons and Veganic World

"As we confront the thorny issue of climate change, we are obligated to look for means of reducing the impact humans have on the environment, especially through conventional, animal-based agriculture. Veganic cultivation emerges as the most planet-friendly solution to growing our food. Drawing upon his rich experiences of both conventional and organic cultivation in several climates, followed by years of veganic cultivation, Jimmy Videle writes persuasively and engagingly about the crucial importance of a whole-system approach that respects the natural world in all its diversity. His book offers a thorough practical guide to anyone wishing to embrace not only a wise but a compassionate lifestyle."

—**Catherine Perry**, PhD, University of Notre Dame

"*The Veganic Grower's Handbook* is an essential resource for independent cruelty-free gardening. Drawing on a quarter century of farming expertise, Jimmy Videle explains how to cultivate healthy ecosystems of edible plants and also clearly details the natural science that makes these methods work. A good choice for those looking to enrich their relationship to plants and the web of life that supports them."

—**Margaret Robinson**, PhD; Coordinator, Indigenous Studies Program

"After years of encouraging meat and animal derivatives on our plates, we realize the impact on our health and that of the environment. Quietly, a balance is returning where plants are more and more at the heart of what we put in our bodies. The same phenomenon occurs in agriculture, where it is realized that feeding the soil with manure and products of animals is not a healthy source of energy either. The soil also needs veganism to regain shape, health and nutrition for the generations that follow. Growing our own vegetables, in a soil nourished solely by plant organic matter is a time-honored principle and respects current and future life in all forms. Jimmy Videle's *The Veganic Grower's Handbook* cultivates these very ideas. In the name of all living beings, thank you!"

—**Mariève Savaria**, author of *La Saison des Lègumes*

"This is an exciting new contribution to the practitioner's literature on veganic production. An experienced grower with conventional, organic, and veganic expertise, Jimmy Videle has responded to the need for accessible, detailed guidance on plant-based cultivation. The handbook is conversational in tone and draws on personal farming experiences and philosophies as well as the research literature to discuss myriad aspects of small-scale, sustainable production. Gardeners and small-scale market farmers will gain not only technical knowledge but also a strong sense of the ways in which veganic growing is based in respect for more-than-human life."

—**Mona Seymour**, PhD., Loyola Marymount University

"With CO2 emissions escalating, conventional and animal agriculture practices continue to be the dominant drivers. We are fast in need of solid solutions. *The Veganic Grower's Handbook* paints a sustainable picture of eliminating exploitation, yet increasing productivity. The potential of small-scale gardening and farming revolutionizes the very way we feed ourselves and nourishes all floral and faunal life in the process. This is an exceptional resource at a critical moment in our history."

—**Dave Simon**, author of *Meatonomic$*

"The way that modern day agriculture functions resemble an apocalyptic science-fiction novel. Billions of land animals exploited, lands desertified and waters turned toxic from chemicals and manures. It is past time for a renewal. Jimmy Videle's, *The Veganic Grower's Handbook* is the breath of life that provides the tools, techniques, insight and vision for human change through small-scale fruit, vegetable and herb growing, that the entirety of Earth's floral and faunal collective deserves."

—**Casey Taft**, PhD, Boston University School of Medicine, vegan author and publisher

"I thoroughly enjoyed reading Jimmy Videle's *The Veganic Grower's Handbook: Cultivating Fruits, Vegetables and Herbs From Urban Backyard to Rural Farmyard*. It provides an elegant solution to the enormous impact of industrial animal and plant agriculture on the environment. Instead of waging war on microbes, insects and animals who are seen as the enemy of agriculture, he shows that farming can be done coexisting peacefully with the many species who keep our planet alive and vibrant. He has taken organic agriculture critical step further and removed all animal products, resulting in the veganic approach. Veganic agriculture eliminates the cruel exploitation of farmed animals. Healthy food, healthy humans and a healthy planet. Thank you, Jimmy, for sharing your journey that makes the world a more compassionate place."

—**Liz White**, leader, Animal Protection Party of Canada

The Veganic Grower's Handbook:

Cultivating Fruits, Vegetables and Herbs from Urban Backyard to Rural Farmyard

By Jimmy Videle

Lantern Publishing & Media • Woodstock & Brooklyn, NY

2022
Lantern Publishing & Media
PO Box 1350
Woodstock, NY 12498
www.lanternpm.org

Copyediting and design by Pauline Lafosse

Printed in the United States of America

Library of Congress Cataloging-in-Publication Data

Names: Videle, Jimmy, author.

Title: The veganic grower's handbook : cultivating fruits, vegetables and herbs from urban backyard to rural farmyard / Jimmy Videle.

Other titles: Cultivating fruits, vegetables and herbs from urban backyard to rural farmyard

Description: Woodstock, NY : Lantern Publishing & Media, 2023. | Includes bibliographical references.

Identifiers: LCCN 2022031757 (print) | LCCN 2022031758 (ebook) | ISBN 9781590566824 (paperback) | ISBN 9781590566831 (epub)

Subjects: LCSH: Organic gardening. | Vegetable gardening. | Sustainable agriculture.

Classification: LCC SB324.3 V53 2023 (print) | LCC SB324.3 (ebook) | DDC 635/.0484—dc23/eng/20220822

LC record available at https://lccn.loc.gov/2022031757

LC ebook record available at https://lccn.loc.gov/2022031758

"A human being is part of a whole, called by us the "Universe," a part limited in time and space. He experiences himself, his thoughts and feelings, as something separated from the rest- a kind of optical delusion of his consciousness. This delusion is a kind of prison for us, restricting us to our personal desires and to affection for a few persons nearest us. Our task must be to free ourselves from this prison by widening our circles of compassion to embrace all living creatures and the whole of nature in its beauty."

—Albert Einstein, February 1950

Table of Contents

Artichokes, Arugula, Asparagus, Basil, Beets, Broccoli, Broccoli Raab, Brussels Sprouts, Bush Beans/Climbing Beans, Cabbage, Carrots, Cauliflower, Celery & Celery root, Chamomile, Chicory, Chinese cabbage (Nappa), Chives and Garlic chives, Cilantro (Coriander), Collards, Corn (sweet), Cucumbers, Dill, Dry beans, Eggplant, Fennel, Flax, Garlic, Greek Oregano, Greens (Asian),

Greens (Mustard), Ground Cherry, Kale, Kohlrabi, Leeks, Lettuce, Lovage, Melons, Mint, Okra, Onions (bunching), Onions (full-size, bulbing),Parsley, Parsnips, Peas, Peppers (hot), Peppers (sweet), Potatoes, Radishes, Rhubarb, Rutabaga, Sage (Common), Savory (Winter and Summer), Sorrel, Soybeans (Edamame), Spinach, Strawberry, Summer Squash (Zucchini), Sweet Potatoes, Swiss Chard, Thyme, Tomatillo, Tomatoes (Cherry types), Tomatoes (Slicer and Paste types), Turnips, Watermelon, Winter Squash, and Pumpkins

About the Author
About the Publisher

Introduction

IT IS THE rhythm of nature that we all follow, whether we consciously know it or not. As the seasons change, we change. There is buoyant expectancy in the spring, as leaf buds break and male birds sing on high. When the summer solstice settles in, so does the solid warmth and long days, the height of our yearly activities. The cooling days of fall trigger us to make preparations for the coming winter, the storing of food and securing our nests. When Yule's longest nights plunge, we lie in a state of dormant reflection, yearning for the return of the light. The solar cycles guide our waking movements. The lunar phases guide us through our nocturnal visions. We are continually humbled by the fact that we are creatures of habit influenced by the flow of the natural whole. More than likely, it is because the entirety of our human make-up is the same macro and micro elements as are found in every other living being on Earth. Humans are simply programmed, or wired, a little bit differently at the atomic level.

Over 95% of the human body consists of oxygen, hydrogen, carbon, and nitrogen. If we add in sodium, potassium, phosphorus, chlorine, calcium, magnesium and sulfur the total eclipses 99.5%.[1] These, along with boron, iron, manganese, copper, zinc, nickel, and molybdenum is what every living plant requires to thrive, which, consequently, exist in us as well, providing some necessary function. We are one with the soil, because in essence we are the soil. When hands touch, and fingers probe into the ground we are caressing microscopic life, a microcosm of ourselves. This is the true connection.

Early *homo sapiens* (humans), more gatherer than hunter, followed the harvests. They traveled to the mild north from the warm south and back again, following the seasonal fluctuations in ripening plant-based food sources.[2] There was a need to become sedentary, in some places, from those migratory beginnings, as the realization became clear that the domestication of plants was necessary for their early survival. There may have been a reliance on grass seeds, including sorghum grasses over 100,000 years ago, perhaps being some of the first signs of cultivation of plant species.[3] There may not have been enough wild harvested food sources to feed the ever-growing clans. Maybe migration and placement of peoples was determined by early climatic change as parts of the southern African continent suffered from a severe drought.[4] Much change was afoot, requiring human adaptations. Trade among tribal groups became vital, domestication of the most passive and curious wild animals followed. And so, it continued to where we are today, where only a mere fraction of the United States and Canadian population cultivate a majority of their own food in season and even less of those who do actually grow a diversity of fruits, vegetables, and herbs.

As the world becomes more technologically advanced and our ever-present smartphones bombard us with news (both real and fake) and overtly happy social media images, we seek to unplug. We desire a return to nature. A walk in the woods becomes a yearning, perhaps the desire to wild harvest mushrooms, yet the key lies right under our feet. The source of all life is the earth we walk upon. She can open the doorway to the deep-rooted relationship that is nestled inside us all. It is possible to interface profoundly, simply by pressing a seed into the soil with bare hands.

What is Veganic?

The word veganic is a combination of the words vegan and organic. Organic, in essence, would be anything of natural origin, derived from living matter. Vegan is best defined in this context as a way of growing that impacts all life as little as possible. A person who considers themselves vegan would not kill or use any animals (animals include humans) for food or clothing, allow experiments on, use for entertainment purposes, enslave, exploit, or abuse. With specific relationship to gardening and farming a veganic grower would not use any manures, or meals (like bone, blood, or fish) in the cultivation of plants and like organic growers would not use any chemical fertilizers or sprays.

A concise definition would be:

> Vegan organic gardening and farming is the cultivation and production of food and fiber crops with a minimal amount of exploitation to all animal and plant species. In addition to the National Organic Standards, veganic growing methods use no animal products or by-products, such as blood meal, bone meal, manure, urea, fish meal, fish emulsion or any other animal originated matter, because the production of these products either harms animals specifically or is connected with the exploitation and subsequent suffering of those beings. Furthermore, while organic cultivation allows for the use of organo-pesticides and organo-fungicides veganic growing would not, as spraying highly disrupts the native floral and faunal balance of the farming and gardening systems.

In conventional agriculture the use of chemical fertilizers, insecticide and herbicides are the normal in cultivating fruits, vegetables, and herbs. This manner of growing utilizes 99.6% of all farmable acreage in the United States and 98.5% of all farmable acreage in Canada.[5] Organic farming, which constitutes 0.4% in the United States and 1.5% in Canada, outlaws the use of all herbicides. However, propane-powered flame throwers are allowed among the two countries organic standard regimes. The organic standards also allow for organo-pesticides and fungicides. Some are so powerful, like the popular Organic Material Review Institute (OMRI) product AzaGuard, that it obliterates over three hundred insect species. Asking the question, how is this devastating practice organic?

Veganic growing allows nature to do the work of controlling as she sees fit. By allowing for a diversity of both cultivated and native flora among the gardens, edges, and hedgerows this method seeks to invite any and all faunal species (insects, reptiles, amphibians, birds, small mammals) that wish to reside there. Maximum biodiversity among the garden area is attained. Spraying of organo-pesticide is never performed, as it disrupts the balance that nature wishes to achieve. Thus, this is the main philosophy of veganic growing, cultivating the gardens for the benefit of all species.

Plants are allowed to mature to their capacity, flowering, seeding and finally composting in place when they finish, leaving homesites for all manner of creatures. The soil surface is never left barren. When a harvestable crop has been exhausted, a cover crop (green manure) is planted to occupy the space, such as buckwheat, clover, and oats, providing more flowers and seeds for those who wish to seek out the nectar, kernels, and canopy and dwell underneath.

Small-scale organic farms try to maximize their space (and profits) by replanting in the same beds, sometimes up to four times in a season. After every rotation, they rototill or plow the gardens, disturbing the microfauna with every successive sowing. Small-scale veganic growing, on the contrary, incorporates a low-till, limited machine approach to preparing the earth for planting. Tractors and the like are highly damaging to the soil structure, compacting clays, and squeezing out moisture from fluffy, sandy loams. Organics and all other forms of farming, growing, and gardening's majority purpose is to grow food for human beings. Veganics allows for a vast amount of space to be utilized for all beings to thrive, from the microscopic nematode to the leggy moose and all creatures in between.

The Manure and Meal Dilemma

All manures come from enslaved animals, who are not free to live as they choose to live and are eventually killed when their usefulness has expired. Female chickens who lay eggs in battery cages, and see their manure pelletized, are eventually culled when their production drastically declines: in their third year of life in small-scale operations or after a mere one-year of laying, in an industrialized one. Cows and sheep provide the vast majority of manure available in the marketplace; it comes from those who are stanchioned (cows and sheep who give milk) or feedlot finished (those raised for meat).

Blood and bone meals come from all animals who are eliminated at the slaughterhouse. Blood is collected during the slaughter of pigs and cows and dried as fertilizer—and is also fed back to the same species of animals as blood meal.

Whole skeletons are transported to rendering plants where the bones are crushed and dried into bone meal, another common fertilizer and animal feed. Small scale animal raising operations, who reside in rural areas too far away from a rendering facility, will commonly make compost of the animals that die prematurely, or mix in dry straw with their manure to sell it as a finished composted product.[6]

Whole fish are harvested from the open ocean (pelagic) such as anchovies, herring, menhaden, capelin, anchovy, pilchard, sardines, and mackerel to be processed into fish meal (70%), the remaining 30% are the fish remains from human processing channels. This meal is sold as fertilizer and farm-raised fish feed.[7] Shellfish meals are fabricated from the shells of trawled shrimp and trapped crab and lobsters. Any soil product that contains the words natural fertilizer means either manure or meals.

Any grower should consider whether or not using the above would conflict with their own morals and standards. Like all conventional growers I did not believe it was possible to grow without the use of chemical fertilizers, then I learned organics. As an organic farmer I thought it was inconceivable to grow without farmyard manure and incorporating animals into the system. Then I realized there was a better way through plant-based composts, amendments, and teas, a markedly less exploitative way. But like all breakthrough moments in our lives, it was a long journey.

From Eager Student to Humble Teacher

After two and a half years living in New Orleans, Louisiana I left on what would become a three-month road trip in a 1973 Volkswagen Bus, throughout southern Texas, New Mexico, and Arizona. Seeking a different life, a simpler country life, thoughts wide open like the skies I was traversing through. It was January 1997. One of the biggest changes happened two weeks into the journey.

Setting out from South Padre Island, looking for a beach along the Gulf of Mexico outside of Brownsville, Texas the bus stumbled along a rutted dirt road. To the north, there was a penned area of cows, then another, culminating in six of them locked together, housing over a thousand individuals. The cows were standing up to their knees and elbows in manure. The smell of ammonia burned my nostrils. Along the side of the road, a slurry of brown sludge streamed down—and eventually, into the Gulf of Mexico. To the east of the pens was a large, windowless concrete building with smoke billowing from the pipes on the roof. This was my first direct experience with a final stage concentrated animal feeding operation (CAFO) and slaughterhouse. I was horrified. I became vegetarian at that moment.

I was fortunate to have bought my first homestead in March of 1998 in a small rural town of Hunt, population one hundred fifty, in northern Arizona. The property was no more than a mile away from the Little Colorado River and the sacred site of Zuni Heaven, where ancient and modern-day Ashiwi (Zuni) people make a pilgrimage fifty miles from their homelands. The upland mesas where the homestead was situated had many meditative sandstone rock outcroppings, where it was not uncommon to find arrowheads and pottery shards. One could envision generations of peoples sitting and flaking spear points. It was a sincere blessing to be able to dwell among the ancient spirits of their heritage lands.

I was a mere twenty-five and thoughts immediately turned to growing fruits, vegetables, and herbs. The thirty-seven-acre property had been extensively over-grazed by the "free-range" cattle roaming the terrain. A spot was chosen in between the sparse stand of one-seed juniper trees. The sandstone soil was rototilled, and garden beds were delineated. The dry Colorado Plateau in the northern Arizona landscape, yields a yearly average of sixteen inches (40cm) of snow and fourteen inches (355mm) of rain, relatively little of which falls during the growing season.

Our big idea (my first wife and I) for our very first growing season was to pick up all the dried cow patties around the property and reconstitute it with water, mix it with some native soil in old tires, and plant summer squash. Watering daily with a soaker hose and feeding the plants with liquid Miracle Grow yielded two paltry squashes from four plants. I had a lot to learn. Just as background information, I did not buy my first personal computer and have internet access until mid-1999. So other than the articles in *Countryside* magazine and Storey's Country Wisdom Bulletins, we were on our own.

In 1999 I built a chicken coop (my first ever construction project) and bought three Barred Rock baby chicks from the local feed store. I was going to take care of them and love them and gave them heat lamps and fresh water and food every day. I built a trap into the house so that when the chickens slept their poop would be collected and I could turn it into compost. At that moment I was not considering what I was going to do with them after eighteen months when they stopped being productive. After two and a half years, I gave them to someone who was to make soup as their usefulness to me ceased. Being vegetarian did not automatically mean that I did less harm.

Monday through Friday, sometimes Saturdays, I would drive into work as manager of a growing rental car company and come home during the long summer days to walk the fields, pulling weeds, checking on tomatoes and beans. Production in the gardens increased greatly when we ditched the old tire idea. On the weekends, thoughts far away from corporate life, I would spend both days in the gardens, hands in the dirt, with a real smile resonating from my soul. With the corporate ladder wearing down my thinning frame from the anxiety and stress, I knew I needed a shift.

In October 2004, a letter came in the mail stating the local Concho Community Center Action Group (a town about ten miles away) was organizing a farmer's market for the following spring. The light bulb flashed, and I saw the prospective life change. We would give it a go and become market farmers turning our one sixth of an acre (7,000 square feet) to a small-scale organic market farm. The transition was made and in early May 2005 every Saturday until the end of October we would sell out of our organically grown produce.

The farm grew to one acre, one hundred chickens laying eggs, and three Nubian goats for their milk over the course of the following four years. We followed all organic protocols, recycling all the manure back into the fields, using low-till methods, mulching, and cover-cropping. We were going to be the most regenerative, sustainable farm in the region. We had dozens of volunteers. We managed part-time and full-time workers all helping us to maintain our twenty-five-member community supported agriculture (CSA) basket program and three farmers' markets per week. We were busy all year long. The growing season spanned from the 1st of April, continuously selling, until the end of November. The winter was for re-construction projects. It was daily care for the animals, year-round. We generated 14,000 lbs. (6,350 kg) of harvestable produce each of the last two years. It was a lifestyle worth living. Yet there were a few variables that were difficult for me to digest then:

- We did not produce enough on-farm fertility, so we had to bring in composted goat manure from another farm where the conditions were not always ideal, although organic.
- After the goat moms gave birth (sometimes to triplets), the male goats were unwanted and either sold or taken to be auctioned.
- When Colorado potato beetles became too infested the potato plants were sprayed with Entrust, an organically approved insecticide that killed every insect living in the patch. The following morning was like a nuclear bomb had gone off.
- When the chickens stopped laying after year three, they were moved into a chicken tractor to the gardens where nocturnal Great Horned Owls would raid the houses. I would say I was "making an offering to Mother Nature."

Maybe I was finally waking up to the cognitive dissidence, or maybe it was simply that my marriage had been suffering for many years, but in October 2009, five years after starting the market farm, we decided to separate. There was much blood, sweat, and tears at that Hunt Valley farm. I really thought that I would be composted there. You just never know, no matter how many plans are made.

I took my knowledge and skills on the road. Not looking back, being well-guided, I left with only a fifty-pound backpack. It contained all my worldly possessions, after taking the rest of my life's accumulations to a Salvation Army thrift store. The first stop was to be the Big Island of Hawaii and would end up becoming three and a half years on the road. The challenge was trying to apply what I learned from growing in the arid, sun-filled Arizona days, 330 days a year, and using those techniques in humid, tropical extremes. Diseases were different. Insect pressures were different. Growing seasons were vastly different. Eggplant, pepper, and tomato plants were actually perennial. I had no idea. "But organic is the same everywhere," I told myself when I lacked confidence—which happened more than once along the journey. For the first 2+ years I worked, consulted, and managed on nine different farms in five different tropical countries, including Hawaii.

I learned how to maintain those perennial eggplant, pepper, and tomato plants. I harvested bananas, cassava, chaya, jackfruit, papayas, plantain, and sugar cane. I climbed coconut trees with the aid of a scaffold to harvest the nuts, and scaled breadfruit, lychee, and rambutan trees without one. I managed work crews in the harvesting of galangal (a type of ginger) and turmeric. I foraged wild avocados and mangoes from two-hundred-year-old growth forests. I created garden beds with mango soil from the Hawaiian forest which consisted of decomposing leaves, branches, and mangoes. Native soils from the Yucatan scrub forests were used to create raised beds for fast-growing greens. All this became my first glimpse into the possibilities of vegan compost and garden planting, even though I would not make the connection until later.

I saw vegan permaculture firsthand, in Costa Rica and Ecuador, as formerly clear-cut forests were transformed into lush, albeit chaotic, layered paradises where nitrogen-fixing trees were planted to canopy the shade-grown edibles that they were feeding, as well as leguminous bushes planted underneath stoic trees like jackfruit and mango. I built raised beds for the planting of native beans in the upper slopes and planted rice in the wallows of tropical Panama. At the base of the glacier mountain Cotopaxi in the Ecuadorian Andes, I planted and maintained potatoes and quinoa. From the most humid lowlands to the highest peaks, I experienced all that I could along that Central and South American route, thinking that my life would end up in a place where it never froze. Yet, for the summer of 2012, I found myself as an immigrant farm worker on a large-scale organic farm in the magnificent province of Québec.

During that hot, sunny, dry summer I realized that everything that was being grown on that farm was exactly the same as what I had grown in Hunt, Arizona over 2,300 miles (3,700km) away. Hunt is 34 degrees north, Ripon, QC is 45.7 degrees north, and many of the varieties were identical. The two main differences being: one, in Ripon with the cooler nights on average, greens could be grown all season long with less problems, and two, it rained frequently enough during the growing season. After vowing to never live where it was cold again, here I was looking at the rolling, forested, warbler-rich hills of the Outaouais landscape and falling in love all over again just like I had when I saw the northern Arizona homestead for the first time.

The following summer in 2013, and for the next one as well, I consulted and volunteered on another Québec farm on the island of Montréal. Taking what I learned the summer before and applying those practices yielded much success. Could it be that my next farm would be in a place where the winter lows can drop to -30F (-35C)? You never know where your life will lead you. Sometimes an old friend's email changes everything.

Kip Anderson, lifelong friend and college roommate, sent an email in October of 2013 asking, "Do you know about vegan gardening?"

"Seems great," I responded, "but it is impossible to grow fruits, vegetables, and herbs productively without animal manures and meals."

"Think again," he wrote back, and linked me to two different organizations online. The Vegan Organic Network was from the U.K. and the Veganic Agriculture Network was right there in Québec. Could it be a sign? Still skeptical, we debated back-and-forth for eight months by phone and email while he and co-producer Keegan Kuhn put the finishing touches on their award-winning documentary Cowspiracy. It finally clicked that it was worth opening my mind to the possibility that veganic farming could work.

According to the film's statistics,[8] animal agriculture was using 50% of the world's arable land, responsible for at least 14.5% of carbon-dioxide-equivalent emissions and possibly up to 51%. It was the greatest factor destroying the Amazon rainforest. It created ever-growing vast ocean dead zones in the Gulf of Mexico. It was causing desertification of once-lively soils with poor monoculture farming practices and overgrazing of ruminant animals. Manure pollution was toxifying groundwater, streams, rivers, lakes, bays, and oceans. Cancers, cardiovascular diseases, and diabetes were on the rampage, affecting hundreds of millions of American and Canadian people, and it all was probably perpetuated by raising animals, fishing the seas, eating them and their products.

What did I have to lose?

In October 2014, La Ferme de l'Aube (Farm of the First Light) veganic farm was born when we (Mélanie and I) found a six-acre mixed forest with three-quarters of an acre open land for growing in the small hamlet of Boileau, Québec. This majestic property was once harvesting grounds of the Weskarini (Wàwàckeririniwak) Algonquin Nation whose traditional territory was harnessed by the Lièvre River in the west and the Rouge River in the east. The apparent signs of those first nation peoples are not as pronounced as at my former Northern Arizona haunt. Even though they remain hidden from my eyes within the deep, densely foliated terrain, I can imagine them reaping the bounty of maple sap, wild berries, and mushrooms that permeate these lands.

In a stark contrast to the Arizona climate, Boileau receives on average one hundred inches (255cm) of snow and thirty-three inches (850 mm) of rain per year. The part of the land that was open was so because the previous owner had scraped away the top twelve inches (30cm) of topsoil so that he could purchase the raw materials to make the road leading to the house. So, for the second time I was to take denuded soils and attempt to turn them to something vibrant and alive. Could it be possible, viable, or even productive in a small business model? If not, I could always go back to exploiting animals for my own existence and sell to others, right? There was no way I could go back, with all that I had learned. So veganic it started and will always be, and as I write this in December of 2021, the answer to whether or not it could be productive and viable is a resounding *ABSOLUTELY*!

It has not been without its challenges, as there are relatively few of us in North America that are growing in this manner. The last count was less than seventy-five veganic farms. A big thanks to the work of Veganic World in mapping them all.[9]

Starting a small farm from scratch is always filled with obstacles and hurdles, as I have now experienced twice. Starting a garden for the first time can be daunting, and doing so with methods that few are using makes it even more complicated. That is what this Veganic Grower's Handbook is for, to help everyone from the small urban backyard grower to the farmyard grower achieve success and to pull away the shroud of mystery surrounding this method of cultivation. I believe that small-scale farms, specifically one acre and less, to be the key to the future reparation of our collective planet. More so, I believe that there is no better way to ensure local food security and independence than for all of us to grow some, if not all, of our own food. With time, patience, experience, and this handbook as a reference guide in your bookshelf, we can begin to cure the anthropogenic mess modern agriculture has created. I became an organic farmer because it was the only occupation I could think of that was the least exploitative to the environment in this ever-modernizing world. I am and will stay a veganic grower because it is infinitely more compassionate.

Whether this will be your first garden or your thirtieth, my twenty-five years of growing experience, all wrapped up neatly in this guide, will aid you in cultivating fruits, vegetables, and herbs. To reiterate: I started my gardening journey in 1998 as a small-scale conventional grower, turning into a professional organic market gardener in 2005 and veganic in 2015. I have experience in growing over four hundred different plant varieties in North America. Here at La Ferme de l'Aube, we have actively consulted hundreds of people on veganic growing techniques through our artisanal seed company and our past selling of vegetable seedlings. We provide forty families with produce throughout the growing year. Just to show further that this manner of growing is possible for the community gardener as well as the small-scale market grower.

Following Nature's Beat

A thick blanket of snow hides the garden beds, but it does not deter us from the thoughts of seedlings and first greens. When the leaves burst their leaf buds and the surrounding forest pulses with iridescent green foliage, both deciduous and evergreen, the natural world shifts into its highest gear. As growers, we follow, working the land, preparing the beds, and planting with all the hope and intention we can muster. The bird migrations come in waves as temperatures fluctuate wildly, rising or dropping forty-nine degrees Fahrenheit (twenty-seven degrees Celsius) in twenty-four hours. Early seedlings brace against the roar of the wind as the pressure between the arctic north and the southern warmth squeezes through a sieve.

The warm and settled date lands when nesting happens in vigor, mothers sit on nests and keep eggs turned and warm. Snakes come out to bask in the sun's rays and toads emerge from their deep hollows. Gardener thoughts turn to maintenance and insect pressures while first zucchinis form. Peas begin to swell, tomatoes set their first green globes. The summer heat and long days tax watering systems and creatures of all types seek solace in the shade of the growing canopies. Days climb over 90F (32C), fueling the most vibrant growth. Cucumber vines run as flowers bloom profusely. Mid-summer rains arrive in spurts, sometimes in deluge as ever-increasing floral blossoms entice bee, fly, and wasp colonies along with fluttering butterflies and moths.

The harvest time begins in earnest as the transformation of fruits, vegetables, and herbs becomes the central focus. Baby flycatchers ease the pressure of mosquitos and black flies. Swallows, alongside dragon and damselflies, eat scores themselves and screen hats disappear as short sleeves yearn for farmer tans. Nights turn cool and the scramble to store for the winter reaches a fever pitch. Jays cache sunflower seeds from ten-foot-tall plants and goldfinches reach for dill heads as we try to clip some to dry off for pickles. Freezers and cupboards bulge from the bounty, bins of root vegetables are stacked in cold storage. Piles of winter squash and garlic crowd cellar rooms. The stovetop brims with bubbling tomatoes, hot sauce, and zucchini relish. Late afternoons in the waning days of summer see us pulling off dried seed for our own genetically diversified seed banks. Tomato seeds sit and ferment on the windowsill.

Like an arctic flame thrower, the first fall frost blackens tender annuals and the decline speeds in intensity. The shift in the gardens is apparent as decaying plants cover garden beds and bird numbers dwindle, songs hidden. The exalted north-south passage of the Canada Geese "V" formations honk in prolific numbers. A smattering of late greens and brassicas under protective cover last until mid-fall, but as early snow blankets the landscape with its metamorphic beauty, thoughts turn to the kitchen and reflection on the season that was.

Thus, is the cycle: dormancy broken, a flourish of activity, thriving growth, diminishing and dying, only to revive again. Even the carrots, beets, and parsnips that will survive in cold storage until the beginning of the following summer, push up their shoots and feel out with their roots at any sign of temperature fluctuation.

For those of us that have grown from frost-to-frost, had our hands in the dirt, face cowering from the winds, upturned to the sun's warmth and embracing summer rains, we know that we follow the heartbeat of the natural world. For those of you that have yet to live this majesty I invite you to come along and experience, in your own way, the blessings awarded to this current existence. May this handbook act as a guide to you as you hone your skills in the cultivation of fruits, vegetables, and herbs with all beings in mind and the least impact possible.

How to Use This Guide

This comprehensive guide seeks to give the veganic grower all the tools and techniques to be successful. From planning to seed-starting in the early season, to garden preparation and transplanting when the weather warms. Composting and maintenance of seedlings in the heat of summer, harvesting and post-harvest handling when the nights begin to cool. Ideas are offered in long-term storage and closing down the gardens when the nights become long. In addition, it provides crop profiles for over seventy different species of fruits, vegetables, and herbs, planting and yield charts, as well as a vast resource section, expansive index, and bibliography for continued learning opportunities. This book is the most comprehensive book to date on all facets of veganic growing for the small-scale grower. I have not included, however, fruiting vines, shrubs, and trees like apples, blueberries, grapes, haskap, raspberries, etc., nor mushrooms even though we do cultivate them, simply because I do not feel I yield enough expertise to consult anyone on the cultivation of them. But if you have the means, space, and knowledge by all means foster them.

Every chapter and topic can be flipped to, depending on where we are in the season. If and when it is necessary to link one chapter to another, I will clearly state that in the description of the section. It is meant to be a reference guide for your use on your personal veganic growing expedition. Everything I know, primarily because of the frequent and continuing challenges I have faced and climbed out of, has led to this work.

This handbook will be most beneficial to those that have a frost-to-frost season in the United States and Canada (see Annex C for a list of selected cities). My experience has led me to the tropics as I have stated already and I currently consult growers in California, but this is not the bulk of my proficiency. There are many techniques, however, that can benefit growers in those climes, though it is not specifically geared to year-round outside growing. Small-scale gardeners in other parts of the world where a frost basks the terrain dormant, including many rural towns and metropolitan cities in Asia and the European Union, can also benefit from the approaches herein.

The proof of the vegan pudding is in the eating of it, so my introductory statements may fall on deaf ears. Flip to a chapter, read and study it, see if it resonates. Practice the techniques that lie within. Cultivate for yourself, with patience and diligence, and before long, all of you who read through the subsequent chapters will be enjoying the bounty. Wishing you all the highest good on your path.

Jimmy and Mélanie enjoying the fruits (bulbs) of our labor in the July sunshine after the 2018 garlic harvest

1

The Land and the Soil

BEFORE THE LAND ever took the form of gardens, she had been through many incarnations. At one point she was wild, growing native flowers, grasses, shrubs, and trees that adapted over the millennia based on changing climate and topography. Closer to a water source more vascular plants established, over drier terrains they became woodier. Plants are low-growing and tough when in a wind-swept location, lusher and fuller when sheltered. Topsoil is more profound when there is less wind erosion.

The creation of the backyard or farmyard landscape to gardens can be very damaging. There had already been a whole community of life in relationship with the specific area. The plants, from low creeping to huge diameter sentinel trees, as well as the insects, birds, reptiles, and amphibians that feed among their specifically needed ecosystems. The smaller mammals scurry and tunnel about and the larger ones hop, waddle, prance, and gait. To build a garden upon any existing land is changing the identity of that already unique environment. So maybe we should not initiate gardens at all? In some cases, no. As important as it is to design space for human food, it is equally, if not more important to leave a vast amount wild or even re-wild. The idea of plowing from fence line to fence line needs to be put to rest. Before the ground is ever broken a working knowledge of what already resides there is imperative.

The backyard urban garden is less damaging than one acre in the country, for in the cities and suburbs human hands have already done extensive damage on the grasslands, edges and forests that were once thriving there. It would be safe to say that 100% of the time a diverse urban garden system would be a vast improvement for the neighborhood's inhabitants. Many back and front yards are cultivated grass, gravel, or woodchip mulch upon native soil. This is a vibrant opportunity to construct very fertile garden spaces.

According to a 2016 University of California at Santa Barbara study by Cleveland et al, it was revealed that, "Turning lawns into vegetable gardens reduces greenhouse gas emissions. For every one kilo (2.2 pounds) of vegetables produced, two kilos (4.4 pounds) of emissions can be cut." Interestingly, the more productive the gardens, the more carbon emissions are decreased, as the grower is buying fewer fruits, vegetables, and herbs. Additionally, by composting all vegetable waste and recuperating greywater into the gardening system, we can further slash emissions. The authors go on to add that, "Our hope is that this research helps motivate households, communities and policymakers to support vegetable gardens that can contribute to mitigating climate change."[1]

The farmyard is more complex because the community of beings that dwell there are already quite extensive, so decisions need to be carefully thought out prior to breaking ground. When looking at the countryside there are three types of land that have the best possibility of cultivation: Grasslands (can be native or cultivated), forest clearings and forest edge, which is where open land meets the forest. There are others that should never be cultivated. Forests, wetlands, and all lands bordering water courses should be left to be as they aspire to be.

Grasslands today are either wild or cultivated. Wild grassland or prairie is easy to understand. It is open land that contains many different species of low-growing flowering plants and seeding grasses. Most of the time, these lands remain untouched all year. In the spring the perennial grasses and plants push from their extensive root systems and green the terrain. Depending on moisture, sun and heat they grow accordingly. Their flowers bloom, seed pods form and scatter before completely turning brown after the hard northern freezes, eventually crushed by the winds, heavy rains, and snows. The residues become compost for the following years' growth, thus, completing the cycle. Wild grasslands sequester 34% of the global terrestrial stock of carbon, while forests sequester 39%.[2] Thus, grassland ecosystems provide a significant amount of carbon sequestration.

Cultivated grasslands are those that have been cleared of trees and shrubs many years ago for the specific purpose of ranging ruminants (mainly cows, horse, sheep, and goats) or, to produce a leguminous-type hay like alfalfa, clover, or trefoil, or grass type like timothy, brome, rye, fescue, and others, for the same animals raised in confinement. These grasslands are cut one to four times per year, depending on region and climatic conditions. Most of the organic matter is balled and transported away. However, since the cultivated grassland is never plowed the soils remain relatively undisturbed, highly fertile, and microbiologically rich. These are fine to transform to gardens, while letting a good portion re-wild.

My first farm in the high mesas of Northern Arizona was a thirty-seven-acre property that had been a section of a 640-acre overgrazed pasture. The land was fenced off eight years before I bought in 1998 and I could barely see the height difference looking down the fence line of the gamma grasses and black and white sage brush that were the predominant flora on either side. To make the market gardens I eventually cordoned off a one-acre segment of the most stripped land. The remaining was left to continue re-wilding. By the time I left in 2009 the gardens were a verdant sea among the native landscape. The wildlands continued their restoration. After nineteen years excluding the still ranging cattle on the other side, the difference along the fence line was dramatic. My side saw grasses and shrubs five times taller with three times as many tufts on the grasses (per square foot). In that extremely arid terrain, it would still take decades to heal properly, but the exclusion of the cows to the state of the grassland was readily apparent.

In addition to cultivated grasslands, cultivated monoculture farmlands like soy (legume), barley, corn, oats, and wheat (all grains), yield golden opportunities for a transition to small gardens. In the United States and Canada, these farmlands span from highway to forest. By cultivating a mere percentage more diversely and allowing the rest to restore to their former glory, would greatly enhance floral and faunal biodiversity. These lands can be fertile due to the yearly composting of crop residues and within a few years all the toxic remnants of chemical fertilizers and sprays would dissipate.

Forest clearings (glades) are those natural phenomena where the forest parts and reveals an open, exposed area. In a forest system these can be fine places for the gardens, with caution. Usually, the clearing is low in biodiversity compared to the surrounding edges and forests. Sometimes it had been created by an intense forest fire. The clearing has good light penetration and can be quite vast. Even though ideally situated, it should only be cultivated if a homestead already exists nearby. I am not suggesting we start creating gardens in large tracts of undisturbed forest chains at random.

Forest edges are the lands that are becoming the most exploited by animal agriculture, particularly by those who raise free-range cows, goats, pigs, and sheep. They are seen by human eyes as low value, not good for timber (forests) and not good for hay (grasslands), yet they are the most biologically diverse ecosystems on the planet.[3] They are short-grass prairies, leading to tall grasses, shrubs, smaller deciduous trees, eventually giving way to larger deciduous and coniferous ones. This is the exact type of layered planting system that permaculture systems and food forests attempt to emulate.

Our six-acre Boileau farm/homestead lies on the forest edge. The mountains to the north, south and west are undisturbed mixed coniferous/deciduous forest, for at least seventy years. The wild edge has low growing native clover and strawberries, as well as bushes of blue, black, goose, and raspberries. Alders course along the permanent creek. Chokecherry, elderberry, and elms grip onto the granite/crystal outcroppings. The forest rises with white birch, red maple, Douglas fir, blue spruce, pines, and cedars. All are watched over by towering sugar maples and oaks. These are the areas that should not be touched. So why is there a one-half acre of gardens? The previous owner had ripped the land apart. The south sloping open terrain had been scraped of twelve inches (30cm) of topsoil to be sold to create the roadway to the house, five years before we bought. Very little native flora survived. So, in this very unique case the land was ideally suited for creating gardens. In 2015 when we started working the land it was in desperate need of diversification and renewal. So, for the second time for me, in as many farms, human-caused devastation was to be converted to a fulfilling, flourishing dream.

To summarize, there is already enough cultivated or human-destroyed (by their hands or the animals they raise) lands that it is unnecessary to cultivate any more healthy, native terrain whether in the grassland, clearing, edge or forest. The world is already producing 1.5x more fruits, vegetables, and herbs than we can possibly eat every year. The problem is not space or the ability to grow enough it is simply plant-based diversity and getting it into the hands of those that need it most.[4]

The Soil

It all begins with the soil; this is where all life springs from. Without the soil there are no plants, bushes, or trees. There are no flowers, fruits, or seeds for any organism to eat. Without a healthy soil nothing thrives. For a quarter of a century, I have had my hands in the dirt, experiencing, observing, and trying to understand the complexities that lie right under our feet. Seeing how the earth reacts to the winds and rains, colds and heat has become an obsession. In all that time of reflecting, what I have come to know as an absolute truth, is that all life begins and ends with the soil, and it is that relationship to her that makes us healthy and strong.

Like all of us the soil is a living, breathing entity. In one teaspoon (one gram) of healthy soil there are one billion bacteria, several yards of fungal filaments, several thousand protozoa, and dozens of nematodes.[5] They all interact together having symbiotic associations with one another. The soil under our feet is teeming with life, but also decaying with death. Does that word bother you? It is interesting how we have a strong affinity with the word life and negative connotations affiliated with the word death. Everything lives and everything dies, no one entity in the plant or animal world is immune. No one immortal. Just as there is day, there is night, it is simply a transformation.

The minerals and elements that are specific to every soil system provide the nutrients for the bacteria, nematodes, and arthropods that eat them. Those soil creatures will feed on each other and even members of the same species. As they excrete, die, and decompose, more soil is created. Filaments of mycorrhizae create vast neural networks transporting food, in the form of macro and micronutrients to the associated plant life.[6] Where the decomposition and excretions of bacteria, nematodes, and arthropods create the elements and minerals plants need, it is the underground superhighway of fungi that transports them from place to place. A healthy soil requires bacterial and fungal composition to thrive. The larger the faunal being, the more excrement. However, far more decomposition and soil building occurs when the plant's vegetative growth dies in the winter. The living organisms within the soil are omnivores, eating both plants and animals, as well as being cannibalistic at times. Manure is deposited by carnivorous, omnivorous, and herbivorous creatures alike but, again, the vast majority of organic matter comes from the plant kingdom.

For an example let us consider a healthy eleven acre (4.45 hectare) northern mixed forest ecosystem, like one that borders the northwest of my current home. There are low-lying plants, shrubs, small and large trees. When the first fall frost approaches plants begin their decay, leaves turn colors and fall, snows and winds break brittle branches, and they return to the forest floor. All will rest under the thermal white blanket. In spring, the moisture from the thaw, combined with the heat of the lengthening days accelerate the composting activity. This happens every year without fail. There are herbivorous animals, like mice, voles, squirrels, and deer that will forage and browse and deposit bits of excrement here and there. Omnivorous moles, skunks, raccoons, and red foxes do as well. A pack of wolves will pass through once per year or two and leave small piles after the meal of a young moose, whose body is left to decompose. So, there are animal manures and meals, but in relationship to the whole the decomposing plant material is the vast majority of the above ground organic matter.[7]

The University of Washington states that to provide one hundred pounds of nitrogen per acre, which is barely enough to satisfy the fertilization requirements to grow sweet corn they claim, it is recommended to use three tons per acre of poultry manure to two hundred tons per acre of dairy manure into the gardens. This is 6,000 pounds (2,720 kg) of poultry manure to 400,000 pounds (181,400 kg) of dairy manure or separated dairy solids.[8] Going back to our healthy forest example, is it feasible to consider adding up to two hundred tons per acre of manure into that setting. No, it is ridiculous, and also ridiculous to think about applying that amount of manure onto a one-acre vegetable patch. Far better would be to add three tons per acre of composted plant materials into the gardens, which is more natural and better assimilated by the plant community. Grassland systems function in the same manner. The majority of fertility comes from the decay and death of the above ground grasses and plants. There would be a smattering of bird and mammal excrements but by no means even anywhere near three tons per acre. This recommendation is simply a result of too much manure created and nowhere to put it. When building soils for the gardens, the only animal inputs that are necessary are the ones that occur naturally by the microorganisms of the living soil.

Soil Types

My favorite test for understanding native soil type is to take a handful of wet earth in hand, squeeze, and make a ball. How it holds together will determine whether the soil is mostly sand or silt, or mostly clay. Whatever shape it remains in will determine the relative structure. If the ball immediately begins to crumble away from the outer edges or cracks in the middle, the soil has a higher percentage of sand or silt. If it is completely solid, holding its' form, the soil has a higher percentage of clay. No matter what the soil type, all crops can be grown, from the most porous sand to the hardest clay. Care, however, must be taken with all.

Sandy soils tend to be deep, well-draining and ideally suited for root crops and plants with extensive root systems like beans, corn, peppers, squash, and tomatoes. They are usually low in fertility as the water drains quite rapidly taking nutrients deep into the soil base layers. It can be difficult to keep a sandy soil wet for small seeds, like carrots and greens.

Silt soils are similar to sands but are denser and more fertile. By their nature they will compact more readily than sand, as they are water retentive but not as much as clay. Silt soils are created when rock is eroded by water or ice. Former glacial valleys and receded former flooded river plains would yield silt soils. This soil type is highly beneficial for many crop families.

Clay soils tend to be compact, water retentive and high in fertility. Clay soils usually have a high presence of earthworms, as their castings (excrement and decomposition) help compact the soil and retain water. Because of the structure of clay soils, aeration can be an issue. Clay soils need infrequent watering. *Brassicaceae* family crops (broccoli, cabbage, kale, and others), eggplants and greens benefit from a more clay soil.

There are other main soil structures. Peat soils have high water retention and are more acidic. If the ball of wet earth feels spongy there may be a quantity of peat. Chalk soils are rich in calcium carbonate and are highly alkaline, these soils would look slightly gray, and the consistency would act clay-like. Loam soils are the best of all worlds as they contain a combination of sand, clay, and silt soils. More sand would be called sandy loam, more clay, clay loam, more silt, silty loam.[9] For the majority of us growers our soils will be either sandy, silty, or clay, with sometimes some peat or chalk tendencies and if we are really lucky, they will be loamy.

Knowing what we are starting with is imperative no matter the size of the growing space. A professional soil test is an inexpensive way to gain scientific knowledge. It will reveal levels of organic matter, element and mineral percentages, as well as the all-important pH (power of Hydrogen) of the soil. The pH will determine which garden plants will grow well as it influences completely the ability for the plants to uptake nutrients.[10]

PH is the relative acidity or alkalinity of the soil. Neutral is 7.0. Below seven, the soil is deemed acidic, above seven it is alkaline. The optimum range of pH for all garden vegetables is between 5.7-7.2. If it is slightly above or slightly below it is ok for most. No matter where the soil is before planting this range can be achieved (more to come in Chapter 5: Garden Preparation). Check out the Annex A: Crop Profiles for the optimum pH range for each fruit, vegetable, and herb. For a more comprehensive chart on pH ranges for all trees, shrubs, vegetables, and flowers check the Old Farmer's Almanac, "Soil pH Levels for Plants."[11]

Here at La Ferme de l'Aube two soil tests were taken from two different sections of the fields in June 2016. From marginally amended soil, it was revealed that:

- pH was 5.1
- Based on CEC of 12.7 (Cation exchange, which is the relative ability for soils to hold or store positively charged ions and influences nutrient availability) the soil type was deemed to be silty loam, most likely due to the never-before-amended fields sitting in a former glacial valley.
- Based on the soil organic matter content of 5.2% the fields were deemed fertile.
- Potassium, sulfur, and iron were high in presence.
- Zinc and copper were medium in presence.
- Phosphorus, calcium, boron, magnesium, and manganese were low.

All of these elements can be read about in Chapter 6: The Major and Minor Elements.

Because of the pH being below 5.5, aluminum, which is present in all soils, was severely phytotoxic to the cultivated plants, causing a severe lack of nutrient uptake. So, just because the gardens were tested to be fertile does not mean that they were healthy to grow cultivated varieties of plants, unless they liked very acid environments.

In summary, soil is the life blood of us all. Combined with air circulation, heat, and water, the system flourishes to create all ecological systems. All these systems thrive by letting bacteria and mycorrhizae live and proliferate. The very best above ground mechanism for letting this happen, whether in a cultivated garden, forest clearing, edge or grassland is the composting of plant-based residues.

La Ferme de l'Aube's one-half-acre gardens in relation to the forest edge and northwestern mountain range in Boileau, Québec.

2

The Garden Plan

A<small>S THE SNOW</small> continues to fall at the beginning of the calendar year, increasing her protective thermal layer on the earth, our thoughts turn to the first shoots penetrating the surface. We inventory the seed stock we have on hand, making a comprehensive list of all varieties and the approximate number of seeds in each open packet. Before we ever order more, we commence with the garden calendar and vision (maps) for the coming growing season. The first time is the most daunting, as the majority of the work comes in year #1. Afterwards there is simply some tweaking to coincide with planting dates and what worked, failed, and what is wished to be tried new.

The best way to start is to make a list of the fruits, vegetables, and herbs you like to eat and consequently wish to grow. Do you want to have cherry tomatoes, cucumbers, and summer squash every week in season? Lettuces and/or mesclun salad mix, every week? Do you like beets, carrots, and peas? How about fresh herbs? The sky is wide open and there can be no limit to your culinary imagination and the planting possibilities.

How Much Land is Necessary to Grow Your Own Food? (Probably less than you think)

At La Ferme de l'Aube we grow on twenty thousand square feet (0.46 acres, 0.186 hectares) cultivating over four hundred varieties of one hundred different species of fruits, vegetables, herbs, grains, and flowers. The breakdown is thus:

- 9,875 square feet (1/4-acre, 0.10 ha) are cultivated for sale
- 5,875 square feet (1/7-acre, 0.058 ha) are cultivated for our own consumption
- 4,250 square feet (1/10-acre, 0.04 ha) are cultivated for all other beings in the form of flowering shrubs, plants, and green cover crops.

From the 5,875 square feet that is for us, we cultivate fruits, vegetables, herbs, and grains outside, starting the first week of May and continuing the outside harvest until the end of November, with the help of season extension practices (see Chapter 8: As Soon as the Soil Can be Worked). With a hundred square foot bed in the passive solar heated greenhouse dedicated to spring and fall greens, we start eating fresh in late March and harvest up till the winter solstice, five weeks earlier and three weeks later than outside.

In-season, we are abundantly eating the entire diversity of produce, from artichokes to zucchini. In addition, we cold-store fresh, can, freeze and dry the following:

Fresh Storage:
- 100 pounds (45kg) each of onions and potatoes
- 75 pounds (34 kg) carrots
- 50 pounds (22.5kg) each of beets, cabbage (red and green combined) and winter squash
- 25 pounds (11kg) dry beans
- 25 pounds (11kg) each of kohlrabi, parsnips, and rutabaga
- 10 pounds (4.5kg) each of celery root, turnips, and winter radish
- 150-200 bulbs garlic
- 1 quart (1L) flax seed

Canning:
- 50 quarts (1L) tomatoes
- 40 pints (500ml) Mexican style salsa
- 15 one-half pints (250ml) hot pepper sauce
- 6 pints refrigerator pickles

Freezing:
- 10 quarts (1L) bags each of celery, greens (like chard, kale, rapini and spinach), shelling peas, shredded summer squash, strawberries, sweet corn, and sweet peppers
- 4 quarts (1L) bags each of edamame, parsley, and rhubarb

Drying:
- 2 quarts (1L) each of basil, chamomile flowers, cherry tomatoes, ground cherries, lemon balm, mint, nettle, oregano, and summer squash
- 1 quart (1L) each of marjoram, rosemary, savory, and thyme

This is the vast majority of the food we consume all year for a family of two. The only main staples we purchase are chickpeas, flours (we prefer buckwheat, chickpea and spelt), lentils, nuts and seeds, oats, plant-based milks, and rice (basmati and brown).

This handbook is not intended to give advice for a small veganic farm business.

However, what I can say is that any growing space over 7,500 square feet (roughly 1/6-acre, 0.068 ha), with 6,000 square feet being for two people's nourishment and 1,500 (around 20% of the total land available) being for the benefit of all other inhabitants, could result in a portion of the land being used for sale or barter. In addition to feeding ourselves well and selling to forty families per week for fifteen weeks, we exchange garden produce for organic apples, blueberries, pears, raspberries, kimchee (fermented cabbage), veganic compost, building materials, acupuncture treatments, and more. The ceiling is boundless and entirely based on your level of community-building interest.

For the last four years our production totals from 2018-2021 keep increasing as we become more experienced and soil health and fertility increases. We needed to keep track of all harvests due to National Organic Program rules. Thus, the following yields:

2018: 5,181 lbs. (2,350 kg)
2019: 5,318 lbs. (2,412 kg)
2020: 5,531 lbs. (2,509 kg)
2021: 6,132 lbs. (2,782 kg)

In December 2018 I authored a report for the Humane Party, USA titled, "The Productivity of Vegan-Organic Farming"[1] that was based on eleven different crop species selected for their importance to farmer and consumer diets. La Ferme de l'Aube was found to be 2.3% and 41.6% more productive than conventional and organic practices respectively. Why is this important? It shows without a shadow of doubt that completely veganic methods of production can compete with and even exceed conventional and organic forms of farming. Even after only a few years of cultivating the land.

As you think about what it is you want to grow, it will be limited by the amount of space you have. To help with your individual field plan, Annex B: Crop Spacing and Approximate Yields has been specifically designed with the small grower in mind. Most planting recommendations found online and in seed catalogs, for example, recommend more space per crop species, mainly to accommodate spacing so that tractors can pass. This chart has been crafted from my own personal experience on the small-scale and consulting advice to the backyard grower.

All 160 of our garden beds are 50-foot (15.24m) x 2.5-foot (75cm), or 125 square feet. The length is not terribly important, though for ease of planning and purchasing of supplies like row covers, screens, and irrigation (if deemed necessary), I do counsel for all beds to be uniform. More importantly is the width. I believe 2.5-foot (75cm) is the ideal width. Throughout all the years of gardening and working on professional farms, this is the easiest to maintain and harvest. We can comfortably kneel or squat from each side, whether it is ground level or raised garden bed. Three feet (90cm) is fine too, but any larger and reaching the middle becomes a strain on the back and shoulders. Throughout the rest of the book, I will refer to "bed foot," which will mean 2.5-foot (75cm) or 3-foot (90cm) by 1-foot (30cm) long. Now that we have all of our planting desires, as well as the information listed in Annex A: Crop Profiles and Annex B—which includes variety, direct seed or transplant, rows, distance, plants/bed foot, approximate yield, and when to plant—we can make our calendar.

Garden Calendar

Learning how to use a google or word excel spreadsheet, or newer application will aid in the calendar plotting process and keep everything nice and orderly. It can also be done with the dependable method of graph paper and kept in a three-ring binder. The decision on how to function is entirely your preference. In some cases, the date of first seeding is self-explanatory and easy to plot. If the "when the soil is open" date is the first week of May, then the first carrots, kales, peas, rapini, and salad greens for example can be seeded on that date. In other cases, it is necessary to work backwards from the desired transplant date. Even though we all want to eat tomatoes as early as possible, the outside transplant date is no earlier than the week of the average frost date. Below are four different examples to consider.

Magenta lettuce (heads) are a 48-day variety from direct seeding, as listed in seed catalogs. But lettuce for heads can be started inside to be transplanted outside as bigger seedlings. By doing this we can deduct 14 days from the total. 48-14 days would yield 34 days from transplanting. We would like to start eating lettuce heads in the last week of June. Counting back roughly five weeks, would reveal a transplant date of May 24. Since the seed takes about four weeks to reach transplant size, the seeding date inside would be April 26. We want to plant six heads, which would require two bed feet.

Peacevine cherry tomatoes are harvestable sixty days after transplant. Knowing that we can only transplant out after last frost, the transplanting date would be around May 24. Counting back exactly four weeks, the inside seeding date would be April 26. Harvest date would be sixty days from May 24, approximately the end of July. We want to plant four plants, which would require two bed feet.

Scarlet Nantes Carrots can be direct seeded outside as soon as the soil can be worked around May 3. They are a sixty-five-day variety, our harvest date would be roughly July 7. We want to plant two bed feet, for a total of a hundred and twenty carrots.

Maxibel bush beans can be direct seeded outside after the last frost, on May 24 as well. They are a sixty-day variety; our harvest date would be roughly July 23. We want to plant thirty-six over two bed feet.

From the four examples our garden calendar/chart would look something like the following:

Variety	# of Seeds	Seeding Date	Transplant Date	Bed feet	Harvest Date
Magenta lettuce	7	April 26	May 24	2	June 28
Peacevine cherry	5	April 26	May 24	2	July 24
Scarlet Nantes carrot	120	May 3 (DS)	n/a	2	July 7
Maxibel bush bean	36	May 24 (DS)	n/a	2	July 23

It is always a good idea to seed inside an extra 15-20% than the plants you want, as germination rate standards are 80% in bought seeds. For Magenta lettuce, seven seeds would be sown for six plants. Peacevine cherry would be five seeds for four plants. The number of seeds is also important for ordering. The seeding date is in bold because this is the date that should be set in stone. The transplant and harvest dates can shift, if necessary, based on germination and temperature fluctuations. When the calendar day opens to April 26, we know it is time to seed Magenta and Peacevine.

Not too difficult? A little complicated? Either way, it will get easier after the first few varieties. With patience, the whole calendar will come to form. But how much to grow? Based on the approximate yield of each species, it is entirely up to you. The key determining variables are how much you eat and the space you have.

Succession Planting

Above is a very simple model and chart, but it can be scaled up to sixty or even six hundred heads of lettuce if desired. Not that we would want six hundred heads at the same time; we want them to come in phases over the summer. Using Magenta lettuce as an example again, let's say we want to start eating lettuce on the 28th of June and eat three heads per week until mid-September, or 12 weeks. 12 weeks x 3 heads of lettuce/week = 36 heads. We would need twelve bed feet for all our lettuce needs. But we do not want to plant them all at the same time, as they will all be ready within a two to three-week window. We would need to plant in succession. To put it simply, Magenta lettuce would be seeded every two to three weeks until the desired number of heads are reached (in this example, thirty-six). From our four examples, Maxibel bush beans and Scarlet Nantes carrots can be succession sown two to three weeks after the initial seeding date as well to extend the harvest.

Once the dates, plants desired, and successions (if applicable) have been entered into our desired calendar model, the map of the gardens can be developed.

Garden Map(s)

For four consecutive years we sold seedlings for people's gardens in Montréal. The one-day event would bring hundreds of customers, buying up over two thousand plants. Over one hundred different varieties of fruits, vegetables, herbs, and flowers were sold. We would consult on varieties and veganic planting methods as clients planned their gardening dreams. Some would browse the selections, rubbing their chins, pondering how they would fit into the space they had allocated. Others were a step ahead. Young and old, new and experienced alike came with their garden maps, even if the size was a community garden plot no bigger than 4-foot (120cm) x 8-foot (240cm). They had delineated the dates of direct seeding or transplanting and space for each variety. No matter the size of the garden, a map is encouraged and highly beneficial.

After we have compiled all our wants and needs for the growing season, that information gets plotted on the map. Like all of us, it is assured that you will also run out of space before you plot all garden aspirations. At the end of this chapter is a sample map with our four examples in a 2.5-foot (75cm) x 8-foot (240cm) bed, with four-year rotation.

Rotation

To rotate or not rotate, that is the question for the modern-day Hamlet. Some of the species that we grow as annuals, like eggplant, ground cherries, peppers, tomatillos, and tomatoes are actually perennials in places where it does not freeze, feeding from the same patch of ground year after year. Like the nine-year-old snowy eggplant bush I was harvesting from in Kapoho, Hawaii. Others like members of the *Brassicaceae* family (broccoli, cabbage, cauliflower, kale), carrots, beets, spinach, and Swiss chard are biennial, meaning they will flower and seed in their second year. Others like chamomile, cilantro, dill, greens (Asian and mustard), lettuce, radish, and rapini are self-seeding annuals, meaning they will produce seed in the first year and will sprout in the same area later in the year or the following spring. Others still grow back from root division, like garlic, onions, and potatoes. If some are not harvested, they will divide and multiply, sometimes even healthier than the re-planted ones. Looked at this way, from a nutrient perspective, rotation may not be necessary.

Some insects are very damaging, like Colorado potato beetles. The larvae will defoliate a plant in a matter of days, limiting the underground potato yield. One reason to rotate potatoes is the claim that it will decrease the presence of these beetles. They will winter over under plant residue, go dormant, and then re-emerge when the spring weather warms. This is just the first generation. They can have up to four, and this does not account for the adults that will migrate in. So, in the case of potatoes, no matter how far away they are planted, the beetles will find the plants.

The most compelling reasons for rotation are to prevent disease and nematode (microscopic roundworm) pressures. Bacterial blights, wilts, and fungal molds live in all soils and are expounded by climatic extremes during the season. When the temperature changes abruptly, mostly due to unseasonably cold and wet weather, these pathogens and pressures materialize. Nematodes, cutworms, and wireworms live in most soils and have their most active periods when soils begin to warm and seedlings are small. While all these issues, to a certain degree, exist everywhere, there are certain bacterial diseases that prefer tomatoes, fungi that prefer *Cucurbitaceae* (cucumbers, melons, squash), and worms that prefer carrots, garlic, and onions. Changing the position of the family groups can be a preventative and sensible response.

In addition to the calendar, plan, and maps, it is a wise idea to keep a daily activity or observation log. As the plants are growing, jotting down observations such as growth rates, insect and disease pressures, and temperature fluctuations will provide valuable data. Noting varieties that worked and failed will make the following year's planning less time-consuming and ultimately more fun. Space has been provided in Annex A: Crop Profiles for observational field notes if you wish to document them directly in this handbook. The more data you collect, the better gardener you will become—based on your own experiences in your own specific ecosystem.

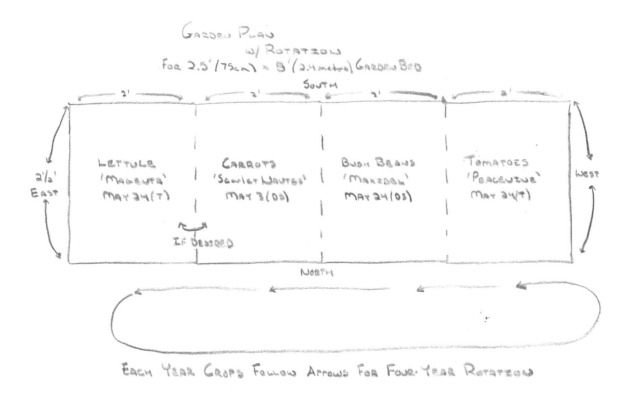

Drawing of garden map (four crops)

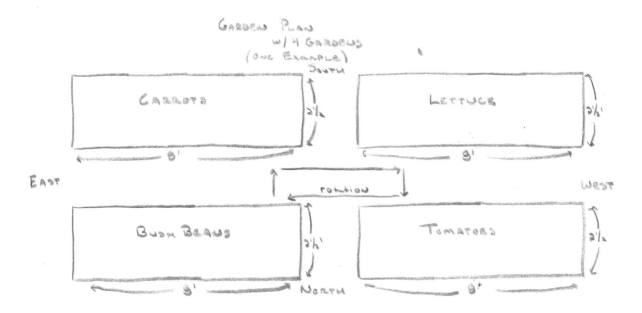

Drawing of garden map (four varieties)

3

Seeds

THE MID-WINTER RESTS cold but warms up briskly in our hearts when the seed catalogs arrive, usually landing in mailboxes before the end of the calendar year. Colorful images of new and tried-and-true varieties grace the coffee table. From the first delivered edition of W. Atlee Burpee's seed catalog in 1896 to the current 300+ page Baker Creek Whole Seed catalog, all planting yearnings lie within these colorful pages. There are many companies, local and global, to choose from.

After the garden plan has been scrutinized, knowing the space allocation for the number of plants of each species type, our thoughts turn to the varietals. There are vast choices and characteristics for each one. Most important to understand is that there are two main ways in which seeds are produced: F-1, which means first generation hybrid, and OP, which means open-pollinated source.

F-1 Hybrid

If there is an F-1 in front of the seed variety listed in a seed catalog, then this is a seed type that has been crossed by a plant breeder. It is the first-generation hybrid of two or more different plants within the same species. The breeder has taken one type of broccoli plant, for example, and pollinated it with another. They do this to isolate a particular trait, such as (but not limited to), disease resistance, heat or cold tolerance, plant vigor (growth), color, or size of heads. F-1s can be produced either conventionally or organically. In order to be listed as "certified organic" an outside, usually for-profit organization, must conduct a yearly inspection to verify that the breeder and/or farm is in accord with National Organic Standards, as written by governmental administrations and ministries. The standard is a twenty-five-to-forty-page set of regulations explaining which practices and inputs are permitted. Conventional seeds do not require certification, even if it is treated with a hazardous chemical fungicide.

(OP) Open Pollinated

If there is no F-1 listed, or (OP) in front of the seed, then the seed is derived from the same plant species. A Scarlet Nantes carrot seed comes from Scarlet Nantes carrots that have gone to seed in their second year (biennial). Like F-1s, open-pollinated seeds can be conventional or organic. Sometimes, seed companies—especially artisanal ones—sell seeds that follow all organic standard protocols but do not have "certified organic" on the package. In addition to the certification process, there is a substantial fee to pay to the certifying body to receive the right to call seeds "organic." While the small grower may be committed to the organic standards, the costs are sometimes prohibitive. Within the open-pollinated seed type, there can be another designation, Heirloom (HL), which means that the seed has been saved and passed down from generation to generation for at least 75 years.

Which is better?

To take another example of F-1s, let us look at hybrid sweet corn. In the last ten to fifteen years, sweet corn plant breeders have been developing corn seeds that are tolerant to cold, late-spring soils. Corn is a heat-loving crop and has a difficult time germinating in soil temperatures below 65F (18.5C). The creation of F-1 sweet corn seeds that will germinate in soils at 55F (12.5C) has allowed northern growers an opportunity to effectively germinate corn earlier and easier than before.

Seeds of Knowledge

I will attempt to explain what I believe is happening from my experiences in seed-saving with an example of an open-pollinated, heirloom seed type.

Let's say in year #1, I plant five heirloom Jaune Flamme tomato plants. It is a saladette type of tomato, roughly two inches (5cm) in diameter, orange, juicy, and sweet. The plant is an indeterminate variety, meaning it will be more than eight feet (240cm) tall and produce fruits all growing season, starting sixty-five days after transplant. The five plants grow well, production is good, and the size of the fruits is typical. The first fruits begin to ripen in fifty-eight days, a full one week earlier than the seed package specified. It has been a hot growing period, many days above 85F (29.5C), and dry with a lot of sun. The plants had some early bacterial wilt on the lower leaves, but grew out of it and shot up past eight feet. I take the first ten tomatoes from the most productive plants and save the seed.

In year #2, I plant the seeds, transplant the seedlings, and in this year, the first fruit ripens even faster at fifty-five days. The summer, however, has been drastically different. It has been cool, most daily highs barely reaching 70F (21C), with many cloudy days and frequent rains. The same wilt appeared on the lowest leaves, this time probably because of the higher levels of humidity, but like the year before the plants grew out of it. Production was good on three out of five plants with some fruits bigger than two inches (5cm) in diameter. I harvest from the three most productive plants, choosing the smaller of the fruits, as this is my preference, and save the seed again.

In year #3, the seed knows all the past information from former growing conditions in its 75+ year history. Now after just two years of seed-saving at my own specific location, it knows how to grow in, but not limited to: two different soil types (one more clay, one more sandy, because of the rotation), times of drought, times of heat, cool conditions, and wet ones. It knows how fast to produce and how productive to be. It would know how to outgrow early bacterial blights and even create defenses from insect pressures. Where an F-1 seed has genetic information from the parent plants and specific criteria breeders have attempted to breed for, the heirloom seeds have over three generations of genetic data as well as new knowledge of our very specific soils and climatic elements. As far-fetched as the idea may be as to the thought processes of a seed, my ideas may have scientific validity. For further reading check out, "Seed Traits and Genes Important for Translational Biology".[1]

So, which is better? Heirloom and open-pollinated, hands down.

Genetically Modified Seeds (GMO or GM)

Based on the most current data available, in the United States, 99.9% of all sugar beets acres planted were GMO, 95% for canola, 94% for soybeans, 94% for cotton, and 92% of planted acres for grain corn.[2] In Canada, 95% of all Canola and 80% of all soybeans were GMO.[3] 99% of all the world's GM acreage is utilized for four crops: corn, soy, canola, and cotton. Currently, the producers of this type of genetically modified seed, like the Bayer-Monsanto mega-conglomerate, have focused their operations on herbicide-tolerant (most commonly glyphosate and/or dicamba-based) or insecticide-treated (most commonly BT-*Bacillus thuringiensis*) alfalfa, canola, corn, cotton, soy, and sugar beets. The vast majority of which is grown to feed animals raised for their meat, eggs, and milk. 70% of harvested GM crops are fed to the world's livestock, making them the largest consumers.[3] It has recently been proven that manure used from poultry animals that were fed glyphosate-resistant genetically modified crops saw the residues "persist throughout the digestive process of production animals and accumulate in their excretion products, causing a decrease in plant growth and vegetative reproduction".[4] The best way to eliminate GMOs from being planted is to stop raising animals. The best way to eliminate GMOs from your diet is not to eat them, drink their milk, eat their eggs, or utilize any of their excretions and fluids.

In lesser supplies, seed companies are working on genetically modified apples, papaya, potatoes, squash, and wheat. Other than papaya, these crops are infrequent visitors to produce departments. The seeds or plants of GMO varieties are not available in most seed catalogs. In fact, most seed companies take a safe seed (non-GMO) pledge. But despite this, there are vast quantities of genetically modified ingredients in processed foods on supermarket shelves. Canola oil, cornstarch, corn syrup, corn oil, cottonseed oil, granulated (beet) sugar, and soybean lecithin and oil are found in many products. If you wish to avoid these, carefully read the packaging labels. Some companies have taken the extra step to label their products as GMO-free. Any grocery store item that is labeled "organic" is also GMO-free by law.

There are a few seeds that are sold by Seminis and DeRuiter seeds, both subsidiaries of Bayer-Monsanto, that may be in some seed catalogs. If you wish to avoid supporting this company completely, shun the following F-1 varieties that can be found at some seed houses. Seminis owns "Minuteman" Cauliflower, "Fairy Tale" Eggplant, "Candy" Onion, "Gypsy" Pepper, "Red Knight" Pepper, "Big Beef" Tomato, "Celebrity" Tomato, and "Sun Sugar" Cherry Tomato.[5] DeRuiter owns "Favorita" cherry tomato, "Beorange" tomato, as well as tomato rootstock seeds DRO141TX and Maxifort.[6] Large agri-business will not get into OP/Heirloom seed production because it is all about profit and control for them. If a genetically modified (again, an F-1 hybrid) variety is planted, the seed can be saved, but the future plant outcome is not guaranteed because of the different parent plants. It is necessary to re-purchase seeds every year, whichever varietal the company chooses to breed. They also patent every F-1, making saving their seeds illegal and punishable by both hefty fines and jail time. As of 2013, Monsanto had raked in over $23 million from these lawsuits.[7]

The other knock against F-1 hybrids is their price. In the 2021 High Mowing Organic Seed catalog, for instance, the Toronjina F-1 cherry tomato costs $7.50 for ten seeds—while the Jaune Flamme cherry tomato (HL) costs $2.95 for thirty seeds. This is consistent with all comparisons of similar F-1 and open-pollinated varieties. If you are cost-conscious like me, this is another reason why OP/Heirloom is the clear winner.

Of the hundreds of varieties we currently grow at La Ferme de l'Aube, 95% are open pollinated and/or heirloom. Of the few varieties of F-1 we grow (all organic or non-treated), three are sweet corn and twelve are in the *Brassicaceae* family. Corn because of the cool soil emergent characteristics, and the *brassicas* because F1s tend to require less nutrients and form more uniform heads, crowns, and shoots. So, in my opinion, the best option for the vast majority is to grow open-pollinated and/or heirloom seeds, especially if you want to save your own (see Chapter 18: Letting plants go to Flower, to Seed, and Saving them).

So how to choose? That is the fun part.

Choose for color, shape, size, early or mid-season, cold or heat tolerance. In most larger seed catalogs, there will be a resistance legend, showing what diseases each F-1 variety is resistant to. As I have stated before, I believe heirlooms and even open-pollinated seeds are already resistant to most things, based on the fact that they have been grown for so long and experienced many different growing conditions. In addition, heirloom slicing tomatoes are unequaled in flavor. Hybrids try to match the exquisite nature of these gems, but fall well short, for a Brandywine Tomato is a spectacle for the eyes and the palette.

Keep a good list of the varieties purchased and make notes in the forementioned observation and activity log. This will be of great help with the following year's seed ordering. It is best to try and order seeds as soon as possible after the catalogs arrive in print or online, as popular varieties do sell out. Seek out regional artisanal seed growers, through the internet or seed festivals. The seeds procured from them will be 100% OP and have a genetic leg-up over a seed company thousands of miles or kilometers away. In addition, you will be continuing the ancient tradition of small-farmer seed saving. Check out the Annex F: Resources section of this handbook for my favorite larger seed houses.

Our offerings of open pollinated (OP) and Heirloom (HL) seeds at the Ottawa seed festival. Seek out one near you!

4

Seed-starting and the Growing Medium

IN ORDER TO achieve proper germination, all seeds require heat and moisture. Soil temperatures for germination vary from 55F (12.5C) to 90F (32C) depending on species. For example, lettuce aspires for a range between 55F (12.5C)-75F (24C), while hot peppers seek a range of 70F (21C)-90F (32C). Trying to achieve that extensive range can be quite tedious even for an experienced professional grower. To simplify the process, I will confirm that all seed species will germinate well in a range of 65F (18.5C) – 75F (24C). Focusing on creating this temperature range will ensure positive results. Monitoring can be easily achieved with the help of an indoor/outdoor probe thermometer, a seed grower's best friend.

Seeds require constant moisture for proper germination. If a seed wishes to germinate in four days like all *Brassicaceae* varieties, any day that the soil dries out will diminish germination rates and increase the length of time the seed will take to sprout. Most seeds will germinate in the dark or light, but sometimes specifically require full light to break through. Ground cherries are a perfect example. For them, the soil should be dimpled with the fingertip, the seed deposited on top and left uncovered in the sunlight. Careful watering must be scrutinized to make certain the seeds stay moist and that too much soil does not float over them.

Some varieties wish to be stratified, meaning to put in the refrigerator for a period of time. Others wish to be scarified, scratched with a fingernail or sandpaper. Some other seeds wish to be soaked for twenty-four hours before planting in the growing medium to accelerate the process. If any of these additional actions are required, seed packets or descriptions in catalogs will usually specify their unique needs.

My favorite method of seed-starting is in fifty-cell plug flats. Each cell is roughly 2 inches (5cm) x 2 inches (5cm) x 2.5 inches (6.25cm). The flats have holes in the bottom of every cell for water drainage. Each plug flat snugly rests in a 1020 seedling tray, also with holes for drainage, which is roughly ten inches (25cm) by twenty inches (50cm). The whole system is highly durable. For the small garden system, the structure of the plug tray permits them to be cut in any increment of five, if desired. I find this method the tidiest, uses the least amount of soil, allows for labeling and organization, quick to clean and easiest for winter storage (as all are stackable). I purchased most of my current stock seven years ago and have yet to put one in recycling. If one cracks, a bit of tape can be placed to extend its life.

At my farm in Arizona, I had used soil block makers for many years. They are specialized metal tools that are pressed into a soil medium to create a stand-alone block of soil. While they use less plastic, what I discovered is that the result can be unforgiving, for the soil medium mix must have the perfect combination of ingredients and water to form non-crumbling and not-to-tight blocks. Only certain recipes seemed to work well. I have used water expanding peat pellets, but fertility was low, and transplanting needed to happen too quickly. Coconut fiber mediums never seemed to decompose. I still have coconut fiber pots that migrate from one compost pile to another for six years running. But like every other topic I touch upon in this handbook, each gardener/grower/farmer has their own philosophy. But from my experience, growing over ten thousand seedlings per year, the fifty-cell plug tray and 1020 flats are the best solutions and assure the highest level of seedling success.

> ## Innovative Regenerative Business Idea
>
> All the plastic items I discuss throughout this handbook could be fabricated regionally, with recycled materials. Some already are, but the entire operation could be. They could even be made from recycled ocean plastic. There are already companies fishing plastic from the seas. Oceanworks, a California-based company, states that they have the capability to produce fifteen thousand tons of recycled sea plastic materials per month.[1] There is no need to produce more virgin plastic, and our earth deserves a hearty clean-up with all industries taking the lead. There are over two hundred fifty million tons of plastic produced worldwide every year and only 10% is currently recycled. We, as a responsible global community, need to work together to achieve the possibility of clean oceans and oil left in the ground for future generations of all species.

Soil Medium

Whatever pots or trays you decide to use, the proper soil starting medium is an imperative. Since it can be difficult to find a well amended 100% veganic soil growing medium, here is the recipe I have created. All of the soil ingredients can be found at a well-stocked nursery, garden center, or hardware store except for organic soybean meal. The most reliable company for this product is Down-to-Earth, and it can be purchased online in the US and Canada.

The mix should be uniformly wet, not soaked (no water standing). This is enough for six separate fifty-cell plug flats or three hundred seedlings total. The mix can be stored in a large Rubbermaid bin indefinitely. The recipe can be halved or quartered if space is an issue. This seedling mix is good for all seedlings, as well as plants that like to be "potted-up" (discussed later in this chapter) to a larger transplant size. If I am making up a batch of seeding medium for "potted-up" transplants, I will add three cups of homemade (screened) compost (see chapter 7: The Compost Pile) and an extra 1/5 cup combined soybean and alfalfa meal. Because of the seaweed, soft rock phosphate, soybean, and alfalfa meal this formulation has enough nutrients for the baby seedlings throughout their growing period inside. There is no need for a liquid fertilizer when watering them. The only seedlings that I give supplemental fertilizer to are the leeks and onions, which reside in the same soil for eight weeks before outside transplanting. For them, I give a light side sprinkling of organic soybean meal before watering after four weeks.

Recipe

To mix efficiently, you will need:

- spade-type shovel,
- wheelbarrow
- 5-gallon (20L) bucket
- 1-cup measure.

Steps:

1. Combine a 5-gallon (20L) bucket of **peat moss** with 1/2 cup **dolomite lime**
2. Mix together and water thoroughly.
3. Add:
   - 3 cups **perlite**
   - 1.5 cups **vermiculite**
   - 1/4 cup **granulated seaweed**
   - 1/5 cup **colloidal soft rock phosphate**
4. Mix together and water thoroughly.
5. Add 2.5 gallon (10L) of **potting mix**, any kind without fertilizer added, **_or_** a well-finished **veganic compost**
6. Mix together and water thoroughly.
7. Add:
   - 1/5 cup organic **soybean meal**
   - 1/5 cup organic **alfalfa meal**
   - 1/5 cup **mycorrhizae**
8. Mix together and water thoroughly

Another Innovative Regenerative Business Idea

There are currently very few places in the United States and Canada where vegan seeding/potting medium are available. There is no reason why these cannot be produced regionally, using the ingredients listed in the potting mix recipe. Mixes can even be fabricated using more sustainable components like composted chipped branch wood, plant-based compost, and shredded dry leaves. Currently, all "organic" mixes that are specifically formulated for seed starting and potting use many of the same ingredients as above. But instead of using plant-based fertilizers they use either dried poultry manure or rendered animal parts. There is a need for a commercially available bagged mix, and it would be quite easy for the same companies or newly founded ones to generate them.

Peat Moss or Coconut Coir?

There is some concern about the environmental impact caused by harvesting peat moss—for good reason. Peatlands are the largest natural terrestrial carbon store. They hold more carbon than all other vegetation types in the world combined.[2] These wetlands are drained when heavy machinery creates a ditch. The surface vegetation is removed by more machines to extract the underlying peat. It had taken thousands of years for these peatlands to form. Once extracted, it can take many years for them to be restored. The current available substitute is coconut coir.

Coconut coir or fiber is a natural fiber extracted from the outer shell of the coconut and is produced commercially, mainly in southeast Asia. On my travels throughout Vietnam in 2013, I witnessed in many instances that the main fuel for cooking was coconut fiber husks, while the locals ate the nut meat and made meals with the liquid. By harvesting the coconuts and selling the fiber to the West, we are effectively eliminating the ability for inhabitants in these countries to eat and cook their food with this regenerative source.

All of the peat moss in Canada and 98% in the United States comes from northern Canada's peat bogs. According to the industry there are 281 million acres (113.6 million hectares) constituting 25% of the world's peatlands. Less than 0.03% of Canadian peatland have been harvested to date. The industry has created a responsibly managed peatlands initiative, for what it's worth.[3]

By creating veganic mixes regionally, the best practices of obtaining all these harvested (alfalfa, mycorrhizae, peat, seaweed, and soy) and mined (dolomite lime, perlite, rock phosphate, and vermiculite) materials could be achieved. Other more sustainable ingredients could be investigated. All industries and communities must align to adopt best practices for this rapidly growing industry.

The Seeding Process

Here is a quick reference breakdown of seeding:
- 50-cell plug flats are perfect for starting inside all fruits, vegetables, and herbs except leeks, onions, and shallots, which should be planted in 1020 flats that are doubled for durability.
- Cucumbers, melons, summer and winter squashes, and nasturtium should be planted in final three-to-four-inch pots.
- Beans, beets, carrots, garlic (in fall), kale (baby), lettuce mix, mesclun mix, mustard greens, peas, potatoes, radishes, spinach, and turnips all should be direct seeded (DS) outside at the appropriate times. Cucumbers, summer squash (zucchini) and green onions could also be direct seeded if desired.

For more specific information on individual crops and whether to direct seed (DS) and/or to pot up to transplant (T) see Annex A: Crop Profiles and Annex B: Crop Spacing and Approximate Yields.

To plant in plug flats, fill the trays with soil to level, make small dimples in the medium with your fingers, place one seed per cell, sprinkle soil over the top, and water gently. A general rule is to plant the seed twice as deep as the diameter of the seed. Tomato seeds should be shallower, squash seeds should be deeper. As mentioned previously, plant 15-20% more seeds than plants you will want to transplant into the field, as germination rates usually average 80%. If a second seed is planted in a cell, do not fret, wait until germination and remove the seedling that is the least vigorous. Once the tray is planted it should be labeled. We like to use a permanent marker and green masking tape, but popsicle sticks work also. With planting completed, it is time to give the potential babies a nice warm home.

My favorite mechanism for obtaining optimal germination temperatures are the seedling heat mat and thermostat. There are many different models for both, and the mats come in two sizes. The 20-inch-long x 10-inch wide (50cm x 25cm) mat is good for one plug flat, the 48-inch-long x 20-inch wide (120cm x 50cm) is good for four flats. The heat mat is plugged into the thermostat, which is plugged into a standard 15 amp, 120-volt outlet. A probe from the thermostat rests on the heat mat to sense the temperature. The thermostat can be regulated to any temperature in one-degree increments. Empty bags of peat moss, perlite, or potting soil can be used to cover the trays completely, trapping the humidity and moisture. On a larger scale, I designed and built a Styrofoam-insulated double germination chamber. Each chamber is governed by individual heat mats and thermostats. By stacking the trays with the help of wood shims, each chamber can house twenty plug flats, or forty in total. Meaning we can germinate up to two thousand seedlings at the same time. So, no matter the scale of your gardening operation, the heat mat system functions efficiently.

Another of my favorite heating systems is the heated cable sand table. If you have accessibility to a small greenhouse or extra room in the house, this system can be utilized. For my system, I built wooden tables 3-foot wide (90cm) x 8-foot long (2.4m), with sides that come up 6 inches (15cm). Inside the table I placed a one-inch (2.5cm) sheet of Styrofoam-type insulation used for wet environments. The boxed table was filled with sand halfway and then layered with one quarter inch hardware cloth mesh. The heated cable was snaked throughout and attached to the cloth with small cable ties. The rest of the box was filled with sand. There are many scale models you can find online by searching "propagation table." Like the heat mats, the cord is plugged into a thermostat and a probe is nestled in the sand to control the temperature. This table rests in our unheated outdoor greenhouse.

Seeds that need light to germinate or that germinate very rapidly, like all in the *Brassicaceae* family, are put directly on the sand table. Where we live, it is not uncommon for the temperatures to plummet to -4F (-20C) when we are starting our seeding season. However, on the sand table with the aid of a thermal row cover (Agribon-40, provides 5-7 degrees Fahrenheit frost protection) and plastic sheeting, the temperature can be conserved at a comfortable 70F (21C) on those frigid nights. For any method you choose, it is imperative to maintain a consistent source of heat. Once the seeds germinate, the more intricate part begins: growing the seedlings.

Growing the Babies (Seedlings)

Seedlings can be grown up in a greenhouse—even minimally sized, 6-foot wide (1.8m) x 7-foot long (2.1m) x 7-foot tall (2.1m), would be suitable—or somewhere in the house. Whether inside the house or outside in the greenhouse, the temperature recommendations are the same. During the day, the temperatures should rest at a comfortable 70-81F (21-27C). More importantly, at night, the temperature should be 61-70F (16-21C), being very cautious to not let the temperature drop below 60F (15.5C) while the seedlings are small.

If space is available, I highly recommend constructing a small permanent greenhouse. A greenhouse will capture heat on even the coldest partly sunny days. I have witnessed temperatures in the low 80's F (high 20's C) when it is -4F (-20C) outside. All aspects of growing can be done in the greenhouse: soil mixing, seeding, potting up (transplanting), and watering. Low-energy systems can run on two 15amp 120V outlets, with the use of the forementioned heating cable or small 120V greenhouse forced-fan heaters. The larger the greenhouse constructed, the more energy needed, but heating just the space necessary and capturing the heat at night with the help of thick frost blankets is more ecologically friendly, than heating the entirety of the greenhouse, from an energy perspective.

In a small greenhouse, where one 3-foot x 6-foot (90cm x 180cm) table with anchored PVC hoops is constructed, ten 50-cell plug flats (500 seedlings), or eleven 18-port 3.5-inch pot trays (198 transplants) can live. They can be covered at night with plastic sheeting and frost covers to trap the heat. A 1500W heater can be placed underneath the table to keep the temperature at night at a comfortable 61-70F (16-21C). The tables are skirted to ground level with recycled plastic sheeting (from soil amendment bags) to hold in the forced heat even when the temperature takes a drastic turn downward. This is a more advanced system that requires decent knowledge of construction and electricity, but it has yielded fantastic results for us. In addition, because we do not heat the whole greenhouse like many growers in northern climates do, our electricity usage remains minimal. All the heat stays where it should: around the plants.

If growing transplants inside a home, the difficulty will be giving the seedlings enough light. If there is a south-facing window, this will be perfect. If none, a system of lights on shelves, determined by the number of trays of seedlings, can be used. I have used this system before, and I am not a huge fan as it can be quite expensive both in materials and electricity costs. However, I know other growers who use it as their primary system and are quite happy. Ensuring the seedlings ten to twelve hours of full light per day as they are growing should be the goal.

No matter where the seedlings are growing, guidance for watering is the same. The smaller the seedling, the more frequent watering needed. The larger the seedling, the less frequent watering needed. When babies put on their first true leaves (out of the dicotyledon stage) the plug/pot can go completely dry before watering thoroughly. The major problem most amateur gardeners have is "loving" their plants too much by giving them too much water. Doing this will cause two major problems: damping off and nutrient uptake.

Damping off is where the seedling rots at their base, at the soil level. They eventually fall over and die. This is caused by the funguses (*Rhizoctonia, Fusarium, Pythium sp.*) that live in all soils. They rear their heads when the earth is too cold and too wet, generally below 60F (15.5C), for an extended period of time. The *Brassicaceae* and *Solanaceae* varieties are particularly susceptible. Once a seedling gets damping off, it does not recover. However, even if some seedlings harbor this condition in their plug trays, it can be completely halted by immediately keeping the rest drier and warmer. The bigger the seedling, the smaller the problem.

Nutrients are only assimilated by the roots at specific moisture levels. If the earth stays too soggy for too long, they will not be able to uptake any of the macro or micro-nutrients (see Chapter 6: The Major and Minor Elements). The roots will continue to push, even through the bottom of the flats and trays, seeking drier, more nutrient-rich terrain. The answer, like damping off, is to water less frequently.

Transplanting or "Potting Up"

The majority of seedlings can live in the fifty-cell plug flats until transplanting outside. However, certain plants wish to be potted-up or transplanted into larger receptacles (three to four-inch pots), like all varieties in the *Solanaceae* family (eggplants, ground cherries, peppers, tomatoes) and most herbs. My preference is 3.5-inch (9cm) pots, but any size between three to four-inch (7.5-10cm) is suitable. We use 3.5-inch durable plastic pots that fit snugly in trays of eighteen. The potting mix recipe delineated earlier will be enough for seventy-two 3.5-inch transplants.

The process of potting-up is quite simple. Fill the pot with soil, but do not pack it. Dig out the middle, creating enough room for the plug and roots to fit. With a fork, pop out the whole seedling and soil block from the cell tray, being careful not to over-disturb the roots. Place the transplant in the pot, keeping the soil level the same. Sprinkle earth into the pot, filling to the rim, and press down lightly with your fingers. Water thoroughly. As the seedlings get bigger, they will want even less frequent watering and resist temperature extremes, especially lower nighttime temperatures. This is a process called "hardening off'."

Hardening off is the practice of getting the seedlings accustomed to being planted outside. When a kale plant, for example, is growing inside at a comfortable 61F (16C) at night it will receive quite a shock when planted in soils that are closer to 50F (10C). Our intention is to alleviate the shock. The best way to do this is simply to diminish the heat. An acclimation space outside will allow the babies to get accustomed to the feel of the natural world like rain, true sunlight, wind, and wind chill. Bringing in the seedlings at night and incrementally lowering the temperatures will aid the transplants' recovery time. A good general rule is to acclimate all seedlings for a week to ten days. I have created acclimation tents outside, using recycled pallets as the flooring, PVC hoops, and frost row covers— just like in the greenhouse.

This is complicated and technical information, and I have tried to simplify the process as much as possible. However, I believe anyone who is serious about trying to produce their own food must become an excellent seedling grower. While there is an investment in trays, flats, mats, etc., considering that the cost of an organically grown fruit, vegetable, or herb seedling can run anywhere from $3-$5 per seedling per year, the costs of these highly durable materials will pay for themselves quickly. Not to mention, that you will experience the profound joy and sense of accomplishment in planting a tiny tomato seed and seeing it become an eight-foot, loaded tomato bush! While I believe that the one-acre veganic farm and less is the answer to the agricultural waste in our world, I believe stronger in the individual or familial production of one's own food. Everyone should, within their capabilities. It is in our genetic make-up. Intuitively, we have the skills—and there is no other hobby or occupation in this modern world that connects us more fully to the earth.

Greenhouse tables full of baby seedlings, covered with plastic sheeting to keep the heat right where it's needed.

Uncovered seedlings of eggplants, peppers and tomatoes growing joyously.

5

Garden Preparation

THE SPRING RAINS fall in warm torrents and the snow decreases her depths. Where once a seemingly impenetrable pack shrouded the landscape, puddles form and rivulets run. Every spring we ask the same question to the earth: How is it all going to melt? With the lengthening, warming days and nights and the steady pelting of rain, it always does. Suddenly, the gardens are revealed.

Over the years, I have worked and tried many bed preparation methods. I have used Farmall, John Deere, Kubota, and Renault tractors with harrow, moldboard, and spring tine plowing attachments. I have created row after two-hundred-foot (61m) row with bed maker attachments. On smaller scales, I have used BCS rear-tine rototillers and craftsman front-tine tillers. I have made garden plots with the arduous task of double digging. I have followed both low-till and no-till philosophies. I have laid cardboard and plastic mulches, both temporary and permanent. The process I prefer is an amalgamation of many small-scale trials.

All our beds are permanent every year. They are built up with the addition of veganic compost and the previous year's garden residues. Each bed is different, with more or less plant matter depending on the previous crop. For example, rapini plants will yield five-foot (150cm) tall stalks and seed heads that when dry create an abundance of straw residue. A late-season carrot bed will be covered with the fern-like carrot leaves that have been popped off from their orange spears. As we approach beds for spring planting, we determine from the garden plan which beds need preparation and what crops will be planted there. We only work the beds that will be planted within a week or two to discourage native flora (some growers call them weeds, but they will herein be referred to as native flora) from taking over the bed. Attention must be made to never work soaked soil. If the soil structure is sandier, the soil will be more forgiving. However, if the soil is more clay-like, simply moving the earth around will create solid masses that become hardened clumps when dry and could remain that way for months.

Here is an example of the bed preparation process:

For a fifty-foot (15.2m) bed of Cascadia Snap Peas, we start by observing the condition of the garden bed. If the bed has straw organic matter, like the above example rapini bed, we will pass with a long-handled rake to gather up the straw and put it aside for the cultivars that benefit from straw mulch. If all has been in-bed composted over winter, like the former carrot bed, we continue on with the process.

With a long-handled four-tine cultivator, we pass the entire length and cultivate the bed. This will free up any large mats of native flora root systems that will impede the growing of the peas. All large root balls are removed and put in the hedgerows to compost or grow as they wish. All small native flora seedlings that were dislodged will be left on the bed surface. We continue by passing with a five-tine broad fork. Most instructions show demonstrations of people walking in the garden bed, pushing in the fork with their foot and walking backwards. I never understood the benefit of walking in a nice fluffy spring bed only to compact it. Walking in the paths and sticking the fork into the bed from the side yields less disturbance. The purpose is to create aeration in the garden bed to a depth of twelve inches (30cm) for the roots to find breathing room.

The broad fork step is optional. It is not at all necessary for small gardens, and up to the individual grower even in larger ones. After passing with the broad fork, we scoop up any loose dirt from the path with a spade-type shovel and place it onto the bed. The topsoil from the paths is very fertile, from compost that had fallen the previous garden season and our recent working of the beds. Because our soils are very acidic—our first soil test revealed a pH of 5.1—I dust four cups of wood ash (dolomitic lime can also be used) per fifty-foot bed, or 1.5 tablespoons per bed foot (2.5 square feet). After this, we rake the bed smooth, and it is ready for seeding. In the case of peas, a nitrogen-fixing, light-feeding cultivar, that's it. In the case of mesclun or lettuce mix, there is an additional final step before direct seeding: the addition of veganic compost.

Veganic Compost vs. Composted Animal Manure

The majority of bagged composted cow manure available at garden centers and nurseries comes from one of two places: the stanchions of stationary dairy cows or concentrated animal feeding operations (CAFO's), where cows raised for meat are finished before slaughter. Pelletized chicken manure comes from battery caged hens raised for their eggs. This is the vast majority of manures available and used by growers and farmers.

Dairy cows are fed a grass/hay feed mix. Feedlot—finished cows are fed a mix of corn, corn silage, and soy. The battery caged hens' feed is a highly processed soy-based, high protein (16-18%) feed. All manures commercially available are from conventional forms of animal agriculture. All alfalfa, corn, and soy fed to these animals is genetically modified. "Organic" and/or "free-range" animals deposit their manure in the pasture, no one is collecting and bagging it for sale.

After the animals are fed the grains, silage, and hay, manure is created through their digestive processes. Once collected, the cow manure needs to cure/compost for six to twelve months, because it is too toxic for use when fresh. Imagine planting a cucumber seedling directly in a fresh pile of cow dung. The dried chicken manure is a relatively new system, where large scale chicken warehouses are fitted with conveyor belts underneath the battery cages and the feces is transported to an industrial drying chamber, where it is flash-dried to retain high nitrogen content.

Large tracts of land (sometimes farms of one hundred thousand acres) of monocultures of corn and soy are plowed and planted. The alfalfa, corn, and soy are harvested by large tractor combines. Large backhoes, forklifts, loaders, and trucks are required for the transport of feed as most is not grown on farms where the animals are raised. More heavy machinery is required to move and turn the cow manure and large surface areas of land are necessary for the six-to-twelve-month compost process. When ready, plastic bags are filled and palleted to be distributed to garden centers, hardware stores, and nurseries around North America. Large storage sheds and warehouses are an imperative, independent of other stored consumer goods, as a single ripped manure bag will allow the smell to permeate the entire enclosed space. Because of the vast number of animals raised in the United States and Canada, there is an overabundance of manure.

A report I co-generated with the Economic Transition Team of the Humane Political Party, "Distribution of Animals Used for Agriculture and Manure Generated: Ratio of Manure to Land Application", found shocking results. Over nine billion animals raised in the United States produce 8.74 billion pounds (3.96 billion kilograms) of manure per day, or 3.19 trillion pounds (1.45 trillion kilograms) per year. All university cooperative extension experts give an annual recommendation as to how much manure can be deposited onto an acre of land and be considered safe. The United States produces enough manure in *just five days* to cover the entire continental United States land territory with this annual recommendation.[1]

The latest assessment of livestock manure production in Canada, from 2006, revealed that Canada's raised animals annually produced 198 million tons (180 million tons) or 403.2 billion pounds (182.9 billion kilograms) of manure. The problem of toxicity was concentrated in six provinces and geographical areas: central and southern Alberta, southwestern Ontario, southeastern Québec, southern Manitoba, southern British Columbia, and Prince Edward Island—where, in all regions, intensity eclipsed 21,700 lbs./acre (4,000 kg/hectare).[2]

Manure is toxic to use, as expressed by Ifeanyi, Ogbuewu, et al. in "Livestock waste and its Impact on the Environment:"

> Careless dumping of livestock waste on farmlands and direct discharge to waterways and percolation of groundwater, usually in by-pass flow via cracks and fissures, is a great risk to human and animal health because livestock waste contains myriads of pathogens, some of which may be zoonotic and can cause systemic or local infections. Highly contagious and pathogenic diseases, such as Foot and Mouth disease and Swine Fever may spread with animal effluent through waterways and, when one farm is infected with the disease, farms downstream will be at considerable risk for infection.[3]

Based on the two above assessments, it is not a reach to say that manure production and subsequent distribution is *careless*. It is polluting all nearby watercourses, and the source of the manure is animals enslaved—for the lack of a better word—and given highly modified feed.

Veganic compost is made up of five main sources: home kitchen vegetable waste (from most city collection bins), grass cuttings from regional parks, field grass (green or dry), dried leaves and/or chipped branch wood. Any combination of one-part dry (brown) matter and one- to two-parts green material, will make an effective compost. Some machines are necessary for cutting, gathering, and transport. However, all the ingredients are 100% sustainable, meaning they are always available. Trees and grass always grow. People always cook, leaves always fall. Veganic compost can be used in some capacity in as little as a month with no toxicity. Fully composted, it can be ready for use in three to six months and provides good nutrition for every fruit, vegetable, herb, bush, and tree. The means to develop it are also less time-consuming, non-toxic, and require no farmed animals.

(Yet Another) Innovative Regenerative Business Idea

The brown municipal collection bins for kitchen waste could consist of only plant-based sources. Grasses from city parks could be cut and incorporated. Dried leaves, which are collected every fall, could be utilized. Farmers could sell their grass and hay, not for animal feed, but for the compost process. Chipped branch wood could be corralled when tree trimmers trim around power lines, which is another annual occurrence. Because there would be no animal-based materials, the toxicity level is basically nil. Every town could have its own composting site. Every municipality already has all the equipment necessary for transporting materials and turning compost. Converting some of the space over to a veganic composting operation would provide all residents with cheap and easy access to a high-quality, non-toxic gardening product.

A well-known Québec farmer once said to me, when I was just getting started into veganic growing, that "it is not easy farming vegan". I would hope you agree that the procedure of generating, obtaining, and using manure is infinitely more complicated.

Continuing the process, once veganic compost is obtained, it is spread on the lettuce mix or mesclun bed at a rate of nine to twenty-four cubic feet per 125 square foot bed depending on the level of fertility prior (a standard size wheelbarrow is six cubic feet, so 1.5 to 4 wheelbarrows). The compost is raked smooth, and the seeds will be planted directly into the finished bed. The only cultures that I do not apply compost to are the above-mentioned peas, dry beans, and potatoes; the rest will receive a yearly application.

Preparing Beds for the First Time

But what if it's a first-year garden? How do you prepare those beds or patches for the first time? Don't worry, I have answers.

Site selection is one of the primary considerations for the gardens. Ideally, the area should receive at least six hours of full sun every day during the growing season. It is possible to grow certain fruits, vegetables, and herbs with less—specifically those that like colder temperatures—but most crops really wish to have six hours or more. The earlier in the day that the garden site starts receiving full sun, the better, as the heat will burn off the morning chill and dew faster, limiting fungal and bacterial pathogenic problems. Any site that is flat or with a slight south-sloping orientation is preferable. Because of the rotation of the earth, the south-sloping direction will receive the maximum amount of sunlight, warming up quickly. There are two schools of thought on which way to orient the garden beds.

The north-south direction is what we chose to incorporate at La Ferme de l'Aube. Our beds follow the contour of the land. Because we receive ample rainfall during the season, the majority of problems that we encounter result from the beds staying too wet, not too dry. Aligning the rows in this direction allows excess rainwater to run down the paths and get caught in the native green strips that flourish from the excess water. The east-west direction, which would run perpendicular to our southern slope, would be considered terracing. The benefit is also with rainfall, collected in the paths, where the water then gradually seeps into the planted beds. In areas where growing season rains are more infrequent, this is something to consider. Either direction is completely up to the individual grower, based on the realities of the specific region.

Whether small urban plots or larger scale garden areas, my preference when cultivating a new site is to lay five-eight mil (.001 inch per mil) black plastic sheeting, weighted down with rocks or sandbags on the edges. Leaving a solid black plastic cover for four weeks will compost all prior vegetative material, whether vegetable plant residues, cover crop, native land, or former grass-planted yards. The fast-working heating process warms the soil, suppresses seeds and regrowth from root systems, and gets biological activity moving.

Where we grow, we find that gopher snakes, field mice, earthworms, ground beetles, and spiders all like to make their homes underneath. After removing the plastic, the green matter is well composted (cooked) and the now-dry material can be removed with a long-handled rake, to be used as mulch or composted in the hedgerows. With the help of some twine (attached to stakes) and a measuring tape, the desired bed or plot is then delineated. Cultivate with a four-prong cultivator, remove large roots, broad fork (optional), scoop paths, then compost—and the beds are ready to plant. The plastic is movable, storable, durable, and can be procured at any hardware store and can even be located by the dumpsters, as building materials are wrapped in it. All tools mentioned can be located at any hardware store, the broad fork can be found online if sought. Like all other plastic products, maybe someday soon all will be made with recycled ocean plastic.

If the native root systems are very pervasive (like clover, couch grass, or sorrel) and your planting area is large enough, a small gas-powered tiller can be highly beneficial for initial cultivation. I have used a 5 hp Craftsman front-tine tiller for the duration of my gardening and farming life. My first one lasted twelve years and was still alive when I left the Arizona farm. My current one is on its seventh season and going strong. If using a rototiller, wait two days after removing the plastic to give all the little friends that have lived there time to relocate. To aid them, I usually fold up the plastic not too far away on the edge of one of the gardens where I do not wish the native flora to take over. They will seek it out and make residence. All those large root systems that come out with the tiller can be left to compost or regrow in a wild part of the backyard or farmyard.

If making raised beds is in your urban garden plan, I would recommend building them directly on native soil and still compost the native flora as demonstrated above. The compost will mix with that native earth and provide long-lasting nutrition. My preference in building materials for these raised beds is untreated wood. Depending on moisture in your specific region, the wood should last five-ten years. If it begins to deteriorate, a new frame can be built around the one that is decomposing. Raised beds can also be made with heavy duty recycled plastic decking materials. It is very expensive but could last ten years and more. It is completely up to the budget at hand. No matter whether they are raised beds or plots, small urban gardens in the backyard, community garden plots, or the one-acre rural farmyard, all growing spaces should be permanent. When allowing plant residues to compost in place and applying veganic compost in the spring, the beds will continue to build up. What was once a flat area can become up to twelve inches (30cm) high over time. This practice greatly increases growing area for all plants' root systems.

Averse to plastic mulch or tilling in the garden plot? In order for fruits, vegetables, and herbs to grow and thrive, native flora must be removed. With the aid of a spade shovel, the top layer can be cut out, revealing the native soil underneath. Expect some physical exertion. However, with diligence, the garden space will manifest and be ready for planting.

The veganic compost is the key, whether starting from scratch or transitioning a former garden to a plant-based one. My first year as a veganic grower, I planted directly into double dug or rototilled soil without composting and the results were paltry. Upon addition of veganic compost, the fertility rose the following year and the yields drastically improved. Because of its make-up, this type of compost is sometimes called "living mulch" in that it continues to compost in place. Even though it is considered "hot," it can be used directly. Since there are still pieces of chipped branch wood or filaments of dried grass still needing to breakdown, compost makes more compost.

A good source of veganic compost can be challenging to find, but it is becoming easier. Here in Québec, I have three sources that deliver or allow pick-up in small or large quantities. Contacting growing centers and nurseries that sell bulk soils will also reveal availability. Growers I have consulted in California, Texas, Manitoba, and Ontario have been able to find sources of either compost materials or already finished veganic compost without too much trouble.

Good observation is crucial. Survey the gardens before working the soil. When the snow disappears and the paths are clear, I begin to walk the fields and plunge my hand into the earth, feeling for moisture, feeling for the relative temperature of the layers. Even though there is a first seeding date set to plant, if the gardens are too wet, they are not ready. Nature ultimately dictates planting the gardens. Follow the flow, don't fight against it. The first plants to green in our garden green strips are the white clover, wild strawberries, and yarrow—telling us that the time for planting is close at hand.

First we pass the spring bed with a four-tine cultivator to bring up roots and native flora.

After which we pass with a five-tine broadfork to help aerate the soil down twelve inches.

6

The Major and Minor Elements

THE FOLLOWING INTRODUCTORY excerpt was captured from the June 2010 issue of *Annals of Botany*, "Plant nutrition for sustainable development and global health" by P.J. White and P.H. Brown: In addition to carbon (C), hydrogen (H) and oxygen (O)

> Plants require at least 14 mineral elements for their nutrition, these include the macronutrients nitrogen (N), phosphorus (P), potassium (K), calcium (Ca), magnesium (Mg) and sulfur (S) and the micronutrients chlorine (Cl), boron (B), iron (Fe), manganese (Mn), copper (Cu), zinc (Zn), nickel (Ni) and molybdenum (Mo). These are generally obtained from the soil. Crop production is often limited by low phyto-availability of essential mineral elements and/or the presence of excessive concentrations of potentially toxic mineral elements, such as sodium (Na), Cl, B, Fe, Mn, and aluminum (Al), in the soil solution.[1]

Just like in our own bodies, too much of one mineral or element in the gardens can be as detrimental as too little.

Major Elements

Carbon (C), hydrogen (H), and oxygen (O) are required by plants in large quantities. In addition, there are six major elements that all plants need: nitrogen (N), phosphorus (P), potassium (K), calcium (Ca), magnesium (Mg), and sulfur (S).

Carbon (C) as CO_2, or carbon dioxide, is vital for the plants' photosynthetic process. The plants effectively take carbon out of the air and assimilate the element into carbohydrates. Plant growth and development requires the uptake of soil nutrients by the roots; however, the concentration of nutrients in soil can vary and plants must adapt to the environment in order to fulfill their nutrient requirements. Sugars produced from photosynthesis are transported into roots where they can assist in regulating nutrient uptake via sugar sensing.[2]

Hydrogen (H) is the most widely distributed element in the world, making up more than 75% of the mass of the universe, and is also the most abundant element in the human body. Hydrogen also has an important regulation effect on plant physiological function. This element is involved in signal transduction pathways of plant hormones and can improve the resistance of plants to stressors such as drought, salinity, cold, and even heavy metals.[3]

Oxygen (O) is vital for respiration throughout the plant.[4] By effectively breathing in CO_2, or carbon dioxide, the plants will take in what they need and breathe out the rest. Through the process of photosynthesis, plants use the energy in sunlight to convert CO_2 and water (H_2O) to sugar and oxygen. The sugar is taken up by the plants as food and then they release oxygen into the atmosphere, which all animals (including humans) require to live.

Nitrogen (N) plays a critical role in the structure of chlorophyll, the primary light-harvesting compound of photosynthesis. It is considered to be the element that provides for the vegetative growth of the plant.[5] If you have ever witnessed gardens, grasslands, and forests on a sunny morning after a nighttime rain, the plants seem to vibrate in their verdancy. This can be the result of nitrogen-fixing molecules from the rain foliar feeding the vegetative growth of all plants. The nitrogen molecules also fix into the soil and the root systems assimilate it into a digestible element.

Phosphorus (P) is like the plant's immune system nutrient-builder, allowing all other elements, major and minor, to uptake through the root systems.[6] By default, it is phosphorus that helps to create an expansive root system network. Simply put, phosphorus is responsible for the storage and transfer of energy through the plant.

Potassium's (K) main role is for the production of flowers and fruits. As the plant reaches the flowering stage of maturity, potassium comes into action and sends the necessary information from the roots to the flower bud to form, open, and set fruit. Potassium does this by moving water, nutrients, and carbohydrates (energy) throughout the plant.[7]

N-P-K ratios are the most commonly seen numbers on boxes of fertilizers and bags of compost. For example, Down To Earth's organic Alfalfa Meal has an N-P-K ratio of 2.5-0.5-2.5, which means 2.5% nitrogen, 0.5% phosphorus, and 2.5% potassium by weight.

Calcium (Ca) is responsible for holding together and strengthening cell walls and membranes of plants. Calcium deficiency can be observed by dark black lesions on the blossom end of members of the *Solanaceae* family. Calcium also acts as a messenger to inform the plant of fertilization and biotic stresses, among others.[8] Simply stated, if there is a disease or insect attack or the plant is lacking in a nutriment, calcium sends out the alert signal.

Magnesium (Mg) is responsible for the element, nitrogen, to uptake into the plant. Without sufficient amounts of magnesium, there would be no nitrogen assimilated, and thus no synthesis of chlorophyll.[9] In short, without magnesium there would be no green in plants, no matter how much nitrogen exists in the air or soil.

Sulphur's (S) main functions are to aid in the formation of chlorophyll and production of plant proteins. Without sulfur, essential proteins (amino acids) including methionine cannot develop and would allow disease in, affect growth, and limit nutritional qualities in plants. It is an essential element in the protein building of our very important bean crops.[10]

Minor Elements

There are eight minor elements that all plants need: Chlorine (Cl), boron (B), iron (Fe), manganese (Mu), copper (Cu), zinc (Zn), nickel (Ni), and molybdenum (Mo).

Chlorine (Cl) functions in plant growth and development by osmotic and stomatal regulation, which is the movement of water through the plant. Chlorine aids in the evolution of oxygen in photosynthesis and helps to make the plant more tolerant and resistant to disease.[11]

Boron (B) is an essential micronutrient for optimum growth, development, and crop yield and quality, especially among all members of the *Amaranthaceae* and *Brassicaceae* families. Boron is primarily responsible for the size and shape of a cell, or cell wall synthesis and overall structure.[12]

Iron (Fe) plays vital roles in plants including respiration, the metabolizing of nutrients, transporting of oxygen, repairing and stabilizing DNA at the cellular level, as well as aiding in photosynthesis.[13]

Manganese (Mu) is an essential element for fulfilling two different functions, acting as an enzyme cofactor or as a metal with catalytic activity; meaning manganese is necessary for other enzymes or proteins to perform their biological activity (catalysts), accelerating chemical reactions within the plant.[14]

Copper (Cu) also functions as a cofactor. Copper plays an essential role in cell wall metabolism of proteins, signaling to the other nutrients where they are needed within the plant, specifically iron and the synthesis of molybdenum (Mo).[15]

Zinc (Zn), like manganese and copper, is an enzyme cofactor. Zinc plays a pivotal role in regulating the plants' response to biotic stressors, specifically insects and herbivores, and can aid in the movement of enzymes to aid in that response.[16]

Nickel (Ni) is an essential micronutrient in that it acts as an activator of the enzyme (protein) urease, which hydrolyzes the urea (two forms are found in plants) found in the seeds and plant tissues. The urease carries away excess elements out of the plants.[17]

Molybdenum (Mo) is another cofactor enzyme specifically used by the plant to participate in both reduction and oxidative reactions, which means that an ion, atom, or only certain atoms in a molecule will gain (reduction) or lose (oxidative) electrons.[18]

These are the seventeen elements that are required, to varying degrees, in all plants for them to grow, flower, fruit, and seed well. Just like in our own bodies, these elements—for they are all required by us as well to be healthy—come from the foods we eat. The food that the plants eat reside as minerals in the soil. They effectively "mine" the nutrients with their roots. As difficult as it may be to understand the functionality of all the elements in relation to plants, the easiest way to create the balance is by creating and maintaining the healthiest soil possible. This is what is referred to as soil fertility, but maybe would be better stated as soil health. For more reading information on all major and minor elements, I have cited a journal article for each in the bibliography of sources. There is a wealth of information, explaining more in-depth the function of each of the elements, as well as the plant's responses to deficiencies (too little) and toxicities (too much).

Chemical and water-soluble organic fertilizers, high in whichever elements, feed the plants, but do nothing for the soil's health and fertility. The plant will take what it needs, if anything, and the rest will be flushed away by rain and irrigation. Only applied composts or in-bed composting really do the job in soil-building. The compost interacts with the native and previously amended soils and fuse them together. Compost added every year gives the seedlings a sufficient nitrogen boost for their initial growth spurt. As the plant grows, especially as the root system expands, the complexity of the compost mixed with native soil can provide all the essential major and minor elements. The healthier the soil, the larger the root systems, the more elements can be sought and transferred throughout the plant. This is the underground world we don't see but can witness as it is reflected in the plants. If all the plants that we are cultivating are green, leafy, and produce flowers and fruits in abundance without disease, it is assured that they are receiving every element they require. Even if an individual plant does get attacked by a pathogen, insect, bird, or mammal the plant can heal itself, much the same as our bodies' immune system.

In Arizona, I used primarily an alfalfa hay residue goat manure and urea compost from goats I used for milk at the farm. The compost yielded very good results. If I did not produce enough, I procured it from an organic goat farm fifteen miles (twenty-four km) away. I did not know it then, but the alfalfa straw wastes (the parts the goats did not eat) had probably more to do with the fertility of the compost than the manure and urea, as the original distribution of weight was probably 10:1 in favor of the leftover alfalfa straw.

At La Ferme de l'Aube in Québec, we only use veganic compost in the fields with the yearly addition of wood ash, which alkalinizes the soil, because the soil pH started well below neutral (7.0). In addition, wood ash provides the macroelements calcium, magnesium, phosphorus, and potassium, as well as the microelements boron, copper, iron, manganese, molybdenum, nickel, and zinc.[19] Don't have a wood stove or a neighbor that does? Dolomite lime, which can be procured at any nursery, has some of the same elements—albeit in lesser quantities with the exception of calcium and magnesium, which are higher in concentration.

The plant-based compost also yields very good results. With the addition of in-bed composting, or decomposition of crop residues from the finished fruit, vegetable, and herb plants, as well as cover crops (both of which I used to a lesser degree in Arizona) it appears that this is all that is required for the gardens to thrive. As observed, they are healthy and vibrant from seedling to seed production.

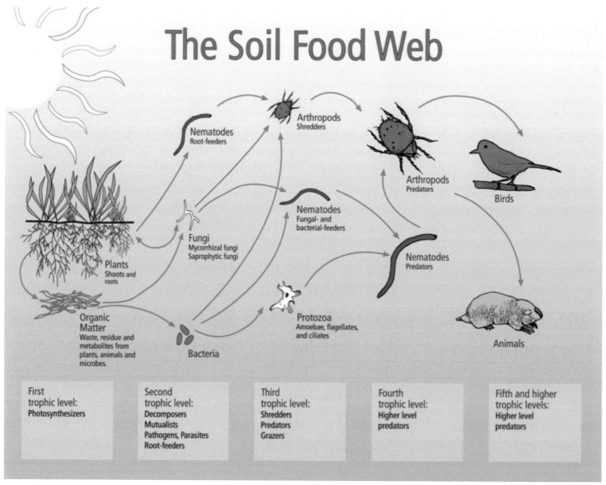

Soil food web courtesy of Dr. Elaine R. Ingham via USDA Natural Resources Conservation Service Soils

7

The Compost Piles

THERE IS SOMETHING miraculous about taking branches, dried stems, grasses, leaves, and kitchen wastes of cabbage leaves, coffee grounds, potato peelings, tomato pomace (and all other vegetable trimmings), adding some water and seeing all that turn into friable black gold. My personal composting adventure was not smooth, however. It has taken me a long time to realize that crumbly, sweet-smelling dream.

I have had varied success, mostly mere attempts at compost making. I remember the first compost bin I built, back in 1997 in northern Arizona. Based on the Storey Publication "Easy Composters You Can Build"[1], it was a cube bin with a 2-inch (5cm) x 4-inch (10cm) recycled lumber frame, stapled with one-half-inch hardware cloth. It was installed with hinges for opening and closing, with the additional benefit of ease of transporting it to another location. This rotted out in a few years. The second attempt was a three-bin system made out of cement blocks, where the older compost was flipped into the adjoining bin and then the new compost started. But other than the middle, I could never get it fully composted. In addition, I had a double-barrel rolling compost bin, purchased from a garden center. It was an expensive investment for more of the same result.

Traveling and working on small farms throughout Hawaii, north, central, and south America, compost piles became more haphazard. The best piles were simply heaped in an out-of-the-way place and turned every so often. Because of the heat, humidity, and rain in the tropical regions, the compost would cook and be usable within weeks. A spade shovel plunged into the middle would reveal rich, hot earth. The idea for the best method was revealed, using all reference materials and experiences—as always, a potent combination.

At La Ferme de l'Aube, our compost piles, of which we always have at least three active piles, are low-tech, highly productive systems. Here is the process:

In a somewhat sunny spot, an area should be cleared of all native flora to reveal bare earth. Directly on top of the soil, small twigs and woody stems are placed in a crisscrossing pattern. This will allow the pile to sit slightly off the ground to allow for airflow and small mammal travel. Alternating layers are placed, starting with nitrogenous green matter (wet): grass clippings, green garden plant residues, and kitchen waste. The more diversity the better. After which, a thin layer of native soil is sprinkled on. The soil brings in the microorganisms native to the environment to aid in the decomposition. On top, a layer of carbonous brown matter (dry): dried garden residues including their root systems, dry leaves, and straw. Again, the more diversity the better. Sometimes the root systems of the garden residues will have enough residual soil that the slight soil layer is not necessary. If possible, there should be a 2:1 ratio of green, wet, nitrogen material to brown, dry, carbon material. So, if six inches (15cm) of greens are placed there should be three inches (7.5cm) of browns. If it is less greens, it will still function. A 1:1 ratio has yielded good results, for it is the layering that is important. The brown carbon is layered between the green layers, and the hot action of the decomposing greens will break down the fibrous browns. The native soil will act as an activator with the microorganisms moving up, down, and throughout the pile.

If we wish to be more scientific about the process, we can create compost piles by using carbon-to-nitrogen ratios. The ideal C/N ratio for composting is generally considered to be around 30:1, or 30 parts carbon for each part nitrogen by weight. Why 30:1? At lower ratios, nitrogen will be supplied in excess and will be lost as ammonia gas, causing undesirable odors. Higher ratios mean that there is not sufficient nitrogen for optimal growth of the microbial populations, so the compost will remain relatively cool, and degradation will proceed at a slow rate. From our examples above dry leaves are, on average, 55:1, straw 70:1. Vegetable scraps are 17.5:1 and grass clippings are 20:1.[2] If we took one part of each for our compost, the mixed ratio would be roughly 40:1, very close to the ratio we seek. Eventually the finished product will have a C/N ration of 10-15:1. Once you have a width, length, and height to your liking—my preference is 5 feet wide x 6 feet long x 4 feet high (150 x 180 x 120cm)—with the help of a garden fork or shovel, create a crevice in the middle of the pile so it resembles a volcano. Pour five to ten gallons (twenty to forty liters) of water into the volcano spout. Then, and this is very important, cover with clear plastic. The plastic will block the rain from leaching out the nutrients, diminish the smell during primary decomposition, and trap heat and humidity, which will greatly expedite the vegetative breakdown. Then do nothing for one month. In the meantime, start a new pile.

After a month, remove the plastic and create another patch, starting again with crisscrossed stems and branches. Using a garden fork or spade shovel, turn the top of the pile onto the bottom and continue until you see the twigs again from that original pile. If the pile is too juicy and/or smelly, simply add some dry material as you go. If it is too dry and not hot, add some green material. If working

66

correctly, the middle of the pile should be quite warm with even some brown matter that has turned ashy. Like before, make a volcano, water, and cover. Each subsequent pile is turned onto the older pile, which will have an increased amount of biological activity from the aggressive microorganisms working them. Don't be surprised if there is usable dirt after only a month. If it has been made well, between the 2:1 and 1:1 ratios, the majority may be ready. After two months, all of the original pile should be ready for use in a typical warm, sunny summer. There should be three piles, sometimes four. The space we require is roughly 5 feet wide (1.5m) x 20 feet long (6m) for three piles. 25 feet long (7.6m) for four piles. The original compost heaps will decrease in width, length, and height by half or more. If space is a concern, the cubic dimensions are not set in stone; the key is the layering, ratios of greens to browns, and subsequent covering. Check out the line illustration at the end of this chapter for a visual perspective.

I screen some of the compost with the help of a one-quarter inch (1cm) hardware cloth-lined wooden box, to be stored and used for the potting up of the spring seedlings. The rest, I wheelbarrow to the gardens. Because it is considered "new compost," I let it sit on the garden bed for about seven days to let it fuse with the established soil. If I am planting a green manure or cover crop, I seed immediately.

The overwintering piles have the extra benefit of providing shelter for mice and mole families in our harsh climate. One early spring, I found a mama star-nosed mole with four babies suckling in the dark, warm environment. I lovingly relocated the family to the adjacent pile. Raccoon, skunk, and raven families sometimes frequent the compost when there is still very little wild food available. All garden and kitchen waste is recycled for the benefit of all species in the floral and faunal realms.

This may or may not be all the compost necessary for your purposes. If space is available, larger compost piles can be constructed. At a neighboring farm, for three summers I co-created a veganic compost of chipped branch wood (delivered for free by the town) and native grass hay from the farm's adjacent grasslands. That particular compost mound was 10 feet wide x 25 feet long x 8 feet high (3m x 7.6m x 2.4m) and was enough for two one-acre farms' entire seasonal compost needs.

Thinking back to some of our earlier examples of how forests function, specifically soil building and protection, branches and pieces of branches are a major soil additive. When the heavy late winter snows fall, or the harsh spring winds blow, older branches break off. During every year's seasonal cycles, they wither away slowly and decompose. Insects and microorganisms aid in the process, breaking down the fibrous lignin material until, after a few years, it has become forest floor earth. Composted chipped branch wood (CBW, defined as branches no more than three inches (7.5cm) in diameter) placed onto the garden beds yields the same results.[3] When using CBW, the same process of layering the browns and greens on bare earth is followed, as well as watering and covering, no matter the scale. Because of the fibrous nature of the chipped branches, the compost requires a longer period of time to decompose; however, a pile made in the early summer is usable the following spring. In places where there is more sun and less snowfall, it may be ready even sooner.

Human Waste

What about human waste? There are ideas for using both. Human poo, like animal poo, needs a long time to decompose enough to eliminate harmful bacteria (six to twelve months). Our dry toilet (outhouse) has a five-gallon (twenty liter) bucket that, when full, is emptied and layered with pine needles (for smell control) and dry leaves. Even though, when fully composted, I can pick it up and it smells fine, I have never been happy with the results. So, it stays in the forest edge where the native plants, animals, and insects will use it. For an exceptional resource, check out *The Humanure Handbook: A Guide to Composting Human Manure* by Joseph C. Jenkins[4] if you are interested in this 100% self-sustaining material.

Human pee is also 100% self-sustaining, solely determined by how much liquid one takes in. Human urea is a high source of nitrogen. Diluted 20:1, twenty parts water to one part pee, it makes an exceptional liquid fertilizer. I have used it in trials on overwintered garlic when their shoots pop out, and on bushes of blue and haskap berries with what seems like good results. I have even added it, though more concentrated, to the compost piles for a trial when I felt that they needed some high-nitrogen activation. Thinking of alternative ways of re-using a plentiful resource, rather than flushing it into rivers and oceans with potable drinking water, seems rational.

Composting should be considered as necessary as seeding, planting, and watering. Plant- based compost materials are readily available as greens and browns everywhere, all the time, and regenerative. Theoretically, the more diverse the plant materials in the compost, the more diverse the result. Furthermore, since plants are miners of necessary nutrients for optimal plant growth (as we learned in the previous chapter) then the decomposition of those plants should yield a compost that has all fourteen essential elements as well as carbon, hydrogen, and oxygen.

In June of 2017, I submitted a sample of our homemade veganic compost for a soil test analysis. The main ingredients were as outlined above, twigs and branches, garden plant residues, kitchen waste, grass clippings (a diverse indigenous mix), native soil, dry leaves, and dried vegetative materials from the gardens, plus wood ash from our winter wood burning. The N-P-K ratio was 0.9-0.4-5.96. Organic matter was at 22%. Carbon to nitrogen ratio (C:N) was 14.5:1. Potassium levels were high because of the added wood ash. There were high levels of calcium, magnesium and sulfur (the other major elements, or macro nutrients). Additionally, boron, copper, iron, manganese, and zinc (the minor elements, or micronutrients) were at high levels. Chlorine, molybdenum, and nickel were not tested for. This provides further ample evidence that a 100% plant-based homemade compost can yield essential nutrients in good supply and, because of the diversity of ingredients, could very well be superior to all other forms. For further studying, check out *Veganic Fertility: Growing Plants from Plants*, published by the Veganic Agriculture Network.[5]

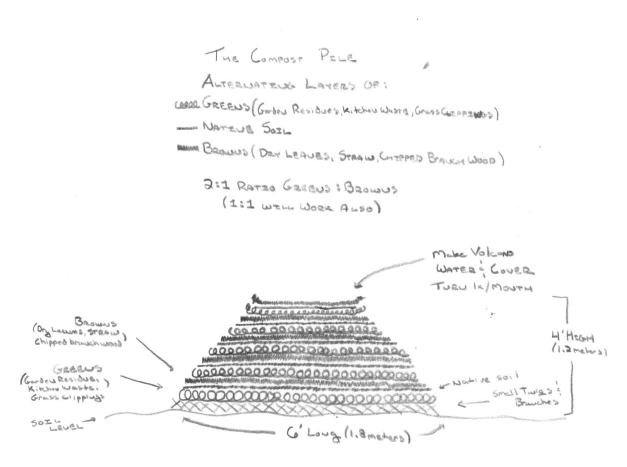

Drawing of compost pile by the author.

8

As Soon as the Soil can be Worked

THE GARDENS ARE open. The last patches of snow have melted away, and the lengthening days warm the rich beds. Garden sorrel, red clover, wild strawberries, and yarrow green up and expand their ground covers. Beetles forage while leaf hoppers dance among the foliage. Bird migration is in full swing, with the male's calls reverberating throughout the canyon forests. The green frogs and American toads bounce among the canopies. At night, the peepers chant, the woodcock males make their nasal *preen,* and the *chirplets* of the bats grace the diminishing light of the night sky. Gardeners' thoughts turn to the first sowings.

"As soon as the soil can be worked," refers to the time when the nights freeze or are quite cold, around 33-35F (1-2C), but the topsoil layer is open by at least twelve inches (30cm). The deep soil layers could still be frozen, but there is ample warm earth to seed and transplant the coldest, hardiest plants. The first seeds of arugula, carrots, green onions, greens (Asian and mustard), kale, lettuce, radishes, spinach, and snap and shelling peas can all be sown. All of these cold tolerant crops can be planted with night-time lows hovering around 32F (0C). By planting early, it gives the gardener a jumpstart on the season and extends the growing harvest season. The "as soon as the soil can be worked" date is earlier than the average last spring frost dates of a region, in some cases by five to six weeks.

Planting the Seeds

Seeding is quite simple. The garden bed or plot space is delineated at the proper distance and the seed is pressed into the soil. The smaller the seed, the less deep, with the general rule being to plant the seed two times its' diameter. Snap pea seeds will be deeper than rapini seeds, radish seeds deeper than lettuce seeds, and so forth. The delineation can be done by making small trenches of rows

70

by hand, with a ruler or tape measure, or with the help of one of my favorite tools: the bed preparation rake, sold by Johnny's Selected Seeds. Although not necessary, I find it extremely beneficial if there are multiple garden rows of seeded beds. The rake is 29 inches (74cm) wide with twenty 4-inch (10cm) teeth. Hard plastic tubes slide over the teeth and work as row markers, placed at precisely the distance desired for the variety to be seeded. As the rake is dragged across the bed, it creates small trenches that can be shallow or deep depending on the angle. Since it is basically the same width as our beds, it is the perfect tool. It also couples as a second rake for removing garden debris and smoothing the seeding surface.

Seeds can be deposited by hand or with the help of a seeder. Most large seeds like peas and radishes we will do by hand. My seeder preference for smaller seeds is the same hand seed sower that I use when seeding plug flats in the greenhouse; however, my partner and wife prefers to seed all seeds with her fingers. The hand seed sower is constructed of durable hard plastic, with a small dial that turns open and closed exhibiting different sized holes. It is held with the thumb and forefinger and tapped lightly to create a stream of flowing seeds directly into the trenches created. With practice, a patch or row can be seeded quickly and efficiently. Loose soil is lightly placed over the resting seeds and tamped lightly with the palm or flat portion of the rake. The seed bed is watered in thoroughly and kept as moist as possible until germination. There are more expensive models of seeders (like Glazer and Jang) that are used standing up, but soil beds need to be perfectly flat, rock and debris-free to work effectively. I know many growers and farmers that use them, but I cannot recommend or justify the expense. However, if you use one and it works for you, it is completely your prerogative.

Extending the Season

"Extending the season" is a phrase that market farmers employ when attempting to allow some crops to be planted earlier in the spring and survive later in the fall. It involves certain specific techniques to keep the plants and soils warmer than the outside air temperature. The main ones are greenhouses, caterpillar tunnels, and low tunnels.

The permanent greenhouse is not just functional for the growing of baby seedlings, but also for early and overwintering greens. Because of the way an unheated passive solar greenhouse traps heat, soils warm faster and open deeper than outside. If some space is dedicated for planting inside the greenhouse, the grower can benefit from an early crop. Where we grow, the first planting date is sometimes during the first week of May, depending on the year. Yet we can plant greens like arugula, lettuce mix, mustard greens, and spinach in the warm and open greenhouse beds the last week of March, five weeks earlier. We are eating salads before we ever have sown seeds in the fields. In addition, because we plant a late patch of kale and spinach in mid-September to be harvested throughout the fall, these crops regrow in late February and are ready when the fields are still resting dormant.

Caterpillar tunnels are six to ten foot (1.8-3m) tall moveable garden greenhouses, at whatever width and length desired, that also have the opportunity to extend the season. They can be moved and covered as soon as the rebar anchors have unfrozen, offering a two to four-week earlier planting. Here, we have two that are moved every year in the spring. Both are 14 feet wide x 50 feet long x 8 feet high (4.3 x 15.2 x 2.4m). They are bent aluminum hoops with rebar anchors. They are covered with the same clear plastic every year, going on their eighth season, and held in place with nylon cord and heavy-duty metal ground anchors. Each one has the flexibility of being opened on both sides to regulate temperature. Ours are primarily used for the planting of the *Solanaceae* family of cultivars: eggplants, ground cherries, peppers, and tomatoes. With our very humid nights and frequent summer rains, these crops perform better when we can somewhat regulate temperature and moisture.

My favorite designs are the metal kind, for long-lasting durability and structural integrity during high wind events. However, I have seen well-built ones made out of PVC plastic tubing that can be fashioned at a fraction of the cost, and to whatever dimensions are preferred. There are many different designs available on the internet. I would recommend one that has solid enough bracing to withstand the winds, can be opened on the sides, is tall enough to walk in (if covering multiple rows), and can be moved easily every year.

The low tunnel is by far and away the greatest innovation incorporated by the small grower and should be utilized by everyone. After the bed is seeded, five-foot (150cm) support hoops are pressed into the dirt on each side. They are separated seven to eight feet (2.1-2.4m) apart, the entire length of the row. They are then covered with a frost-protective Agribon-type 17 or 19 row cover or insect netting (screen), depending on the culture planted. The covers and nets are held in place by sandbags, rocks, or shoveled soil. For all greens, I use just the insect screen (similar to a mosquito net). It lets in rain and light at 90% transmission but keeps out or limits the activity of certain early spring insects (see chapter 13: Integrated Insect Management). The screen blocks the heavy early morning dews, as well as the harsh spring winds, allowing the bed to dry out more slowly and keeps the delicate early shoots from being battered by the gales.

A comparative survey I undertook in 2018 showed that an uncovered mustard green bed had spotty germination and insect holes in the leaves so profuse the greens were uneatable. The covered bed had some holes, but markedly less, and germination was nearly 100%. The plants went on to grow green and lush, while the uncovered bed quickly composted upon itself. My stepfather incorporates the insect screen on his frequent sowings of greens and radishes in the Bay Area of California, to guard humidity in the increasingly arid times and keep the overly curious ground squirrels at bay.

Frost protective Agribon-type 17 or 19 row covers can add an extra 2-5 degrees Fahrenheit (1-3 degrees Celsius) in temperature, so even if it is 32F (0C) outside it can still be 37F (3C) underneath. Light transmission is 80-90% depending on thickness. Like insect screens, they block the damaging winds, deter hungry insect species, and still let in rain, although less than insect netting. If the temperature forecast shows a plummeting nighttime low, I will simply put a row cover directly over the screened row of greens, then remove it when the sun pops out and the threat of freezing has passed. Incorporating the low tunnel (highly recommended), caterpillar tunnels, and a passive solar greenhouse (if space exists), will extend the season in which we can all eat from our gardens. There is another way that we can eat earlier, one that is even more effective than season extension: the planting of perennials.

Perennial Plantings

Veganic permaculture is an approach to growing that adopts principles observed in the natural world. It includes a set of designs that are derived using whole-system thinking to cultivate plants, wild animals, and people. From this method of understanding, one would incorporate permanent cultures (permaculture). Explaining this, I have never taken a permaculture study design course, nor am I an expert on the permaculture principles; if you are interested, Graham Burnett's *The Vegan Book of Permaculture*[1] gives a veganic perspective to these processes.

Like the early seeded greenhouse and over-wintered greens, biennial and perennial plants start offering their shoots and leaves as soon as the soil warms. The perennials that can be planted where you live need to survive the lowest winter temperatures. For this we have the United States and Canada plant hardiness zones.[2] There are thirteen distinct zones that are divided by 10-degree Fahrenheit (5.5 degrees Celsius) and two sub-zones (A & B) that are sub-divided by 5 degrees (2.75 degrees Celsius). La Ferme de l'Aube is in zone 4a, meaning that on average our lowest low temperature during the winter will be between -25 and -30F (-31.5 and -34.5C). Any perennial or biennial plant that is rated hardy to zone 4 and below can be planted and has a very good chance to come back the following year.

Here is a partial list of edible biennials and perennials that have grown back every year since we have planted them:

- Vegetables: Asparagus, dandelion, garlic, kale, bunching onions, and sorrel
- Herbs: Chives, comfrey, Greek oregano, lemon balm, marjoram (wild), mint, nettles, savory, and thyme
- Fruits: blackberries, blueberries, goji berries, grapes, raspberries, haskap (honeyberry), Saskatoon berries and strawberries

And there are many, many more flowering plants that we plant, could plant, or that grow wild that survive the harsh winter colds. The point is: the more space available, the more perennials should be planted, and wild ones left to cultivate themselves for the benefit of all beings. A list of more perennials hardy to zone 4, though by no means exhaustive, can be found in Annex D: Flower and Herb Chart.

Before many shoots or leaves form in the perennial patches, trim and cut out old dead growth and dried flower stalks. Using a pair of garden cutters and a rake, all dry material can be added to the compost pile or used directly as mulch. Before using a mulch, adding a nice layer of compost will give the growing shoots a nice burst of nutrients for their spring growth spurt. Every year, it is amazing to me to witness the insect activity abound, correlating exactly with the regrowth of wild and cultivated perennials and biennials. All life, as discovered, follows plant life.

Low tunnels installed with insect screens in foreground of winter squash and background of brassicas.

Pulling the bed preparation rake draws lines for the spacing desired, whether direct seeding or transplanting.

9

Irrigation and Rainwater Collection

WHERE WE LIVE, west of the St. Lawrence and north of the Ottawa rivers, we are blessed with ample precipitation throughout the year. The rainfall season that runs from March until November sees an average (over the last five years) of 29.5 inches (750mm). The snowfall from November until March averages 88.5 inches (220cm). There are months that are excessively dry, made up by months that are exceedingly wet. For example, in 2020, an extremely parched June yielded 1.75 inches (45mm) of rain at an inopportune time when all the garden beds had recently been planted and the seeds and small transplants required frequent watering. This was followed by an inordinately wet July giving 7.75 inches (197 mm). Where a simple average shows consistent rainfall month-to-month, year on year can be quite different—especially in these times of global climate change. Thus, now, this is the cycle of things here in Boileau, Québec, as it is everywhere.

We rely on the rain for watering the fields. Daily checks of the local online weather channel will reveal whether we will receive moisture or not. But what was once a given has become anything but, and a solid irrigation plan has become essential. Collecting the rainfall in the abundant times is highly beneficial, and increasingly necessary. In addition to keeping daily activity and observation logs, I also record daily high and low temperatures and precipitation amounts. I have done so every day since January 2015. Because we are so remote, weather forecasts are unreliable, and I can get a sense of the reality on the ground by tracking daily patterns. The more data and observations one records, the better their understanding.

As soon as the snow turns to rain, I install six 40-gallon (150L) barrels underneath four downspout locations on the barn and house. When it rains one third of an inch (10mm), I am able to collect more than 160 gallons (600L) of water. This is sufficient to water all the baby seedlings and first greenhouse plantings by hand.

When the nights stay above 23F (-5C) I attach three-quarter-inch tubing to on/off valves installed on the barrels. The water travels downhill to a hand-dug 40-foot x 50-foot x 6-foot (12m x 15m x 1.8m) pond which can hold 33,000 gallons (125,000L) of water. In good snow and rainfall years, the pond starts the growing season full. From the pond, a high-pressure Honda water pump capable of discharging 105 gallons (400L) per hour is used to irrigate the garden beds during droughts. Depending on the culture, we use either bobbler sprinklers or drip tape to irrigate. Either irrigation type can be helpful in the backyard or farmyard.

From "Rain Water Collection on a Small-Scale Veganic Farm," which can be found in its entirety in issue forty-five of *Growing Green International*, 2020, I wrote:

> "To collect rainwater is not only advantageous but, may very well be the least exploitative way of attaining water. No electricity needs to be used to collect and theoretically for watering. If you don't currently collect water for your irrigation purposes whether small plot or small farm, now is a good time to start. A simple system is very inexpensive to set up and the results are, well, a bounty."[1]

Irrigation

The bobbler sprinkler system acts like rain showers. Left on for a period of time it soaks the surface and penetrates deeper into the soil. For small seeds (like beets, carrots, greens, and turnips, for example) where multiple rows are planted, it is very effective. This system works well with circular, square, or rectangular plot plantings. One bobbler, supported by a stainless-steel shaft attached to a main-line tubing, can be placed in the middle of the garden patch to cover a ten-foot (3.3 meter) diameter circle.

The drip tape system is low water use and high efficiency. It is very much recommended for growing seasons that witness infrequent rainfall. It can be run off a water pump or house spigot, using any kind of water source. It can run on low-pressure systems as well. The initial system which includes tubing, emitters, drip tape connectors and drip tape is more labor intensive and expensive to set-up, but the benefits are apparent. Transplants that are planted 12-18 inches (30-45cm) apart in one to two rows would have the drip tape placed directly at the plant's base. The slits in the tape are cut every 6 to 12 inches (12-30cm) depending on preference and, when pressurized, the water begins to drip down. After thirty minutes at normal pressure (like an outside home spigot) the water penetrates down 18 inches (45cm) or more depending on the main soil type. Plants with deeper root systems are greatly enhanced by this irrigation practice.

Of course, the old-fashioned way of watering by hand with a watering can is always appropriate. Attaching a hose to the outside faucet with a spray nozzle mimics the same action of rain (and bobbler sprinklers). Putting the hose underneath a plant and letting the water trickle out has the same effect of the drip tape. So, if you have more time than money, use what fits within your individual budget. Depending on the garden's size, a proper system and/or method of irrigation are important points of reflection.

At one Québec farm I worked and consulted on in 2013, we used a surface well to pump groundwater into an above ground pool as the collection vessel and irrigated from there. There was no rainwater collection system on-site, even though there was a 16-foot x 30-foot (4.9m x 9.1m) barn. The barn was within yards of two 100-foot (30m) greenhouses that were used for seedling, early greens, annual tomatoes, and permanent raspberries. When I broached the subject, the manager just about laughed himself out of his chair. "This is Québec, there is water everywhere," he cried. As true as that is, weeks of drought that occur inappropriately cause real grower stress. The added security of water collection capabilities to mitigate the dry times ease the pressure on the well system and the gardener's mind. Obviously, every region, from the driest lands to the wettest parts of the world, can be vastly different month to month.

But how much to water? How often? When during the day? These are important questions, and here are the best answers I can give:

A seed requires constant moisture for germination, whether in plug trays or in the field. Every day that the seed gets too dry, the greater amount of time is required for her to germinate. Every day the germination time is extended, the greater the probability of decreased germination percentages and seed rot possibilities. The best way to germinate seeds in the garden beds is to water immediately after planting and at the end of every day until sprouting. The moisture will rest all night. Even if the next day is sunny the earth should still be wet below the surface at seed level. The amount of water required to soak one bed foot (2.5 square feet) of a freshly seeded patch is approximately 0.29 gallons (1.1 liters) if watering with a watering can; this assumes a well-composted plot. As the seed germinates the less water is necessary like inside grown seedlings. If I am unsure, I dig my finger next to the small shoot. If it is still wet to the third knuckle of my index finger, I leave it alone. If dry, I water. Clay and peat soils will be the most water retentive, silt soils will hold more moisture than sand, which will require more consistent irrigation.

For larger plants, when it has been completely dry and the temperature is over 77F (25C), I water every three to five days when they are still actively growing, and about once a week when plants are fruiting. Depending on the garden beds the varieties are planted in, the soil type here could be silt loam or clay loam with some peaty soils mixed in. Plants' root systems are twice as wide as the plant is tall. A zucchini bush two-foot (60cm) in diameter should have a root system four-foot (120cm) in diameter. There will even be root tentacles reaching further and deeper. Don't be worried about keeping the plants too dry, the roots will find moisture. Always keep in mind that plants assimilate nutrients from the soil best when there is minimal moisture.

Although I am by no means an expert on small fruits, what I have observed is that berry bushes and vines produce much more prolifically when they have sufficient water during flower and fruit set. In 2021, perennial haskap berries (our personal favorite) yields increased dramatically from the year prior with the installation of a drip-tape irrigation system. In both 2020 and 2021, the twelve bushes flowered profusely. But the dry weather in May 2020 left the flowers to dry out and the harvest was negligible. By contrast, with a watering method installed, 2021 saw a harvest of fourteen pounds (6.35 kg). The harvest was even more abundant than recorded, for the cedar waxwings had a buffet of the remaining blue gems every morning for a week thereafter.

"How much water should I give dry soil, if watering by hand?" For an established determinate tomato plant, I will pass five times with a watering can. I will water, let it percolate down, and repeat. Each plant will receive about 1.5 gallons (5L) of water once per week. If using two lines of drip tape, slit at 6 inches (15cm), on a 50-foot (15.25m) bed that harbors 70 tomato plants, I will let the water run for 1.5 hours. The tape is emitting a rate of 0.15 gal./hr. (.61L). Drip tape is by far less time consuming and more efficient than the watering can technique.

At my Arizona farm, the entire one-acre operation was on drip tape. The soil type there was sandstone sand that drained rapidly. I would be lucky to receive five inches (125mm) of rain during the entire growing season that spanned from mid-April to late October. Almost all of it would fall between August and October, when plants were already well established. Watering was on a timer, with every garden bed watering for two hours every morning and one hour every afternoon. The abundant sunshine and summer temperatures frequently reaching 100F (37.5C) dictated the watering schedule. I always wanted to create a water collection system for those dry periods, it just never materialized.

When to water is as important as how much. For small seeds that do not mind colder nights, I will water at night, where the moisture will hold in the soil well into the next day even on the hottest days. For established plants and those seedlings that do not like cold nights, watering after the sun has come out is preferable. The heat of the day will dry out the leaves and stems if watering with a sprinkler system or a watering can that causes splash. If the drought has set in, with no rain in the two-week forecast and nights are over 60F (15.5C), I will exclusively water at night when it is needed.

Nutrient Density of Fruits, Vegetables and Herbs Related to Nutrient Uptake

As the leaves, roots, flowers, and fruits start reaching a harvestable stage, I will greatly limit watering. Too much moisture at this stage causes rots, but also makes all fruits and vegetables taste watery. A tasteless tomato may be a factor of watering when the fruit is blushing. A melon will be unsweet if irrigated when ripening. Lettuce will lose its crispness. Mustard greens will lose their bite. All varieties of fruits, vegetables, and herbs must go through dry times to reach their full flavor potential, especially at the harvest stage. It appears from my observations they may even become more nutrient-dense. I have noticed the difference between the flavor and crispness of a head of lettuce when it has reached maturity during a time of drought versus harvested after a rain. Our customers have noticed a fuller flavor and longer storage life in the refrigerator as well, some claiming they remain in the exact same condition more than two weeks later.

We know that too much moisture in the soil will limit nutrient uptake. We also know that if soils are too dry, the plant will have problems obtaining the nutrients it needs. From Chapter 6: The Major and Minor Elements, we learned that the elements phosphorus, potassium, sulfur, boron, copper, and iron are responsible for moving water and nutrients throughout the roots and vascular body of the plant. The plant's vascular system is similar to animals' nervous systems that transmit information from one body part to another. It would hold that as plants develop, they would communicate their nutrient needs from their roots throughout the plant body.[2] So, what is the effect of soil moisture on plant growth and development on lettuce and tomatoes, for example? Do they become more nutrient-dense when they have higher nutrient uptake, which is best achieved at lower soil moisture levels?

An established lettuce plant, like all other plants, will have a root system that is twice the diameter of the main body. So, if it is one-foot (30cm) wide and tall, it will have at least a two-foot (60cm) wide and deep root system. As the upper layers of soil dry out, the roots will push farther and further searching for the nutrients the plant needs for that specific stage of development. If the lettuce is lush and full, then it is likely that it has assimilated all seventeen elements required for growth. The wetter the conditions in early-stage development, the more stunted the plant. Too much water at the later stages and the head can rot. Only at the correct moisture range will the lettuce thrive.

An established indeterminate tomato plant requires ample water during the initial growth spurt. It wishes to be tall, with good leaf cover to protect the fruits from direct sun which can cause damage. When the plants set their fruit and begin to blush, too much watering will cause them to crack and taste waterlogged. Limiting the water to the plant in fruiting development yields a true to type flavor and higher nutrient yields.

This idea is corroborated by a 2017 study of experts from the Pharmacy Faculty and the Higher Technical School of Agricultural Engineering (Escuela Técnica Superior de Ingeniería Agronómica—ETSIA) of the University of Seville. They published a study that shows that when reducing the water used to water cherry tomato crops by more than 50%, the product not only maintains its quality, both commercially and nutritionally, but it also even increases the level of carotenoids, which is the pigment that gives fruits and vegetables their color.[3,4] While scientific evidence in this regard is lacking, truth on the ground has proven to me that less water can yield tastier results, which in the end is exactly what we are looking for.

Rain-water fed, hand-dug pond uphill from the gardens douples as a cooling off spot with a fruit popsicle on those blistering summer days.

10

The Planting Rush of the Tender Annuals

THE AVERAGE LAST frost date (see Annex C for a North American city close to you) has passed and the nights are staying consistently above 50F (10C). The planting rush begins. It is time to get in all the tender annuals. Because of the long maturity times of some crops like dry beans (90-105 days), red bell peppers (75-90 days), sweet corn (75-90 days), some heirloom tomatoes (80-90 days), and winter squash (90-110 days), it is imperative to get these transplants and seeds planted as soon as the nights turn warm. For it is the nighttime temperatures that we are most concerned about when considering tender annuals. Cold nighttime soils stay humid longer, the more humid the less nutrient uptake can occur. The longer the plants' roots feel cold and damp, the less vigorous they will grow. They can remain stunted, and disease possibilities are higher. But as important as the last frost date is, so is the warm and settled date.

Warm & Settled Date

Here in Boileau, our average last frost date is May 25. But because of the former glacial valley we are settled in, we live in a cold micro-climate. Micro-climate can be defined as the variability of change based on environmental factors like mountains, valleys, tree-lined wind breaks, lakes, and rivers. For us, the colder climate most likely occurs due to the large north-facing hill at the bottom of our south-sloping gardens. It is not uncommon for us to receive a slight freeze of 31F (-1C) the first week of June. In 2019 and 2020, we actually had 30F (-2C) freezes on the 21st of June and the 15th of June respectively, which made planting tender annuals challenging at best. Hardy crops (beets, *brassicas*, carrots, greens, lettuces, onions, and potatoes) seem to take the shock well, but the tender annuals will die back. Regrowth normally occurs, but this can set back the harvest by two to three weeks—if it even comes in at all.

Old-time gardeners I have met at my two established farms over the years, have very firm opinions of when to plant:

"I don't plant nothin' until after Memorial Day."

"After the first full moon in June."

"After the first new moon in June."

"Not until the 15th of June, never earlier!"

All of these statements have one thing in common regardless of region: they are describing the warm & settled date, which is roughly three weeks after the average last frost date. So, you may ask, if my average frost date is also May 25, do I need to wait until mid-June to plant?

All tender annuals can be safely planted earlier by incorporating season-extending techniques that were discussed in chapter eight. Putting wire hoops and frost-protective row covers on eggplants, peppers, and tomatoes at night will keep them a few degrees warmer when the nighttime lows get dangerously close to freezing. For all *Cucurbitaceae* family (cucumbers, melons, and summer and winter squash cultivars) we install hoops and row covers immediately after transplanting. Leaving them on until profuse flower set will not only protect these heat-loving crops from the coldest nights but will create heat traps, causing more vigorous vegetative growth. They will keep the soil more humid, block the battering late spring winds, and confuse insects that seek to munch on the tender shoots. We have saved many plants by draping row covers over them, sometimes even at four in the morning (the coldest times) when the cold air descended unexpectedly. Keeping them close at hand until the region-specific warm and settled date will give the gardener an extra tool in these times of ever-challenging climatic change.

Transplanting

The process of planting transplants is rather simple. With garden preparation, rake or tape measure mark out the distances for each culture. For example: broccoli should be planted sixteen inches (40cm) apart, while heirloom tomatoes want eighteen inches (45cm). The two annexes, Annex A: Crop Profiles and Annex B: Crop Spacing and Yields, detail all the required spacing information.

All transplants should be well-watered before commencing transplanting. Broccoli seedlings are transplanted directly from the fifty-cell flats. The seedlings are popped out of the tray with a kitchen fork, and a small hole is created in the soil with the index and middle fingers measuring the entire length and diameter of the soil block. The small root ball is then set in, ensuring that the base of the plant remains at soil level. Soil is lightly pressed around the seedling, filling all air pockets. When all are planted, they are thoroughly watered.

Tomatoes are transplanted out from a three- to four-inch (7.5-10cm) pot. The pot is lightly squeezed to free up the smaller roots that have clung to the inside. The plant is either gently pulled out of its pot by hand, or the transplant is turned upside down and cupped, pulling the pot away simultaneously. It is wise practice, when pulling the plant, to do so from the leaves as opposed to the stem; for if a leaf tears it is minor, where a stem injury can be fatal. With a hand trowel, a hole deeper and wider than the root ball is created. Tomato stems will create roots, which is why they look somewhat fuzzy or hairy. To help stabilize the rather large and vining heirloom tomato plants, I recommend planting the tomato plant up to the first true leaves. Those fuzzy hairs will readily enlarge and root-in. As with the broccoli seedlings, soil is pressed lightly around the plant and watered in thoroughly when the tomato patch is planted. For both these two examples, we will give a seaweed or kelp-based liquid fertilizer (preferred brand is Bionix) watering at initial transplanting. Kelp is an excellent source of natural phytohormones and macro and micronutrients. It is not necessary, but this fertilizer can help with the transplant shock caused by disturbing the root system.

All transplants, whether from cell blocks or larger pots, want to be planted before the plants begin to turn color. You will notice a difference if a seedling is in its pot too long. The green sheen of the baby plant begins to dull in color and the dicotyledons yellow. Upon removal of the seedlings, the roots will be tightly wrapped around the ball of earth, also known as "root-bound." It is far better to transplant when the roots just begin to show out of the bottom of the cell and/or pot. When set into the garden plot at this stage, they will continue to push out their root systems with the least amount of disturbance.

Companionship Planting

Whether to plant in rows, blocks, or interspersed is completely up to the individual grower. There is historic context for the benefits of all as long as a high level of diversity is maintained. I have always found planting in blocks or rows to be more efficient in terms of maintenance and harvesting than an interspersed system. Additionally, I have found that yields are higher from all plants receiving as much full sun as possible in a well-designed garden. Saying all that, it is possible to position any other plant to another, as long as the distances each variety wishes is kept in place. For example, broccoli wants to be planted sixteen inches (40cm) apart. Large cabbage wants to be planted eighteen inches (45cm) apart. The two can be eighteen inches apart from each other in an interspersed planting system. For another example, peppers wish to be twelve inches (30cm) apart as do cherry tomatoes. In effect, they can be planted twelve inches apart from each other. Interspersed planted gardens have the possibility of beautiful geometric designs like circles and spirals. I would also try to keep in mind that it is best to keep taller plants to the north and/or west to not block the sun of the shorter varieties whenever possible.

Personally, I like the row and/or block system. Like the garden plan map illustrated from chapter two, where there are two feet (60cm) of carrots, followed by two feet of lettuce, then two feet of beans and finally two feet of cherry tomatoes in an eight-foot (2.4m) bed. The harvest will be much better and easier than if the beans are planted under the tomatoes or the carrots are planted under the lettuce. For further imagery, let's think about the following examples:

First, basil being planted under tomatoes. Tomatoes can be planted after last frost, even if the nights dip below 50F (10C). Basil, ideally, wants to experience temperatures no lower than 55F (13C). By the time basil is to be planted, the tomatoes have already grown for two to three weeks. The basil will be growing in part shade under the fast-growing tomato canopy and is likely to be stunted. Pathogens like *Peronospora belbahrii*, which causes downy mildew, can be more prevalent. If planted in blocks, however, with the tomatoes planted to the north, both crops will receive full sun and have all the space they need to flourish.

Another example is mesclun mix, a combination of lettuces and mustard greens. The seeds are sometimes sold together by seed companies as a blend. The mustard greens are faster to baby stage (21-24) days, with the lettuces about one week later (28-30 days). Lettuces are also slower to germinate by one to three days. The mustards will sprout earlier, grow taller, and push root systems deeper than the lettuces. I have always found when planting them interspersed that the mustard greens grow quite lush, but the lettuces make a dismal showing. Like basil and tomatoes, they both prefer full sun. The taller mustard greens provide damp and humid conditions, causing a higher prevalence of damping off caused by *fusarium spp.* (and others) in the lettuce seedlings. A far better way to plant mesclun is in blocks. Planting two bed feet (60cm) of mixed lettuces the first week and then one-week later planting one-foot (30cm) of arugula, one-foot of Ruby Streaks mustard greens, and one-foot of Red Russian kale is a good option. They will all reach the baby stage at the same time, making a perfect-sized mix.

Three Sisters: Exploring an Iroquois Garden by Marcia Eames-Sheavly[1]

The Three Sisters system refers to the planting of corn, pole beans, and squash or pumpkins together in hills. The practice of planting more than one type of crop together is called interplanting. Although this planting system is not common in the United States today, it is in fact a well-thought-out growing method that is used extensively in other countries such as Mexico. Interplanting is coming back into favor for some crops because farmers are finding that large plantings of one crop can have some major disadvantages.

> In the Three Sisters planting system, raised areas are made about three feet apart, both within and between rows. Several seeds of corn are planted in small holes and covered. As the emerging corn plants are weeded, the soil is gently mounded, or hilled, around the corn plants. When the corn is about four to six inches high, bean and squash seeds are planted in the

hills. Bean seeds are placed in each hill, and squash is planted in about every seventh hill. The three crops grow together for the remainder of the season.

The planting of corn, beans, and squash has been more than a gardening activity for the Iroquois. The Three Sisters system also has provided a varied diet, keeping the people healthy for hundreds of years. Customs, stories, myths, and legends have surrounded the agriculture of the Iroquois. Many customs have been carried on as a means of respecting and honoring the plants that have given life to the Iroquois culture. In short, the Three Sisters system has helped support a culture whose people have used the land without destroying it.[1]

There are other interspersed plantings that are highly beneficial. Planting a nitrogen-fixing legume crop under *Brassicaceae* and sweet corn strains, after those plants have grown up with established root systems, works very well. The legume crop like clover, especially one that likes shade, will fix nitrogen in the soil for the other plants' root systems to find and assimilate. There will be more on this idea in Chapter 12: Fertilization (Long and Short Term) as well as in Annex A: Crop Profiles. Flowering plants, planted in an interspersed or interplanted, diverse way, are highly suited for companionship, and develops vibrant ecosystems for all beings to share.

Planting for all Beings

As veganic growers, we are planting not solely for human consumption, but for all other beings as well. The allocation of space for flowering plants and shrubs in addition to fruits, vegetables, and herbs will help to diversify the garden plot. The more diversity the better, and the fewer problems with the different cultures. Insects, amphibians, reptiles, avian, and small mammals are omnivorous creatures. While we as humans can choose to be vegan, which our anatomical and physiological make-ups wish we were[2], all other beings are who they are. Even though some creatures' diets can be varied, if they require small animal or insect protein for example, they have no choice but to consume it. This is nature and how she functions. By incorporating a diverse and layered planting complex into the gardens of both annual and perennials, we will attract the maximum amount of garden creatures. (See Annex D: Flower and Herb Chart for some of my favorites to diversify the garden space.)

All species of the above-mentioned families of garden friends have specific purposes and niches they wish to inhabit. All of them, in some way or another, are beneficial to the garden system. Bees, flies, wasps, butterflies, and moths are associated with pollination. The more flowering plants that are pollinated, the more go to seed, creating greater abundance in the future. Ants corral aphids and aphids provide the sweet juice they ingest. Relationships are reciprocal.

Frogs, toads, and spiders manage beetle and other insect populations when they become abundant. Birds fly through and consume earthworms, caterpillars, and grasshoppers. All beings play a part and make up the natural balance that has existed on earth since the dawn of time. As gardeners, growers, and small farmers we must embrace this natural heaven and plant accordingly, changing our collective speciesist thoughts in doing so.

Just like us, all natural beings feel the rush of the short growing season. They find the spots they prefer, make their nests, feed themselves, and find nourishment for their babies. They are compelled to collect pollen and nectar. They must fatten up for the long journey southward. They glean the last fall seeds and cache them for the long brutal winters. They require (and often must create) burrows deep enough to be warm during long periods of hibernation. There is a whole world among us, one that we can understand if we simply observe nature during the seasons as we grow.

Bulbing onions in the foreground and garlic in the background rooted in and growing after the warm and settled date has passed.

11

Maintenance of Cultures

A S THE BABY seedlings grow, all cultures require different amounts of attention and maintenance. Some plants are fussy when small, requiring extra special care, while others are more independent and robust. When the plants are beginning to root-in and establish themselves, it is very important to keep the area around them free of native flora. Native plants are quite vigorous as they have adapted and evolved to the regional conditions they inhabit. Plants like amaranth, clover, couch grass, dandelion, plantain, purslane, sorrel, vetch, and yarrow have expansive root systems. They are also nutrient miners, reaching deep into the soil to seek out nutrients. If these plants are left to establish in the garden beds, where we wish to grow fruits, vegetables, and herbs, they will strangle and suffocate the newly-planted transplants and emerging seeds.

The Zen of Weeding

Most gardeners have had a similar reaction to the prospect of tearing out weeds as my wife's grandmother. When told that we were starting a small veganic farm, her first comment was *"Maudite chiendent!"* in her thick Québec accent. Politely translated, it would mean cursed couch grass! We approach the act of weeding as tireless, unforgiving, and never-ending work, as we struggle to keep the gardens clear of native flora.

I am going to offer a different perspective on weeding. Firstly, as you have noticed already, they are not to be known as "weeds", they are native flora. For the most part, they were here first; our cultivars are the infiltrators, and we are the invaders to their native landscape. Trying to eradicate the native flora is futile, they will always eventually out-compete and win over the terrain. Couch grass, for example, has a vast root system. New plants emerge from the rhizomes (root systems). It is not uncommon, when pulling out an emergent grass shoot, that the root system travels three feet (one meter) away, making more shoots along the way. When we till or hoe, it cuts the roots into little pieces, all of which become more baby native plants. What we will attempt to do is relocate them (and all other native flora) away from the garden plot.

How is this Zen?

It is in the approach followed by our actions. Zen weeding is about meditation, breathing, intuition, and observing the moment. Zen way can be applied to any task, no matter what wishes to be accomplished. Before commencing, we take a deep breath as we observe the garden bed. We look at the task before us not as a challenge, but as a momentary process. We crouch down into a comfortable position and observe from ground level, all the while focusing on our breathing. With the intention of wishing to give breathing room to the varieties planted, we let all other thoughts go. Our concentration lies only in the moment as we begin.

My favorite tool is the Japanese hand hoe, available from Johnny's Selected Seeds. Working away from us, we glide the sharp blade through the soil, intending on bringing up entire root systems of the plants. By digging deeper than the native flora, the hoe delicately brings up the entire root ball, which is then set aside. Upon completion of the garden bed, all of them are transported into the green strips or edge rows where they can re-establish. By doing as little harm as possible, even to that *"maudite chiendent,"* we are living in as much balance and harmony as we can, being growers, with the plant world.

The most productive gardens, whether organic or veganic, permaculture or row cropping, are the ones where the native flora has been removed when the seedlings are small. Permaculture suffers—from my observational and working experiences in Costa Rica, Ecuador, Hawaii, and Panama—because the native flora suffocates the plants attempting to be grown for our eating. In some cases, the edible plantings cannot even be located. Not to say that veganic permaculture cannot be productive. I believe with the right combination of plantings, and at least some developed pathways for ease of harvest, it can be highly productive due to its whole-system approach.

Sure, hours of crouching can be difficult on the back, but the philosophy of looking at weeding not as a chore, but as a beneficial task, will at least put us in a better state of mind. When and if possible, work in teams of at least two. There is a sense of satisfaction when a bed or patch has seen the native flora removed, leaving only the culture we wish to flourish. It can be an invigorating experience. We, at La Ferme de l'Aube, weed native flora before planting and then return two weeks later to observe the state of things. On average, we weed every garden bed (a total of 160) once per month for four months. Personally, I have spent thousands of hours of my growing and farming life developing the best possible techniques and yogic positions for this task. Some farmers like standing stirrup or spade hoes—and they can be useful, having the extra benefit of being less rough on the back. But for me, there is something about seeing the gardens at ground level that brings our whole existence into clear focus. Whichever tool you incorporate, it is important to work weeding into your gardening routine, not as an afterthought, but in the moment. Breathe in, breathe out, repeat.

Insect Screens and Row Covers

In the last two chapters, I have touched upon the value of screens and covers in our plantings. They are of high value because of their abilities to guard moisture, block wind, deter insect pressures, and protect from frost. Below is a list of the crops that benefit from these two materials.

Crops that greatly benefit from insect screens are: Arugula, Asian greens, bok choy, broccoli, brussels sprouts, cabbage, cauliflower, kale, kohlrabi, mesclun mixes, mustard greens, radishes, spinach, and turnips.

Crops that greatly benefit from row covers are: cucumbers, melons, summer squash, watermelons, and winter squash.

In the early season, just after seeding the earliest bush beans and transplanting eggplants, ground cherries, peppers, and tomatoes, we put wire hoops on the rows immediately. When the nights unexpectedly dip to close to freezing, which they historically have, I will drape the covers over when the sun goes down. Labor-intensive for sure, but it allows the grower the opportunity to get the plants growing, flowering, and fruiting faster. For *Brassicaceae* family varieties, the insect screen is left on for their entire growing period. Because of the very damaging cabbage worm, (more about all integrated insect management in chapter thirteen) it was the only way we could harvest full heads of some of these varieties. Since the insect screen has the added benefit of stretching, the plants' growth is not hindered by being underneath.

Staking

When the warm days and, more importantly, nights have become more permanent (the warm and settled date) and the threat of frost has passed, the matter of staking begins. Peas, which are very cold hardy, are staked when the first tendrils begin to search for something to latch onto. My preferred materials for staking are 1-inch x 2-inch x 6-foot (2.5cm x 5cm x 1.8m) wooden stakes. They are inexpensive, completely compostable when they rot, and small pieces can be used for kindling, further being recycled as wood ash, and put back into the gardens. They are placed every eight feet (2.4m) and pounded into the ground eighteen to twenty-four inches (45-60cm) to support the eventual heavy vines. I tie sisal or hemp twine to the end and pull it taught between the stakes. Depending on the height of the peas, there may be eight to ten lines of twine for the vines to climb.

The same system is used for climbing beans. Each individual tomato plant is staked with the same stake dimensions, with only the height changing. A determinate tomato plant can use a 4-foot (1.2m) stake, a semi-determinate 6-foot (1.8m), while an indeterminate plant requires the full 8 feet (2.4m). In Annex A: The Crop Profiles, you'll find maintenance advice for each crop detailed. The tomato plants, as they grow, are tied with strips of any old cotton t-shirt. The shirt is cut into 1-inch wide (2.5cm) x roughly 12-inch long (30cm) strips and loosely ties the stem of the plant to the stake for support. The fiber does not mar the stem and is forgiving when the plant later increases in girth. When the stakes are removed at the end of the season, the cotton sometimes ends up in the soil—but it all eventually composts.

Mulching

I am a huge fan of dry mulching, whether using dried garden plant material, hay or dry straw. The addition of mulch keeps the humidity up and native flora regrowth low. The straw mulch will also keep fruits of vining and bushy plants from rotting, when touching wet earth. The crops that benefit greatly are the *Cucurbitaceae* family varieties and ground cherries, which are harvested after their fruits have fallen from the plant. In some years, we have straw-mulched potatoes to good results, as well as eggplants, peppers, and tomatoes. After the plants and vines have died from the first frost, the straw remains as a protective layer over the soil. A point of caution for dry mulch: as much as it can be an insulating layer, it also has the effect of trapping the cold ground temperatures. If the straw is placed when soils are still cold (this can be gauged by sticking one's hands deep in the soil) the soil at those levels will never warm up. Here in Boileau, Québec, we wait for dry mulching until two to three weeks after the warm and settled date, just as the vining *Cucurbitaceae* are starting to run. In addition, we like to mulch garlic that is planted in the fall. It provides an insulating layer before the snow creates her own and keeps humidity in the sometimes very dry springs. It is always amazing to me that, the following year, there is very little straw left in the beds. Yet if there is, we rake it up and use it on that year's cultures. Just like the wooden stakes and twine, we re-use as much as possible until it simply becomes composted earth, returning to the source.

On the Fence about Fencing?

Are animals getting into your garden patch that covers and screens are not protecting? Maybe a fence is necessary.

In their book *Living the Good Life*, Helen and Scott Nearing[1], who lived in Vermont, discuss how their neighbors were having their late harvest eaten by deer. It was so damaging to the crops and their collective psyches that they had thrown in the towel and stopped trying to grow anything. After a wildly unsuccessful first growing season here in 2015, the late summer took a turn and saw forty to fifty plants of broccoli, cabbage, and kale looking quite content. One September morning, I noticed a broccoli plant devoid of all its leaves. Looking into the forest a couple of doe eyes stared back at me, before turning tail and bounding off. I put my hands together and said a prayer. I stated to the natural world something like, "here at the farm we don't harm, hunt or eat you, so I ask that you do not eat what we eat." I put my full intention into the prayer and went off feeling quite contented. The next morning, she came back with two friends and ate the entire patch, even pulling carrots out by the tops. I ordered a deer fence that afternoon and installed it when it arrived. It was exactly the same advice the Nearings had told their neighbors: "If you want a harvest, put up a fence."

Here in Québec, as well as in Arizona, I installed fences that were high enough that deer (white-tailed deer in Québec, mule deer in Arizona) would not jump over. They were also buried so creatures could not burrow under. My favorite is a nylon invisible deer fence that is supported by eight-foot metal t-posts, spaced every ten feet, and attached with plastic cable ties. It is durable up to twenty years and it actually appears invisible. From far away, you see right through it to the gardens. I have created fences with poultry wire, but it is less flexible and metal spurs (faults of the construction) can be dangerous. Other farmers I consult have tried electric fences but found that the deer quickly learned to slide under. To date, the only challenge I continue to have is with a resident groundhog who eats through the nylon mesh to enter the gardens. In Arizona, it was the desert cottontail rabbits that would somehow nudge their way through the gate openings. So, I have allowed them to share some of the harvest. I do sometimes chase off the groundhog (who we named Joe) when I see him, as I did the cottontails, for he is quite the glutton. Organic farms I have worked for in the past have used all manner of animal controls. Live trapping and relocation for groundhogs. Snap and sticky traps for field mice. Some farms even used dogs to hunt and kill raccoons. Others shot deer with rock salt in the early daylight hours. In the end, I share the same doctrine as the Nearings: if you want to harvest, after all the work of seeding and maintaining, put up and bury a fence. The fence will greatly eliminate the early morning shock of seeing an eaten patch in the most humane manner by far.

Straw mulching of summer squash and zucchini to protect from rotting on wet soils.

12

Fertilization (Long and Short Term)

THE MAJORITY OF our gardens' soil health and consequent fertility comes from veganic compost, composting of plant residues, and cover crops (green manures). Other than wood ash, to raise pH, and adding macro and micronutrients like boron (which can also be purchased at most grocery stores as "20 Mule Team Borax") to some beds before planting, there are no other soil amendments utilized. Plant-based products like dry seaweed, greensand, rock dusts and powders are fine, but can be expensive and sometimes difficult to locate. I incorporated some of these ingredients into my soils in Arizona, but my observational opinion was that it was the alfalfa-based goat manure that was providing the vast amount of both major and minor elements. Where veganic compost and cover crops benefit is that they fertilize for the long-term, breaking down slowly over the course of the season into nutrients that plants can assimilate and continuing into the following year without eroding or leaching away.

Cover Crops AKA Green Manures

The cover crop (green manure), and even plant residues, are the second most important veganic amendment after compost. The green manures cover bare earth, aiding in water retention. They have vast root systems that control erosion.[1] The grass, grain, or legume cover crops pull nutrients from deeper in the soil strata. When they dry, they become a winter mulch and readily compost to make more earth. Whenever there is an open patch, like when all the radishes are harvested, a cover crop is planted.

In garden areas that are suffering from low organic matter and fertility, a cover crop can be used to regenerate the soil. For an example, a bed is cast seeded with buckwheat. The buckwheat grows tall and flowers, which attract many species of bees, flies, wasps, butterflies, and moths. When they begin to seed and the pollinators have left for more showy sections of the gardens, we walk with long-handled walking scissors cutting down the tall stalks, letting them fall into the beds. Once all cut, we will bring compost (even if it is not fully composted and full of large fibrous material) and spread it directly over the buckwheat stalks, creating a lasagna-like compost (thank you Patricia Lanza, *Lasagna Gardening* for the inspiration[2]). The buckwheat will regrow from the roots and die back at first fall frost, creating an additional layer. The following year, most has been decomposed, and bed organic matter and fertility has greatly improved.

Over the years, I have trialed many different cover crops. What I will caution is, since I am not discussing tractor-based systems, I would avoid all perennial green manures like alfalfa, rye grass, vetch, and white clover in the growing beds. From my experiences, these crops will quickly become invasive and create a heavy burden for the gardener. I have highlighted my favorites below:

- Buckwheat is a fast-growing scavenger of phosphorus and potassium, releasing it to the next planted crop. Flowers bring multitudes of native bees, syrphid flies, wasps, butterflies, and moths.
- Oats are used primarily in late summer and early fall to protect the bed over winter. They are also a scavenger of available nutrients. Oats can be allowed to go to seed (groat), if planted earlier in the season and saved for the following year's planting or collected for eating.
- Crimson clover is a fast-growing, nitrogen-fixing legume. It is tolerant to shade and is the best for under-sowing vegetables, like sweet corn and those in the family *Brassicaceae*.
- Berseem clover is the heaviest nitrogen fixer of all the legumes. Highly beneficial when used on an open patch of ground or after crop harvest where a heavy feeding *Cucurbitaceae* or *Solanaceae* will be planted the following year.

There are others that were very interesting to us that we trialed in the 2021 growing season:

- Lentils are a nitrogen-fixing legume tolerant to cool soils. They created a nice mat of foliage that protected the soil from drying out.
- Cowpeas are another highly adaptable nitrogen-fixing legume, and are well tolerant to drought, and sandy or poor soils.
- Sunhemp is a crop for creating biomass. It has beautiful yellow flowers and will be beneficial as a dry straw mulch the following year.

In a small system, it can be difficult to find space to put the cover crop. It is highly recommended, however, after a crop harvest or when the garden beds are low in organic matter. They give the living soil a chance to regenerate. In the cold north where the growing season is no more than six months, and the dormant season is the same amount of time, it is less critical. But in those areas where the growing season is eight months and longer, incorporating some square footage to the green manure for even a season will yield great results in the future.

Some crops are greatly enhanced during their growth by under-sowing a cover crop like the before-mentioned crimson clover. This is considered "live mulching." Broccoli, brussels sprouts, cabbage, cauliflower, and sweet corn are some that benefit. The root systems of the clover fix nitrogen, which the plants can assimilate. The clover works in harmony with these heavy-feeding cultivars. Clover is formidable, outcompeting other native flora and retaining moisture in the soil. When the garden plants die back, a healthy green cover crop remains.

Compost Side-Dressing and Plant Macerations

For short-term fertilization, compost side-dressing and plant macerations (also known as plant fermented teas) can be utilized. There are certain crops that produce fruits and vegetables over a long season, especially those in the family *Solanaceae*, that benefit from extra nutrients. As the flowers and fruits form, we want the plants to shift their growing process from leafy growth to flower and eventual fruit set. A compost that is balanced in phosphorus, potassium, calcium, chlorine, boron, nickel, and zinc can be of benefit. These are all elements that aid in flower and fruit production, transporting of nutrients from the roots through the plants, and alerting the plants of biotic stresses to then aid them in defense (as studied in Chapter 6: The Major and Minor Elements). Most of the time, the well-composted beds are enough. However, it is a simple process if the grower deems it necessary. Using a spade shovel or trowel, scoop the compost around each plant in a circle (known as side-dressing), leaving it a few inches away from the base of the plant. The next time the plant is watered, the compost will slowly filtrate through the soil down into the root system.

Plant macerations, which can also be called plant-based teas, slurries, or fermentations, are a valuable source of highly soluble liquid nutriment. Native and cultivated perennial plants like clover, comfrey, dandelion, horsetail, stinging nettle, and yarrow are commonly called nutrient miners. Their extensive root systems reach deep into the subsurface soil layers taking up the major and minor elements that reside there. Horsetail and yarrow have the added benefit of being antifungal and anti-bacterial so when incorporated could award the plant with extra protection from certain disease pressures.

From the scientific literature it has been inconclusive that these teas provide much if any benefit, however, further multi-year studies are definitely required. Considering the heavy influence of animal agriculture around the world, it is highly likely that these plant macerations have been overlooked and even shunned. I have read that in France, it is quite common to go to the local nursery and see one-gallon (3.78L) jugs of stinging nettle concentrate available for sale. The Canadian Organic Grower's publication, "The Three R's of Fertility," highlight plant-brewed teas of the same varieties mentioned above.[3] From Cornell

University's College of Agriculture and Life Sciences, small farm program, nettle tea fertilizer is mentioned.[4] Among the small grower communities in The United States and Canada, they are becoming increasingly popular due to their ease of transformations, use, and inexpensive cost. It is up to each of us, individually, to decide their efficacy in our growing situations.

The process of making the plant-based teas is quite elementary. As soon as the plants are growing vibrantly in the spring, take a few leaves off of many plants in different locations you are wishing to ferment. Pack the leaves into a one-quart (one-liter) glass jar, fill with water, and seal tightly. Let the mixture sit in partial shade for two weeks to ferment. When opening, watch out: It smells really bad. Strain into a five-gallon (twenty-liter) receptacle using an old pillowcase, sheet, or t-shirt, squeezing lightly to emit the excess. Fill to the top with water, making a 20:1 dilution. The plant-based tea is ready for use as either a liquid or foliar spray fertilizer. If not using all of it right away, take the same pillowcase or material used to filter the fermentation and drape it over the bucket to thwart the permeating odor. It is important to apply the liquid or foliar spray at the end of the day when the sun goes down.

At La Ferme de l'Aube, we foliar spray all growing crops every four weeks with a 50/50 mix of comfrey and stinging nettles. Because of the smell, I never spray on leafy greens or any fruits or vegetables that are to be harvested soon. For example, broccoli or kale plants when they are heading or tomatoes when fruit is turning. Other than the very occasional compost side-dress, this is the main extent of our fertilization regime. I cannot attest with full confidence that foliar feeding has an impact on plant growth. I have not done side-by-side comparisons. What I can say is that in the eight years I have used them here, I have never seen any adverse effects from using it. It is like a tonic for the plant, simply giving them an application of liquid love.

There are other potential sources of plant-based amendments that can be procured at home, which I have some experience with but do not use widely. Compost tea takes a ratio of compost to water and, with the aid of an aeration pump, breaks out the nutrients from the compost to be used as a liquid fertilizer or foliar spray. The effects of compost tea on certain plants have been studied, yielding good results.[5,6] Biochar is made in a contained fire where organic vegetative materials are burned at high heat, creating a charcoal-like substance by a process called pyrolysis. Biochar can modify soil microbial abundance, activity, and community structure.[7] The same nutrients that are found in the wood ash exist, as well as the elements found in the plant materials, but because carbon has not been allowed to escape, it is captured in the black, porous substance remaining instead of being released into the atmosphere. For those that have space to build an outside fire, this can be a very interesting soil additive prior to planting, like with straight wood ash.

What I have found encouraging on my plant-based growing voyage is that it has proven to me, 100%, that animal-based composts, fished meals, and rendered animal bodily fluids and parts are not necessary. The same nutrients are found in plants. Just like eating a plant-based diet gives the human body all that it needs to create healthy organisms, plant-based composts—and, when wanted, fertilizations—give the plants all they need to expand, flower, fruit, seed, and thrive.

A thick patch of buckwheat in the foreground and sunflowers in the background up to the forest edge. Both plant species are nutrient miners for in bed composting.

Late fall oats being cut down with walking scissors for fall-planted garlic "green manure."

13

Integrated Insect Management

I HAVE CHANGED the name from Integrated Pest Management (IPM) to the above, just as I've changed the name from "weeds" to native flora. Both insects and native flora are integral to successful growing. The native flora arrives before the insects, for it is exactly those plants that the insects require for their existence. The same is true in a forest ecosystem. As trees and shrubs bud and bloom, certain insects awaken with them. The undergrowth of the forest creeps, covering the soil as the soil warms. This growth harbors ground beetles, spiders, and a vast abundance of other ground dwellers. As the green world awakens, so does insect biodiversity.

All insects can be viewed as pests. Ants eat some plants to make way for their mounds. Beetles over-infest cucumber and potato plants. Mosquitoes and black flies seemingly exist just to annoy us. Wasps make their nests under barn eaves and attack us when we enter. Spiders run around the kitchen floor. But they can (and should) be viewed as beneficial, as this is the veganic growers' way of thinking. Those same ants corral aphids, nourishing themselves on the sweet juices left by the aphid colony. They will contain the population to certain plants. Some of the aphids' favorites are native vetches, which thrive in sandy soils. That same soil type is that which some species of ants prefer to make their mounds.

Mosquitoes breed in stagnant water, like ponds and marshes. Directly alongside them are dragon and damselflies, who also require stagnant water. They feed on the mosquito larvae. There cannot be one without the other. The mosquitoes, which are most pervasive at dusk when the dragonflies seem to bed down, are then dined upon by the awakening bats. Small towns are often perplexed at the lack of bats. It is solely because they spray either a synthetic insecticide, like Methoprene, or a biological one, like BTi, into stagnant waters to discourage mosquito larvae. Effectively eliminating the pesky (to humans) mosquito is annihilating the bats' main food source and jeopardizing their survival.

The same organic and inorganic chemicals are used to discourage black fly breeding. But just like how all insect populations work, a healthy population is necessary for those that require them as a food source. They are the main food source of Barn swallows. Once one of the most abundant swallows in North America, they are now considered a threatened species, primarily because of the insecticide used to destroy their food sources.

I consulted and worked on a small organic garden operation in Cuzma, Mexico (close to Merida), where the low dryland tropical forest housed a cenoté (underground lake). This was the main water source for the property owner. Every dusk, an infesting cloud of mosquitoes would attack any living being. No sooner than they would begin to harass us, the nocturnal bats who lived in the cenoté would fly out of their roosts to feed. As I stood with bare arms outstretched—dozens of mosquitoes swarming, wishing for my blood—the bats homed in and delicately picked them off my arms. I could actually feel the kiss of their lips on my skin. At La Ferme de l'Aube, the battalions of dragon and damselflies do the same work on the blackflies. Sometimes landing on our heads to survey the land, scouting their prey. Like in Merida, here the bats emerge at dusk. Some species, like the little brown bat (*Myotis lucifugus),* prefer to course the terrain of the forest edge with their echolocation skills, eating their body weight in flying insects every night.

A main consideration for the veganic grower is to plant as much diversity as possible, to encourage as much faunal diversity as possible. Here we plant no less than 20% of our available growing space to plants for others to enjoy. We are also blessed to live among a highly biologically diverse forest edge. Surrounding us is more than 150 acres of wildlands, including mixed forests, grasslands, marshes, and mountain streams. Flowering plants (see Annex D: Flower and Herb Chart) bring the pollinators that are required to make squash and melons. Spiders make their homes to control thrip and mite populations. Birds nest in forest edges and utilize wooden garden stakes as perches to pick out caterpillars. Nature works as a circle of balance, and all floral and faunal creatures play a role. The very worst thing any gardener can do to upset that balance is spray insecticide, even if the label says that it is "organic."

The No-Spray Principle

Let's look at the least caustic of them all, Safer (brand) insecticidal soap, which is basically an organic, biodegradable type of kitchen soap. This product suffocates the soft-bodied insect, like aphids, by blocking its pores from respiration, eventually killing them. I used it religiously in Arizona as the warm days, cold nights, and humid beds of late spring made exceptional breeding grounds for gray and green peach aphids in our lettuces and mustard greens. All during the growing period, every three days, I would walk into the gardens at dusk, lift off the row covers, and spray. Some would asphyxiate, some would live. Those that survived multiplied, and in the end all that time and expense was for naught.

Just like most insect pressures on cultivated crops, it is the lack of biodiversity and crop maintenance that creates the most problems. The aphids could have been mostly avoided by using an insect screen, instead of row covers. If I would have uncovered the beds at night, so that night crawling spiders entered the patch, I probably could have saved myself months of hassle. Spraying can decrease the population to the point that their predators move on to places where the populations are more to their liking—and don't smell like soap.

From the 2019 article "Declines in insect abundance and diversity: We know enough to act now," in the journal Conservation Science and Practice, authors Forister, Peltonand, and Black, state:

> For variety, abundance and ecological impact, insects have no rival among multicellular life on this planet. The vast majority of bats, birds and freshwater fish depend on insects and humans depend on insect pollination for nutritious fruits and vegetables. Indirect effects of insects are just as consequential, including effects on nutrient cycling and competitive interactions among plants. Although less than 1% of described invertebrate species have been assessed for threat by the International Union for Conservation of Nature (IUCN), approximately 40% of those that have been assessed are considered threatened. The most influential factors driving insect declines are habitat loss and degradation, pesticide use and climate change. All species are worth protecting and preserving for their own sake, but the current crisis is much larger than individual species and rises to the level of losing key functions in terrestrial and aquatic ecosystems.[1]

As small-scale growers, we can make a local impact. By keeping our human footprint small, incorporating a "no spray ever" approach, all the while attempting to adapt to dramatic climate fluctuations around the world by diversifying our plantings, gives these incredibly important creatures their best chance for survival in our garden systems.

Each region will have different insect pressures, and some infestations will be worse than others. But from all my experience with spraying organic and inorganic insecticides, my conclusion is that spraying will exacerbate the problem in the long term. They may provide a temporary relief, but the better solution is to plant for insect biodiversity and let them thrive. So, the crux is: we never spray and have not in any of our growing seasons here as veganic farmers. However, that does not mean that we do not actively manage some insects ourselves. The damage that some cause is fast and furious. I have highlighted those that are the most notorious from my gardening and farming career below.

Flea beetles make up many different species in the leaf beetle family *Chyrsomelidae*.[2] These tiny creatures begin to surface as soon as the soil warms, following the emergence of wild plantain *Plantago major* in the northern part of North America. They will decimate small mustard leaves like arugula, Asian greens, bok choy, kale, radish, rapini, and turnip. They will make the leaves non-storable, for the tiny holes that they puncture grow in size as the plant grows. When harvested and stored in the fridge, they quickly yellow. By keeping the beds plantain-free, and covering with insect screen immediately after planting, we will dramatically decrease the flea beetle populations. They tend to favor early-season, open garden patches. They seem to prefer cool, humid conditions to initially establish, more so than dry and hot environments, usually subsiding by mid-summer. However, they can persist if late summer and fall turn cold and wet. I think that the screens deter them because, when they jump, they hit the top and do not like being trapped underneath.

Colorado potato beetles (*Leptinotarsa decemlineata*) are a striking white, black-striped beetle with orange spotted face.[3] They are an incredible nuisance to the potato patch throughout the United States and Canada. They will also invade eggplant plantings. Some winter-over underground and in hedgerows, while others migrate in. Crop rotation does not reduce their prevalence. The adults find each other, mate, and the female deposits ten to twenty orange eggs on the underside of the potato foliage. When the larvae appear, the problem magnifies as they eat the foliage in dramatic fashion. Untended, they will defoliate a plant in a matter of days. Following the larvae, spined soldier bugs and assassin beetles will enter the patch and feed on them. If given a chance, by not spraying insecticides, nature will create the balance. However, since the problem can quickly get out of control, we do actively pick off the adults by hand and remove eggs and larvae on sight, until the potato plants go to flower. If started when first adults are observed, the process takes roughly five minutes every other day for a 125 square foot patch.

Striped and spotted cucumber beetles are members of the family *Chrysomelidae*.[4] These white to yellow beetles, with black stripes (for striped) and black spots (for spotted) seem to arrive just as the *Cucurbitaceae* (cucumbers, melons, summer squash (zucchini), watermelons, and winter squash) are transplanted in the spring. They also like ground cherries. They are pervasive throughout the United States and Canada. They like to hang out on the underside of the leaves, as well as inside the showy blossoms of squashes and delicate cucumber blooms. The adults eat the flowers and the toxin in their saliva can wilt the plant to death. Their larvae, like Colorado potato beetle larvae, hatch from yellowish-orange eggs and begin to feed voraciously on the foliage. Because of their nature, they will often fly when they see the gardener coming, making them next to impossible to pick off by hand. However, there are preventative measures.

Placing protective row cover over the plantation until all the transplants have blooming flowers will deter them immensely. When they cannot enter through the covers, they will keep migrating until they find an exposed patch. Upon removal of the covers, I will walk the field daily, early in the morning, while they are subdued by the colder morning temperatures. When I have located a particularly infested flower blossom, indicated by the many holes in the petals, I will remove the whole blossom. Because of the damage inflicted by the beetles, it will not set fruit anyway. Over the years, I have noticed that their intensity and resulting damage to the plants diminishes once fruits start setting and the plants expand. Another option is to wait until late spring/early summer to plant these crops, when their migrations have passed. This can be fine for cucumbers and summer squash, with days to harvest at fifty to sixty days, but in some areas this will be too short a season to bring in winter squash. Spined soldier bugs and assassin beetles do work the plants, searching for larvae—they just need the freedom to do so.

Cabbage butterflies/worms (*Pieris rapae)* are white butterflies with faint black spots on their wings, which can be sometimes absent. They are the most abundant and destructive butterflies to cultivated fields in the world.[5] They begin to migrate in and throughout the United States and Canada when the temperatures climb. They hover, specifically seeking out *Brassicaceae* cultivars: bok choy, broccoli, brussels sprouts, cabbage, cauliflower, kale, and kohlrabi. When they home in, they will glide down and deposit their tiny white eggs into the central crown of the plants. A single moth can lay dozens of eggs on multiple plants. When the eggs hatch and the green worm larvae form, they begin to eat from the crown. If infested, the flower head (florets) of cultivars like broccoli will become disfigured and hardly eatable. Since the worms grow so fast, their poo can be just as damaging as their foraging. Cauliflowers, for example, can be forming correctly, but if the excrement drops on the curds, they will blacken and slowly rot out.

The best preventative maintenance is a twofold approach. First, cover all *Brassicaceae* family varieties with insect screens from transplant to harvest. Being diligent with this method will reward the grower with an eatable crop. The screen will block the butterflies from entering, and they will continue migrating on. Second, plant a trap crop. This is a plant in the same family that the insect likes, but instead of covering it with a screen, a few plants are left uncovered to encourage insects to lay there. I like to use bok choy. It is planted early, very fast-growing, and bolts, flowers, and seeds in the first year. The moths will readily locate the ones left for seed and deposit their eggs. The additional benefit is the beautiful and bountiful yellow bok choy blooms, which are attractive to pollinating native bees, flies, and wasps. When worms grow in size on the large bok choy leaves, American Robins, Phoebes, and many other flycatcher species will work the plants for grubs. American toads and green frogs bounce among the canopy, looking from underneath.

Grey worms/cutworms (*Agrotis spp.)* are a yellowish-brownish-grayish caterpillar that live in the soil. "Cutworm," as they are commonly called, refers to the larva of several noctuid moth species (*Lepidoptera: Noctuidae).*[6] When the ground and nights warm, they surface to cut down small seedlings, both native and planted. They chew the stem at the soil base, which will kill the transplant

104

outright. They seem to prefer sandy soils and their favorite cultivated targets are *Brassicaceae* varieties, early onion seedlings, pepper, and tomato plants. In years of heavy abundance, they can also be present in beans, beets, lettuce, and Swiss chard. They are prevalent throughout the United States and Canada. For control of the cutworm, observation is the best prevention.

In the early morning light, after the transplants have been set in the ground, we will walk the patch. When we notice a plant cut or seedling defoliated, we will dig a shallow circle around the transplant with our fingers, about two inches (5cm) deep. The worm is usually located resting at that depth. We then remove and deposit the cutworm out of the gardens. The American Robins, ground beetles, and toads do the rest. Another solution offered by a farmer friend is to set the alarm for an hour before dawn, grab a flashlight, proceed to the plantings where they have been observed, and watch for them crawling around on the surface. The choice is an individual one. I prefer to have a few extra transplants on hand just in case, replanting after the worm has been located, and sleep an extra hour. As the plants get bigger, the stems become too fibrous, and the worms move on to newly emergent native shoots.

Green peach and gray aphids are two species of the superfamily *Aphidoidea*. They are a soft-bodied insect family, found throughout the United States and Canada, and can be very damaging. The green peach aphids[7] congregate in loose colonies, while the gray aphids (or cabbage aphid[8]) congeal into large masses. In our years of growing veganically, they have only caused us 100% loss twice. Both times, it was mid-summer plantings of black and daikon radish and purple top turnip in beds that had not been ideally composted. A mix of humid conditions under insect screen covers and grower mismanagement (me) was the culprit both times.

In 2020, they wiped out one hundred square feet of the crops mentioned above. As a test, in an infected quick radish crop (twenty-eight days) where they were also present in great numbers, I removed the screen. Within a couple of days, the aphid populations stabilized and diminished, most likely due to the green lacewings and spiders moving in. The leaves never reached full growth potential, but the radishes did. Even though for a majority of the time, screens are a grower's trick for protection, what is going on underneath requires diligent surveillance.

Squash bug (*Anasa tristis*) is a greyish-brownish sap-sucking insect of the family *Coreidae*.[9] They were a frequent resident in my Arizona growing days and caused me many summer and winter squash plant losses. They are prolific breeders, laying dozens of eggs. The larger larvae and adults have toxic saliva, like the cucumber beetles, and the leaves can wilt once bitten. Plants will cease growing and eventually die. Management was picking off of the adults every other day, but it was only marginally successful. I did not know of insect screens at that time, but in theory, they could be used for a great prevention strategy as well as planting later in the season. Fence lizards did work the patch and eat the adults. To date, I have not observed them at my own farm nor the others I have worked on in Québec, but it is probably just a matter of time in these days of constant climate change.

Tomato/Tobacco hornworms (*Manduca spp.*) are caterpillar larvae of species of hawk and sphinx moths.[10] They can reach two inches (5cm) long and are a spotted light to dark green, with voracious appetites. The caterpillars, which grow vigorously, have been known to completely defoliate a six-foot (1.8m) tomato plant in two days. The best method of control is to pick them off in the early morning hours, as they seek refuge from the sun on the underside of leaves. We used to find them in Arizona by first locating large mounds of caterpillar feces on the leaf surface; they were usually right above. Due to their aggressive nature, they are mostly impervious to bird predators. When they reach full-size and a threat approach, they sit back on their hind segments and chatter their sharp teeth menacingly. Quite a sight! In my part of Québec, I finally noticed them for the first time in summer of 2021 while walking along the country roads, but they have already made their way into fields in the southern half of the province, as they have throughout the United States.

Integrated Insect Management (IIM) is not simply about predator-prey relationships but about the welcoming of all insect friends. On reflection of insect management, I can say that two things are true. First, the greater the floral diversity in the gardens, green strips, hedgerows, edges, and surrounding wildlands, the less damaging insects are to garden crops. Second, the "no spray-ever" principle allows all insect populations to thrive. Predatory insects control crop-damaging insect species far better than any insecticide.

Planting a diversity of flowering plants and herbs (see Annex D: Flower and Herb Chart) at different points during the growing season is very important to the life cycles of bees, flies, wasps, butterflies, and moths. These insect beings are essential to all varieties of plants that require pollination to set fruits and vegetables. Only through a no-spray approach can these creatures proliferate. Spraying of many chemical pesticides or organocides can attack the nervous systems of these delicate dwellers. I have mentioned which insects to watch for in Annex A: The Crop Profiles, for each crop profiled.

Regionally, there are surely other insects that I have not highlighted that may be quite prominent. The publication "Disease and Pests of Vegetable Crops in Canada" is a comprehensive 1021-page guide to almost every plant disease and insect pressure found in Canada.[11] For the United States, expert-run university extension websites like Oregon State University Extension Service's "Pests, Weeds and Diseases"[12] describe regional diseases and insect pressures. In addition, for knowledge of all insect creatures, one of the most comprehensive websites I have found is Iowa State University's Department of Entomology BugGuide,[13] for all our insect identification pleasure.

Great Northern bee (one of many species of native pollinating insects at La Ferme de l'Aube) seeking nectar on a comfrey flower, one of the first to bloom in the spring.

Mid-late summer floral diversity to attract a plethora of faunal diversity.

14

Managing Plant Diseases

Aᴸᴸ ᴸᴇᴀᵛᴇˢ ᴼᶠ all deciduous plants, bushes, and trees eventually die when the weather turns cold. All of them. When the leaves turn color, like on aspen, birch, maple, and oaks, it is the process where the leaves stop producing chlorophyll, the green pigment made up by molecules in the leaves. This process means that the plant discontinues to transfer food throughout the plant. It is thinking about entering a state of dormancy. When the leaves turn to ceremonious yellow and orange, this is from carotenoids that become the dominant pigment. Anthocyanins are the pigments that causes the majestic pink, purple, and red colors representing the last gasp of life before the fall.

What I have learned, in many different ecosystems, is with the brilliant fall colors abounding, a look at the lower vegetation reveals all manner of bacterial and fungal wilts. This is the nature of things and completely normal. Even some of the leaves that are turning color, those magnificently pigmented, yellows, oranges, and reds have bacterial leaf spots. When the gardens succumb to plant diseases, most of the time it is a natural process. To reiterate: it is part of all plants' cycles to develop disease at the end of the growing season. What we wish to avoid is a plant getting disease before the weather turns cold in autumn. But even if they do, it can aid them in genetic diversity and strength for future generations. From "Evolutionary Ecology of Plant Diseases in Natural Systems," in the Annual Review of Phytopathology, February 2002, Gregory S Gilbert stated[1]

> "...pathogens can help maintain plant species diversity, facilitate successional processes, and enhance the genetic diversity and structure of host populations. Understanding the impacts of diseases in natural plant communities requires integrating numerical dynamics, rapid evolutionary, and spatial structure of both host and pathogen populations, and an appreciation for how destructive actions at one scale can be the foundation for positive outcomes at another."

Surveying the gardens, green strips, and edges, signs of fungal mildew proliferate when the nights start turning cold. Native vetch and yarrow are spotted with powdery mildew. It is only a matter of time before the garden plants will as well. Since it is solely the biorhythm of every cultivated and wild plant to die back, returning all food energy into the root system, there is no reason to panic. Like stated above, perennial plantings can increase their genetic diversity. In annual plants that we save seed from or that self-seed, the same can be true. In cultivated plantings of fruits, vegetables, and herbs there is some maintenance that can be done to deter earlier than expected blights, mildews, and wilts.

Most plant diseases will occur earlier than expected when the soil health (fertility) is less than optimal, just like in our own bodies. When we do not have enough of a vitamin or mineral (not in balance), our immune systems can become compromised, and bacteria or viruses can attack and infect us more easily. The same is true in plants: not enough of one of the major or minor elements to help build the plant's immunity and it could succumb to disease. There is evidence to suggest that an increase of nitrogen fertilization in the *Solanaceae* family of crops can increase susceptibility to fungal pathogens,[2] whether the (N) fertilizer is chemical or animal. And it makes sense. When a high nitrogen fertilizer is applied, like chicken manure, the plant can experience an extreme growth spurt. Growing too fast will stretch the plant's resources, opening up pathways for its immune system to become compromised.

Many times, the bacteria and fungus enter the plant from the soil level because the bottom leaf has received some kind of damage. It could be from an insect chewing on the foliage, or from someone walking by and accidentally bruising a leaf. This creates an additional entryway for the disease to enter.

All fungus and bacteria that infect plants can be found in all soils. They are lying in wait. When conditions are ideal and soil health has the proper amount of all nutrients, these conditions remain at bay. When the plants have ideal moisture, nights are not too cold, the days are warm and sunny to burn off the morning dew, these conditions are minimal. But when torrential rain or a long, warm drought hits, followed by a cold night, these diseases will rear up.

Dry mulching limits the contact of the soil to the bottom underside (moist, humid) leaves of the plant. Dry mulching cucumbers, melons, summer squash, winter squash, eggplants, ground cherries, peppers, potatoes, and tomatoes will eliminate most bacterial and fungal problems. Plants like tomatoes produce prolific suckers (side shoots) that will crowd the central stem and create a very humid environment. Removing them from the base of the plant, as well as removing any bottom leaves that are touching the soil, will decrease humidity and discourage the uptake of fungus and bacteria from the soil. Keeping all crops as native flora-free as possible will also limit humidity-related disease problems.

Even if (for example) fungal, powdery mildew sets in on summer squash plants, or verticillium wilt shows on tomatoes early in the season, it is not the end of the plant's life. From my observations, 99% of the time, the plant will grow out of it if given a chance to recover on its own. The plants will continue living and produce an eatable crop. If a plant does have a growing center that does become wilted and dies, remove the plant and deposit it in the garden hedgerow or wild edge, letting nature absorb it. In Annex A: Crop Profiles there are specific diseases listed for all crops profiled to take notice of. Below are a few that are the most pervasive from my experiences.

Damping off can be caused by any of the fungi *Fusarium, Rhizoctonia, Pythium, Phytophthora spp.* and others.[3] These fungi are particularly pervasive in soil-starting medium and in cold soils outside. Upon germination and shoot production, the stem becomes weak and brown and eventually falls over. A seedling that suffers from damping off will not recover. Management of damping off in the greenhouse is a two-prong approach. First to only water seedlings when dry, and only with warm water, not cold. Second, is to keep nighttime soil temperatures above 60F (15.5C). If a few seedlings in a plug tray have damping off, it does not mean the rest are lost. Simply follow the two steps above, keeping the nighttime lows warmer. Damping off is particularly pervasive in *Brassicaceae* and *Solanaceae* seedlings. In the field, damping off will often affect early seedlings of bok choy, lettuce, mustards, radish, spinach, and turnip. As it is slightly more difficult to manage in the field, if a seedling is affected, it is good practice to remove it, giving the others more room to grow.

White mold is caused by the fungus *Sclerotinia sclerotiorum*. This very pervasive fungus affects over four hundred fruit, vegetable, and herbs worldwide and is endemic in the soil, lasting anywhere from three to eight years.[4] In my experience, this is the most destructive pathogen of them all. Because of its vast host base, crop rotation unfortunately does not eliminate the problem. White mold infects *Glycine, Physalis,* and *Solanaceae* families most readily. White mold is brought on by high levels of humidity after a period of drought and can occur at any temperature range from 50-90F (10-32C). The infected part of the plant develops a white fungus on the stem, leaves, pod, and fruit. Once infected, the plant does not recover. Best course of management is to remove the infected plants and deposit them out of the gardens. Usually, this fungus does not wipe out the whole plantation. An assumption can be made that if a plant does not get infected by white mold, it may have an internal resistance. Seed saving from these plants may help to create open-pollinated and heirloom cultivars resistant to this very prevalent pathogen. Observations from the 2021 growing season revealed that a couple of hot, dry weeks following a cold, rainy spell when white mold surfaced resulted in lightly infected plants healing and new infections declining measurably.

Powdery mildew is a member of the fungal family *Erysiphaceae*.[5] This fungus mostly occurs during times of drought followed by a drastic dip in temperature. So, it appears that powdery mildew may be caused more by the cold than high humidity. Powdery mildew is pervasive on all *Cucurbitaceae* cultivars and will put an end to all *Pisum* (peas) plantings. It presents itself by a fuzzy whitish fungus that covers leaves and stems. Other than the *Pisum* family, it has been my experience that the *Cucurbitaceae* family will live on and grow out of the fungus. The best management when powdery mildew is observed is to discontinue irrigation, letting the plants go as dry as possible; though soil humidity does not seem to initiate the fungus, it does appear to exacerbate it. Dry, warm soils allow the plants to uptake nutrients, to build up resistance, and continue to put on new, unaffected, leafy growth.

Verticillium wilt is caused by the fungus *Verticillium spp.* Verticillium wilt can infect over four hundred host species.[6] This fungus lives on in the soil year after year and shows up on some plants at La Ferme de l'Aube every growing season. *Verticillium spp.* appears to favor specific *Solanaceae's* (potatoes and tomatoes). It is brought on during times of high soil humidity and warm 70-81F (21-26.5C), but not hot, temperatures. It presents itself as yellowing and curling leaves. I have most observed this fungus after irrigation or good rains in mid-summer, after the plants have put on their vibrant growth, followed by a colder than normal night. However, it is rare that it outright kills any plants, based on my observations. Usually, the plants will grow out of the wilt. Best management is to eliminate soil humidity by limiting irrigation and letting soils dry. Dry mulching can also be an effective deterrent to this pathogen.

Bacterial leaf spot is caused by a number of *Xanthomonas spp.* bacterial pathogens and is especially pervasive in *Solanaceae* (peppers and tomatoes).[7] Starting with brown lesions spotted on the oldest leaves, it can cause the whole plant and fruits to become infected if left unchecked. Usually, however, it can be managed by limiting irrigation, effectively drying out the soils. If leaves and stems become too affected, I have had good luck removing the whole stem. Research does show that resistant seed can be planted, if a plant is unaffected or outgrows the condition in a home operation, seeds should be saved to build up the resistance. See Chapter 17: Letting Plants go to Flower, to Seeds, and Saving Them.

Soft rot is a bacterial pathogen caused by *Erwinia carotovora spp.*[8] This pathogen manifests itself when heavy irrigation or rain is applied to plants that are in their final stages of development. Bulbing onions, chicories, and head lettuces are especially susceptible. It presents itself as brown, rotten crowns in heads and in the soft necks of onions when the necks have fallen over, indicating full maturity. I have seen full losses of a run of head lettuces in the field after heavy rainfall. The best management practice is to eliminate irrigation during late-stage development. For onions, allowing them to dry thoroughly in a sunny place after being pulled may destroy the harmful bacteria.

It should be obvious by now, based on a few of these descriptions of plant diseases, that the best management for them all is low soil humidity. We cannot control the temperature outside, even in caterpillar tunnels. We cannot stop the ground from being saturated by rain. We can, however, manage irrigation wisely. The drier, the less plant-killing pathogens. Remember: the bigger the plants get, the less water they need.

Nutrient deficiencies

Different from bacterial and fungal infections, nutrient deficiencies are caused by abiotic factors. Examples of this are fertility imbalances (too much or too little), moisture and temperature extremes, mineral toxicity, and physical injuries to the plant by either human, machine, or wind. What I have observed, however, is that these factors mostly occur when there is either a lack of a nutrient in the soil system or the plants are unable to uptake a nutrient due to extreme drought or saturation. The latter is usually the culprit in the case of small-scale growers in Canada and the United States.

The best way to reveal deficiencies of nutrients in the garden plot is with a soil test. If the soil test has revealed a pH in the ideal range for growing fruits, vegetables, and herbs (5.7-7.2) and shows that all minerals exist from the sampling, then the issue is surely uptake. However, it is also possible that if there were heavy rains during the growing season, there could have been leaching, where the minerals may have washed away.

In my experiences as a professional farmer, mineral deficiencies have generally been very mild problems, for I have always tried to focus on building nutrient-dense soil, as opposed to feeding the plants with a fertilization regime. Yet, even so, there are a few that we must contend with every year.

Phosphorus deficiencies (lack of uptake) in greenhouse seedlings is exhibited by the underside of the leaves turning reddish-purple.[9] If left unchecked, this condition will stunt seedling growth and invite other disease issues—including mortality. Seedlings of Brassicaceae and Solanaceae are the most prone. Usually, this condition follows a colder-than-normal growing night in the greenhouse, with the soil medium remaining saturated. The remedy is to let the plug trays go completely dry before watering and raise the night-time temperature.

Blossom-end rot is a common physiological disorder that occurs on the fruits of eggplant, pepper, tomato, and watermelon. Blossom-end rot can be related to many factors, but the underlying cause is an inadequate amount of calcium in the blossom end of the fruit.[10] This condition presents with dark black lesions on the blossom end, causing misshapen and uneatable fruits. It seems every year when the first fruits form, especially on peppers and tomatoes, blossom-end rot appears. The best solution I have found to clear up the problem immediately and completely is to apply a dusting of wood ash (preferred) or powdered dolomite lime directly at the base of the plants prior to subsequent irrigation.

Boron deficiency in the family Brassicaceae (also known as cole crops) can be exhibited by hollowing in the main stem, decreased curd size, mis-shaped and reduced heads. Boron significantly improves the vegetative growth and quantitative parameters of cole crops.[11] Before planting any of the brassica family of cultivars, we apply powdered boron (which can be found at most supermarkets as "20 Mule Team Borax") at a rate of one-eighth of a teaspoon per plant. Observational data from the years of 2015-2021 at La Ferme de l'Aube have shown that the cole crops uniformity increased when we began application in the 2018 growing season.

Regionally, there are many other plant pathogens (diseases) and deficiencies that I have not highlighted that can be quite conspicuous. Again, the Canadian Phytopathological Society's (phytopath.ca) "Disease and Pests of Vegetable Crops in Canada" is a comprehensive 1021-page guide to most every plant disease, nutrient deficiency, and insect pressure found in Canada.[12] For the United States, university extension websites, like University of Minnesota Extension's "Plant Diseases"[13] and University of Arizona's "Guide to Symptoms of Plant Nutrient Deficiencies"[14] are examples of university extension service websites available online. I have also listed a journal article for each of the plant diseases and nutrient deficiencies, which can be found in the bibliography of sources, if you wish to learn more about these topics.

Rows of snap, shelling, and snow peas, staked and twined in full vibrancy.

15

The Harvest

THE SEEDS HAVE germinated and are growing, climbing, and vining. The transplants are staked, bushy leaves waving in the breeze. Flowers pop and give way to small fruits. Those delicate morsels plump and begin to blush. Greens grow tall, roots take form, onions bulb and potatoes crack the earth. All the work and struggles culminate in these moments. The harvest will start slowly with the first greens, lettuce, peas, radishes, and turnips. Quickly, the bounty will flow with beets and carrots, kales, and Swiss chard. Summer squash is a daily harvesting affair. Snap beans will be picked every other day. Cherry tomatoes, two to three times a week as the sweet fruit quickly over-mature and fall off the plants. Learning to be an observant, competent harvester is as important as any other technique in the grower's regime. It's time to breathe easier as the harvests come in. The most fun part begins.

A plant's purpose, embedded in its genetic make-up, is to go to flower, to seed, and preferably as quickly as possible. It is the desire to propagate, that is why it exists. This is true for all plants. As growers, our desire is to harvest at the optimum moment. We eat leaves (like kale, lettuce, and mustards). We eat seed pods (like beans and peas). We eat fruits (cucumbers, eggplants, peppers, tomatoes, strawberries, and zucchini). We dig up roots (beets, carrots, onions, potatoes, and radishes). We also eat flower buds (broccoli, brussels sprouts, cabbage, and cauliflower). The harvesting of most crops should be self-explanatory, yet each and every variety is unique, and the correct timing of the harvest is an art form.

Mustard greens, when harvested small, have a mustardy flavor that is agreeable—but wait too long as the leaves enlarge, and the mustard flavor is like eating pungent wasabi (Japanese horseradish). Green beans can be harvested thin, which are more tender, or plump, which are better for sautéing and canning. Wax beans will only reach their sweet, somewhat (vegan) buttery flavor, when they are full yellow and thick in girth. Sugar snap peas, if harvested too young, will be crisp but not sweet. Harvested at just the right time, when full-sized with robust seeds but still juicy and tender, they will burst with the classic sugar snap flavor. Cherry tomatoes are only at their most luscious when allowed to vine-ripen. Hot peppers have the same heat at the green and red stage, however they become sweet when red. Summer squash can and should be harvested smaller, at eight to ten inches (20-25cm), for a more tender delicacy. The larger ones are good for breads and muffins. Small beets have the same flavor as larger ones, and carrots obtain their sweetness after the diameter increases. Small radishes are still piping hot, as are overly large ones, whereas the perfect harvest timing yields a crisp morsel with a hint of radish zest. Onions mature in flavor and mellow as they reach fuller size; immature onions can be too piquant for some people's palates. Immature cauliflower curds are sweet and flavorful but if left to overdevelop they become bitter.

At our local grocery store, run by an organic farm, I saw 3.5 oz. (100g) pint containers of ground cherries selling for $4, in season. It is a crop that we also sell and is a favorite among our clients' children. At the farm store, the skins were the classic dry beige color, but the fruits inside were greenish yellow. Their flavor will be tart. When ground cherries are ready to be harvested, they fall off the plant with this coloration. However, this is not the proper color for selling and/or eating. If the ground cherries sit in a room at 55-60F (13-15.5C) for about five to seven days, they will turn a golden yellow-orange and taste sweet and tropical. This is their true flavor. A customer of ours who frequents our farm kiosk brought a pint of our ground cherries to a friend in Montréal. Upon eating them, she exclaimed that in the twenty years she had been eating them, she had never tasted ground cherries so divine. Like the farm store, most other places that sell them do so in the greenish-yellow tart stage. The customer never realizes their true magic. Harvesting and eating at peak flavor is nothing short of a masterpiece.

The best advice I can give about when any produce is ready in the field, is to try it. Take a bite of a bean or pea, cherry tomato, carrot, or radish right there in the field. If it is the flavor you are looking for, then it is time to harvest. If not, wait. Tricks for best harvest practices and tips can be found in Annex A: The Crop Profiles. It will not reveal the optimal time for every variety that is possible to grow, that would be a book in and of itself. Instead, the best way to know is practice and documenting in the observation log. However, there are some basic concepts I will share here.

A good general rule for all leaf crops is to harvest the outer, oldest leaves first. All leaves grow from a central crown and branch out. By harvesting the outer leaves, it will signal the plant to continue to put out new growth. If cutting greens, such as leaf lettuce, with a knife, cutting just above the central crown will ensure strong, fast regrowth.

Fruiting and podding crops will be more productive the more often they are harvested, as it will encourage the plants to produce more flowers. This is especially true with peas, snap beans, and summer squash. Because of their innate desire to produce seeds, they size up fast. By cutting the summer squash a little smaller, we will encourage the plant to produce more bountifully. This will award us with the extra benefit of eating a truly gourmet vegetable, something you will not find at most farmer's markets and grocery stores.

Root crops can also be harvested young. Onions can be pulled as green onions, potatoes as new potatoes, and carrots as pencil carrots, but it is not necessary. These plants will all attempt to reach their full potential based on spacing. If winter storage is our purpose for these roots, then reaching full potential is recommended.

Edible flowering crops are the trickiest. Cabbages are easier than broccoli, which is easier than cauliflower, which is much easier than brussels sprouts (the hardest of them all.) All of these vegetables produce stalks from the central crown, but they will also push up, growing stalks from the joints between the central stem and branch to produce flower buds. If the purpose is to have many florets—like broccoli, for example—we will let all the flower buds form and harvest them before opening. If we want to harvest just the central crown, we remove all the additional flower buds except for the central one. The plant will focus its intentions there. After cutting the main broccoli head, the plant will continue to live on and make more flower buds from the joints. This is true for broccoli, cabbage, and cauliflower. They will not be as big as the main crown but will still be nice and eatable.

A solid harvest receptacle is an imperative, as is a good quality pocketknife. The more rugged these items, the longer they will last. My preference is to use three-gallon (11 liter) Rubbermaid bins. They are highly durable and virtually indestructible. Another excellent, recycled option is the heavy-duty cardboard boxes from grocery store produce departments. For cutting, I have three pocketknives: one is a Felco garden knife, another is an Opinel brand, and the third is a Victorinox (like a Swiss army knife); all three can be sharpened. No matter what you use, choose something that folds closed and can rest in the pocket easily. We use the pocketknife for all greens, *Brassicaceae*, and summer squash. Garden cutters (my preferred make is Felco) are useful tools for cutting the woody stems of eggplants and peppers. We use the harvest bins and recycled boxes for harvesting everything.

Succession Harvest

At some point during mid-summer, the first plantings of greens and lettuces after three-to-four cuttings will begin to tire and immediately put up a flower stalk. The plant is trying desperately to go to seed. Within the garden plan, it is a good idea to plan multiple croppings that will yield a succession of harvests. As a small farm, we are trying to provide our customers with the highest diversity possible every week. Just like us, most of our clients want salad mix, as cut greens or heads of lettuce every week. Just planting one time would not be sufficient to satisfy all of our demands. In our garden plan, we plan multiple sowings (successions). Lettuces we plant every week, mesclun mix every two. We will have three sowings of radishes and turnips, four sowings of beets, carrots, and snap beans. Two successions each of snap peas, summer squash, and cucumbers will allow us to continue the harvest as long as possible. When thinking about your own individual garden needs, consider whether succession planting may fit your wants and desires.

Post-harvest Handling

Post-harvest handling is where most growers lose their crop, and between this and storage, where most farm waste occurs. I have witnessed experienced farmers lose the vast majority of their crop due to inadequate management and harvesting at inappropriate times. The best general rule is this: If a fruit, flower bud, green, herb, pod, or vegetable wants to be stored in the refrigerator (below 40F, 4.5C) harvesting them at the coldest possible moment of the day is the appropriate practice. Even harvesting in the early morning hours, the temperature will most likely be warmer than 40F. So, for all greens and flower buds, immersing them in cold water immediately after harvesting—to "remove field heat"—will ensure longer storage life. After which, they should be shaken and allowed to air dry before packing.

If a fruit, vegetable, herb, or root wants to be stored warmer—like basil, onions, strawberries, tomatoes, and winter squash—they can be harvested anytime during the day. Beans and peas will mold quickly if picked when wet or dewy and then stored at 40F, so these specific crops want to be as dry as possible before harvest. All information on post-harvest handling criteria can also be found in Annex A: Crop Profiles.

On larger scale organic farms—five acres (two hectares) and more—where I have observed and worked, losses of hundreds of pounds of beans, potatoes, summer squash, tomatoes, and winter squash due to post-harvest handling mismanagement were, unfortunately, common. This is why I believe in the one acre and less farm, as well as the backyard to farmyard grower. They are more efficient, meaning they have higher yields per square foot (meter), and the ability to adapt to local conditions more readily to ensure less waste. This is corroborated by evidence around the world.

Land Productivity Efficiency Greater on Smaller Farms

In Thomas Masterson's essay, "Productivity, Technical Efficiency and Farm Size in Paraguayan Agriculture," he concludes that "the relationship between productivity and farm size is an affirmation of the inverse relationship in the case of Paraguay... land productivity is significantly greater for smaller farms (especially the very smallest farms)."[1]

In the working paper "Brazil's Agricultural Total Factor Productivity Growth by Farm Size," the authors, Gasque et al. show that,

> The farm sizes achieving, over the 1985–2006 period (in Brazil), the fastest annual total factor productivity (TFP) growth were the smallest (0–5 ha) and largest (500+ ha), the former having a small growth advantage. Farmers operating less than 5 hectares also achieved the fastest rate of technical change. The slowest TFP growth rate, in the national analysis, was experienced by the 20–100 ha size class, followed by the 100–500 ha class.[2]

The article "Inverse Productivity or Inverse Efficiency? Evidence from Mexico," written by Kagin et al., confirms

> the existence of both an inverse productivity and inverse efficiency relationship in rural Mexico... small farms have more output value per hectare and operate closer to their efficiency frontier than large farms. Overall, our findings offer a guardedly optimistic view of small farms' capacity to produce efficiently...[3]

The Food and Agriculture Organization of the United Nations "State of Food and Agriculture Report 2014" revealed that, "families run nine out of every ten farms (worldwide) or 500 million farms. Additional analysis shows that family farms occupy a large share of the world's agricultural land and produce about 80% of the world's food." Furthermore, the report states that, "worldwide farms of less than five hectares (12.3 acres) account for 94% of all farms and occupy only 19% of all farmland ... and smaller farms tend to have higher yields than larger farms within the same country."[4,5]

The European Union has been taking notice of the presence of small farms. The article "Typology and distribution of small farms in Europe: Towards a Better Picture," by Guiomar et al., states that

> "The contribution of small farms to local food supply, food security and food sovereignty is widely acknowledged at a global level. In the particular case of Europe, they are often seen as an alternative to large and specialized farms. Assessing the real role of small farms has been limited by a lack of information, as small farms are frequently omitted from agricultural censuses and national statistics."[6]

From the most recent study to date comparing smaller farms to larger ones, from July 2021 by Ricciardi et al, "Higher Yields and More Biodiversity on Smaller Farms," stated that, "Our analysis finds that smaller farms have higher yields and harbor greater crop diversity and higher levels of non-crop biodiversity at the field and landscape scales than larger farms."[7]

Even though small farms over one acre (.40 ha), as demonstrated in the above essays and studies, have high yield potential, significant waste as farm size increases gives me pause in any recommendations of continuing along this course.

Waste

While yield is an accurate measure of productivity in our agricultural systems, waste should also be considered. It has been claimed that up to one third of all food is wasted. The food supply chain (FSC) has five component parts: agriculture (during harvest), post-harvest handling, processing, distribution, and consumption. To fully understand where food losses are occurring, it is important to break down the categories specific to North America.

From the study "Global Food Losses and Waste," conducted in 2011 by Gustavsson et al. for the Food and Agriculture Organization (FAO) of the United Nations, they found that in North America and Oceania:

- Approximately 33% of all cereals are wasted. 12% of the loss is attributed to the farmer.
- Approximately 60% of all roots and tubers are wasted. 47% of the loss is attributed to the farmer.
- Approximately 21% of all oilseeds and pulses are wasted. 57% of the loss is attributed to the farmer.
- Approximately 52% of all fruits and vegetables are wasted. 44% of the loss is attributed to the farmer.[8]

Only in the cereal category is some part of the chain (consumers) more wasteful than at the production level; in every other crop category, it is at agricultural production (during harvest) and post-harvest handling where the waste is the largest percentage. To paint the picture more clearly: 60% of all roots and tubers and 52% of all fruits and vegetables are wasted, with 47% and 44% respectively attributed to the farmer's hands. This shows distinctly that farm size must be decreased to eliminate the spoils.

Here at La Ferme de l'Aube, for four years running (2018-2021), we have had around 1% waste that would be attributed to us (agriculture harvest and post-harvest handling). Some of the crops we harvest in September rest in storage until the following May. Even the harvest that does become inedible is always deposited in the compost pile, which is returned back to the gardens to complete the circle. Interestingly, as production increased, so has the loss—with 2021 being our most profligate at 1.4%. So, even for us, we can improve by making the gardens more stream-lined and increasing our growing prowess.

Back at my one-acre farm in Arizona, my recollection of waste from the main commercial vegetable production years of 2006-2009 was that it was also practically nil. The viability of the small farm and backyard garden in relation to efficiency, productivity, and waste in the United States and Canada has yet to be extensively discerned and studied. Yet, what seems to be apparent is that, when we as growers have less production space, we are more cognizant of not losing any single fruit, vegetable, or herb.

The early summer extravaganza of carrots, radishes and salad turnips.

The late summer harvest at the on-farm kiosk at La Ferme de l'Aube.

16

Letting Plants Go to Flower, to Seed, and Saving Them

ALL PLANTS DESIRE, whether cultivated or native, to produce flowers and set seed, either from the mechanism of the fruit in which the seeds are housed or from the flowering stalk. Seed stalks like those on grains, grasses, and greens set their seed on long reedy legs and wait for the wind to carry or rattle them off. They readily germinate if the temperatures are still warm or will lie dormant until the heat returns. Seeds encased in fruits fall off the plant, like tomatoes, or get so large that they split open, like squashes. The following growing season, they will freely sprout. Sometimes birds take seeds like sunflowers or small fruits and either deposit them in a cache or through their droppings where, upon warming, they will create volunteer patches.

Letting plants go to flower and seed is transformative for the garden patch. It provides a lush habitat for all manner of faunal creatures. The low-growing cilantro plants quickly bolt in the heat of summer, creating many branches. Native bees, flies, and wasps frequent the delicate white flowers. Ant colonies and ground beetles work the grounds underneath. Toads hop, lizards crawl, and snakes slither to find shelter from the summer heat. Chickadees and goldfinches glean fibers from the stems for nesting material. Huge heads of dried dill seeds provide late-summer treats for these same bird friends. Mammoth sunflower heads on eight-foot (2.4m) stalks provide nutritious kernels into the fall for them, as well as many jay species. The pollen that precedes seed formation is procured by bumblebees, using it for whatever purpose they wish. As mentioned a multitude of times, the more floral diversity, the more faunal diversity.

It is important to consider planting flowering plants that flower at different times in the season, to create permanent flowering patches from frost-to-frost for pollen-seeking insects. The bees that awaken with the warming temperatures are hungry after their dormancy period. If they live in proximity and do not find a suitable food source, they will travel on, as will syrphid flies, wasps, butterflies, and moths. In late summer and fall, the same creatures are feeding furiously, sensing the cold weather approaching. The bees and wasps will hibernate. The butterflies and moths will, in some cases, need the extra nourishment for their long journey south, like the remarkable Monarch butterflies. Every year, millions of fall migrants from northern breeding areas in southeastern Canada and the eastern United States (east of the Rocky Mountains), fly southwards to overwinter in roosts in a small number of coniferous fir groves atop the trans-volcanic mountains of Michoacán in central Mexico.[1] By planting more variety, we are giving back to those creatures' habitats that which we have so aggressively stolen from as a collective species. The late summer activity is nothing short of a vibrant carnival.

To over-emphasize the point, letting as many plants as possible go to flower will maximize the faunal biodiversity in the gardening system. This is an uncommon practice among market gardeners and small farmers. Flowers and seeds are not a profitable undertaking for most growers. This concept utilizes too much space that could be flipped to a quick-growing "cash crop." It is rare to find a market grower who also saves a majority of their own seeds. There are a few of us who have honed this time-honored skill. I wish to impress upon the urban backyard to farmyard grower that the process of saving seeds is as important a skill as gardening itself. By engaging in this ancient tradition, we will ensure genetic cultivated plant diversity and purity. Without this practice handed down to us from the past generations, we would not have the fruit, vegetable, herb. and flower varieties we do today.

But merely seed saving for our own gain should not be the sole purpose for the veganic grower. Agriculture has caused more land-use change than any other anthropogenic industry except infrastructure and development. "It currently constitutes the largest biome on the planet, occupying a third of the global ice-free land area," confirmed authors Ramankutty et al., in "Trends in Global Agricultural Land Use: Implications for Environmental Health and Food Security,"[2] In reality, for the natural world, monoculture of corn laden with pesticide and herbicide is hardly more biodiverse than a parking lot. Even larger farms that till up crop residues in the fall see very little biological diversity. In comparison, the garden plot of one acre and less can help restore some of that variance that lives in the surrounding natural environment. In large part, by allowing plants to reach their full flowering and seeding potential.

Saving Seeds

Let's take radish as an example. Every year, we direct sow radish as soon as the soil can be worked. Since radishes (*Raphanus spp.*) cross with other radishes (more on this phenomenon later in this chapter), we plant only one type to let go to flower and seed. It changes every year, so we have a continual rotation in our personal seed bank. One year, it will be Cherry Belle (red), the next Pink Beauty (Pink), and the following D'Avignon (bicolor red and white heirloom). After harvesting a few to taste test, we select out the most beautifully formed, uncracked globes and let them continue to enlarge. Soon, the flower stalks shoot up—known as bolting—and start to display their rather showy white blooms. They produce flowers late in the spring to early summer, when there are few other native or cultivated flowers about. The inhabitants of our region in the form of bees, flies, hornets, wasps, small butterflies, and moths come in to frolic. The plants will continually flower until the end of summer. When the flowers have dried, pods form and dry on the plant. We select out all the dry pods and these become our seed bank. The rest of the plant rests in place, and when the heavy rains and snows fall, will decompose. Some of the pods we missed will shatter and the seeds will lie dormant until the following spring. The seeds then "volunteer" germinate when the ground warms yielding extra early radishes.

Certain plants are very easy to seed save from, like any that form in a pod—for instance: beans, bok choy, mustard greens, peas, radishes, and turnips. When the pods are dry, collect them and crack them. The seeds can then be stored in any receptacle you choose. Glass, used Tupperware, or reused envelopes are all good options. Others are somewhat more difficult. Peppers, both hot and sweet, are saved for seed when the pepper is at its most ripe, usually in the red stage. The seeds are extracted and left to dry on a paper towel or scrap notebook paper for a day or so, in a warm semi-dark place. I have labeled collections on top of the refrigerator drying all summer. They are then put into a storage vessel like the others. Melon and winter squash seeds can be harvested from perfectly ripe melons and squash. Cucumbers and summer squash must be grown exceptionally large before seeds will be viable. Summer squash will be a size we would never really want to eat. Cucumbers are ready when the whole fruit gets large, yellow, and soft to the touch. After extracting all the seeds and rinsing them, they are left to dry in a warm semi-dark location. Tomatoes, however, are a little different.

Tomato seeds are all surrounded by a gelatinous casing. This gel-sac should be allowed to ferment for ease of saving the seed. Here is my favorite method, with which I save over forty varieties: A perfectly ripe tomato—whether slicing, Italian, or cherry—is cut right down the middle, through the stem and blossom end. The seeds should be clearly visible. With a knife or by squeezing, I empty the seed and juice into a glass jar. A half pint (250ml) mason jar works very efficiently. Once all the seeds are deposited there, I fill the jar with equal amounts water and let it sit in a warm place in the light. The light and warmth will help ferment (mold) the glutinous gel sacs of the tomato seeds. As soon as a fuzzy black or green mold develops on the surface, I scoop it out into the compost bin and fill the jar with water. Using a chopstick, I swish the watery tomato seed mixture and the rest of the gel sacs float to the surface. I gently pour it all off. The viable seeds will settle to the bottom. I will do this a few times and once satisfied, with the aid of the chopstick, I will pour the seeds onto a scrap piece of copy paper (nice and strong). The seeds will dry out in the same location as the others for a few days. When dry, I pop them off with my fingernail, label (with name, date, number of seeds and characteristics) and package them like all the rest.

There are roughly 2.2 million professional farms in the United States[3] and Canada[4] combined, and of these only a small handful grow a diversity of crops for sale and seed. A look in a seed catalog for heirloom varieties (passed down for at least three generations, or about 70 years) will reveal varieties that have been selected out by small home growers and farmers. Black Turtle bean, Black-seeded Simpson lettuce, Brandywine tomato, D'Avignon radish, and Waltham Butternut squash are a few examples that exist because of the efforts of small gardeners. It is they, and us, who have kept many heirloom varieties proliferating. All heirloom and open pollinated cultivars can be saved by the home gardener. Some need a distance of separation (out-breeding); some can be grown in close proximity (in-breeding).

Those that can be grown in close proximity (about 50 feet apart, or 15.2 meters) are beans, eggplant, lettuce, peas, peppers (hot and sweet), soybeans, and tomatoes.

All of these crops have perfect flowers. The pistil (female) and stamen (male) are housed in the same flower, so they self-pollinate. Being self-pollinating means that they do not require insects to transfer the pollen to make fruits set. The anthers which carry the pollen are located next to the stamen and require only vibration. The vibration source can be insect presence (movement), wind, or us walking by and brushing the plant. This will cause the stamen's pollen to "trip," permeating the pistil.

I have been seed-saving for over twenty years and have never had any of the above cross among varieties, even when planting side by side. For example, seed saving from Black Turtle beans and Jacob's Cattle beans in rows adjacent has yielded true seed every single year for that duration. The same has been observed for tomatoes. A Brandywine tomato planted eighteen inches (45cm) apart from a Cherokee Purple has yielded pure seed. The recommendation by professional seed savers is fifty feet as stated above. However, truth on the ground (for me, anyway) has been that separation is not necessary for any variety with perfect, self-pollinating flowers.

Other fruits and vegetables require separation anywhere from one hundred feet (30.5m) to one-half mile (0.8km) for genetic purity and is achieved by growing just one variety type within those distances, such as beets, the *Brassicaceae* family, carrots, corn, cucumbers, melons, summer squash, and winter squash.

These will all cross. But even then, there are summer and winter squash that may not cross with each other. It depends on the Latin species name. An heirloom Ronde de Nice (*Cucurbita pepo*) will cross with a Yellow Crookneck (*Cucurbita pepo*), both summer squashes, and will cross with Sweet Reba Acorn Squash (*Cucurbita pepo*), a winter squash; but they all will not cross with heirloom Waltham Butternut (*Cucurbita moschata*). Summer and winter squash varieties with the same species names can be diligently saved, however, if planted closer than the seed-saving recommendations. By detaching the stamen and hand-pollinating the pistil, gently rubbing them together in the early morning hours before pollinating insects awake, it will become pollinated. The female flower can then be closed with a twist tie until the squash forms. The seed should be true.

For another example, Prize Choy bok choy (*Brassica rapa*) will cross with heirloom Purple Top White Globe Turnip (*Brassica rapa*), even though they seem like two completely different plants.

Some plants like beets, broccoli, carrots, onion, parsley, and others are biennial, meaning that they will flower in the second growing season. Some, like those in the family *Brassicaceae* (broccoli, cabbage, cauliflower, collards, kale, and kohlrabi) as well as parsley and leeks, can be mulched and wintered in place even if the temperatures reach -30F (-34.5C). They will all readily regrow from their root systems and immediately send up flower stalks. Others like beets, carrots, onions, parsnips, and rutabaga want to be harvested and kept in dormancy between 33F and 40F (1-4.5C) for the winter months. In spring, after the soil opens, they can be replanted and set to go to flower and seed.

Confused? Don't worry, you are not alone. If you are interested in one of our oldest, most indigenous of gardening traditions there is an excellent resource available. Suzanne Ashworth's *Seed to Seed*[5] has been in my bookcase since my gardening adventure began. It can be considered the bible of seed-saving information and techniques.

Here, of the over four hundred varieties of plants that we cultivate, 125+ are perennials, and we actively seed save from 115+ annuals and perennials. It increases every year, for this is food security for all beings here in Québec. Installing perennials and saving our own seeds takes out the importance of the ever-consolidating seed industry and puts the power back into our calloused hands.

For some of my favorite flowering plants, both annual and perennial check out Annex D: Flower and Herb Chart. Another excellent resource is Jenny Hall & Iain Tolhurst's collaboration, *Growing Green: Animal-Free Growing Techniques*. Specifically, chapter nine, "Environmental Conservation," details the many veganic principles to encouraging insects, birds, reptiles, amphibians, wildlife, and the biodiversity of cultivated and indigenous flora.[6]

Open-pollinated and heirloom cherry tomato diversity, all of which we seed save.

17

Preserving the Harvest

AS THE HARVEST starts coming in strong during the late summer days, breakfast, lunch, and dinner meals have healthy portions of home-grown fruits, vegetables, and herbs. No matter what size garden one has, there is a high likelihood there will be too much produce at the same time. Thinking about preserving the harvest while it is still beautiful and bountiful will augment late fall and winter plates, when times are lean.

At La Ferme de l'Aube, the dehydrator makes its appearance early in the growing season, when the fresh herb plants are plentiful. Our preferred model is the Excalibur brand with nine trays. While a little steep in price, the quality and durability are second to none. The dehydrator can be used for all manner of fruits, vegetables, and herbs. It is useful for drying leaves like basil, lemon balm, and oregano. It is good for drying flowers like chamomile and calendula. It is well equipped to handle the dehydrating of sliced fruits and vegetables like apples, ground cherries, peppers, tomatoes, and summer squash. The flavor holds exceptionally well. Once fully dry and cooled, the bounty can be stored in food-grade plastic bags or bins, mason canning jars, or recycled glass containers.

Raw freezing of fruits like blueberries, raspberries, strawberries, and rhubarb is an excellent way to preserve the nutrient content. I used to make preserves from these, but after a year of going nuts and canning twenty-five half pint jars (125ml), I realized that I did not eat that much. By freezing fresh, they can be made into fresh coulis, preserves, smoothies, or added into cakes and cobblers. They can even be eaten directly from the bag as a frozen delicacy. We freeze bell peppers (red, green, and bicolored) and diced celery. The tough upper end of the celery stalks is also frozen to be made into vegetable-based soup stock. End of season cilantro and parsley can be conserved as well to give a lift to winter soups and stews. Grated zucchini is welcome when we yearn for zucchini muffins and/or croquettes. English shelling peas, shucked of their green morsels, are sweet remembrances of the summer. Even those leftover vegetable scraps like carrot ends, garlic and onion skins, leek trimmings, parsley sprigs, and pumpkin and winter squash rinds can be placed in a stock pot, boiled down, and frozen for instant vegetable stock.

For vegetable greens like collards, mustards, kale, rapini, and spinach, it is preferred to quick blanch them. This process involves boiling water and plunging the diced greens in for about one minute. Strain, allow to cool, and then pack them into freezer bags. Edamame pods should be blanched for three minutes. Sweet corn can be cooked thoroughly, as if eating corn on the cob, and then stripped of the kernels with a kitchen knife and packed. Basil and garlic scapes blended together will create that much cherished summer pesto, deep into the winter months. With freezing, the sky is the limit. There are others I know who freeze whole tomatoes and blanched snap beans. I hate waste, whether vegetative or plastic material, so I re-use all freezer bags as often as possible.

Canning is a more complicated process of preservation. It is a heritage practice that historically was passed down from generation to generation. Some of us can remember our parents and grandparents boiling down huge cauldrons of tomato sauce or relish and hot-packing it for year-long storage. There are a few different methods. Great care must be taken in sterilization and sealing to protect against bacterial contamination. Check appropriate resources like from the USDA, "Complete Guide to Home Canning"[1] and the Government of Canada's, "Home canning safety."[2] Canning, however, is my preferred method of preserving all tomato products, like whole tomatoes, sauce, and Mexican-style salsa.

Fresh pickles can be made from cucumbers, green beans, hot peppers, and okra when in abundance, using a simple salt, apple cider vinegar, and water brine. Here is a recipe I have used for years: Mix 1.5 cups organic apple cider vinegar, two cups water, and two tablespoons salt in a sauce pan and bring to a boil. Set aside to cool. Cut cucumbers lengthwise or in circles, as desired. Green beans and okra can be packed whole. Hot peppers can be sliced or whole; if whole, poke a few holes in the pepper with a fork to allow brine to enter. Pack clean pint (500ml) jars with the fruits and vegetables and pour the liquid over the top. Leave half an inch (1cm) of head space. Secure with a canning ring and lid. If making dill pickles or dilly beans, I will add a clove of garlic, one-half teaspoon of whole peppercorns, and one teaspoon of dill seed. Place in the refrigerator and wait six to eight weeks for proper flavor infusion. They can all store for up to one year. Because of the high vinegar content, there is almost zero percent chance of contamination.

Lacto-fermentation, through its process, creates (among other things) probiotics through lactic acid. Lacto-fermented products will regulate gut bacteria and be a valuable source of vitamin C.[3] Cabbages as sauerkraut or kimchi (a Korean staple), carrots, daikon, garlic, ginger, and onions, as well as hot peppers are responsive to this method of preservation. *Wild Fermentation: The Flavor, Nutrition, and Craft of Live-Culture Foods*[4] by Sandor Ellix Katz is a fantastic resource on these and many other fermentation ideas.

When crops are coming to an end, preserving the harvest in all the above-mentioned ways, plus others that I have not, will allow the grower to capture the summer flavor. Will Bonsall's *Essential Guide to Radical, Self-Reliant Gardening* is truly an exceptional excursion for the literary senses. Chapter 17: Freezing, Fermenting and More provides some of those other ideas in preservation.[5] In addition to harvesting at the perfect, full-sized time, the practice of "gleaning" the last fruits, leaves, and stems will increase the pantry and freezer storage no matter what the size or quality. Before the last frost arrives, "gleaning", or stripping the plants of the last beans, eggplants, peppers, and tomatoes (even when all green) will lengthen the time of fresh consumption. Most, if not all, green tomatoes will turn color when left at 55-60F (13-16C). They are not fantastic to eat fresh, but are a wonderful addition to chilis, sauces, soups, and stews.

Cold storage is the process of keeping fruits and vegetables in a dormant state for long-term keeping. When it is time to pull out the roots, like beets, carrots, parsnips, and rutabaga, they will want to be stored at less than 40F (4.5C) as soon as possible. For the small garden, one refrigerator is usually sufficient; however, for the bigger garden, a second refrigerator may become necessary. For the 6,000 square foot garden space (the amount needed to feed two people in season and throughout the late fall and winter), a root cellar, unheated basement or insulated cold room would be required. All roots are alive when stored. If the storage area gets too warm, the tops will begin to leaf out and small filaments of roots will begin to appear as their dormancy breaks. Long-term cold storage seeks to pause the process. Using the methods described below, I have been able to store root crops for nine months in an insulated cold room kept between 33-39F (1-4C), when outside temperatures have plummeted to -35F (-37C), with the use of a simple forced fan heater, with thermostat set on just about the lowest setting.

All roots should be dry at storage but not clean. The dirt acts as an extra insulating layer. The dirty outer skins of onions act in the same capacity. We pack all beets, cabbage, carrots, celery root, kohlrabi, parsnips, winter radish, rutabaga, and turnips in three-gallon (eleven liter) Rubbermaid bins. The same ones we like to use for harvesting. These heavy-duty bins are easily cleaned and disinfected at the end of the season and can last a lifetime. All of the above-mentioned vegetables wish to be stored with a slight level of humidity, and the bins are excellent for that purpose. The only caution is if the temperature climbs above 40F (4.5C), the bins should be opened, and the excess moisture wiped away with a cloth.

Potatoes and onions are stored at the same temperature, but are instead kept in recycled heavy duty stackable cardboard boxes. Usually, these can be found in great quantity by the dumpsters of grocery stores or in produce departments. These two crops like to have slight air circulation. All cold room, basement, and root cellar areas should be dark, like a refrigerator when closed.

Long-term storage requirements of garlic, pumpkins, and the whole assortment of winter squash are slightly different. The minimum temperature should be no less than 50F (10C) and not raise much higher than 60F (15.5C). If colder, winter squash will eventually develop cold rot and garlic will mold. The pumpkins and squashes can be stored in cardboard boxes, while the garlic prefers a closed paper bag.

Proper post-harvest handling and preserving techniques will eliminate garden waste and reward us with fine wintertime meals. With some forethought, and using the skills provided in this handbook (see Annex A: Crop Profiles for individual crop storage requirements and preservation recommendations), you can ensure all the blood, sweat, and tears of obtaining the actual harvest will be, well-preserved.

Our portion of the potato harvest (Agria, Caribe and Yukon Gold) to be placed in cold storage for the lean winter months.

18

Putting the Gardens to Bed and Reflections on the Season that Was

A T THE END of the growing season, when plants are starting to die from the frosts, bacterial, and fungal pathogens, a tangle of vines and piles of organic matter remain. It's time to clean up, raking out the residue, right? Not so fast. The best way to protect the soil from erosion and carbon loss is to leave it all where it is. As discussed briefly in chapter six, this is a process called in-bed composting. The fall rains will flatten the plants and the snowpack will keep it all in place. A new study from July 2021, conducted by a team of researchers from the University of Copenhagen and the Technical University of Munich, explains their findings on letting crop residues rot directly in the fields. In the journal article "Particulate organic matter as a functional soil component for persistent soil organic carbon," they state:

> We demonstrate that agricultural crop residues are absolutely central to carbon storage and that we should use them in a much more calculated way in the future. Plant residues make it possible for carbon, in all likelihood, to be stored in soil for roughly four times longer than if they aren't added.[1]

As important as it is for carbon sequestration, soil fertility, and health, it is also very important for the creatures that inhabit the gardens. Small mammals will make burrows under the snow layer through the plant residues. They will eat the seeds and shred the dried vegetative matter for warmer dens. Moles and voles will make tunnels in the topsoil, creating airflow and reconfiguring the terrain. In a way, like a beaver attempting to shift streams and rivers to create wetlands, these small burrowers are terrestrial engineers. I am not experienced or scientific enough to understand exactly what they are trying to accomplish, but what I am assured of is that they are doing it for specific purposes. Maybe they do what they do for the benefit of others as well. In addition to them, gopher and ground snakes will burrow deep into the soil underneath, as do toads and frogs. All that thrives during the growing season seeks a warm winter home to hibernate. But don't moles, voles, mice, and kangaroo rats eat the seeds and seedlings? I am sure they do. But in all my time of small-scale organic and veganic gardening, I have never observed great destruction. They are eating some seedlings, but I believe the damage rests as minimal as long as they have hedgerows, green strips, and weedy piles to make their lives. From my experience, only in less diversified fields and gardens do they devastate seedlings and roots.

When the spring thaw comes and the garden beds begin to peek through, the transformation is quite astounding. Beds of plant detritus have composted more than two thirds of their residues. All leafy green matter has been digested by the bacteria, worms, insects, and small mammals that live on and in the soil. Really only the toughest and woodiest stems remain. Like I mentioned before, in Chapter 5: Garden Preparation, the beds are either raked of the remaining stems to be put in compost piles or set aside as dry mulch. This approach, taken straight out of a healthy forests' playbook, is the gardener's cheapest and easiest way to increase soil fertility. The only real effort we sometimes make at the end of the season, when the plants have discontinued growing, is to pull them out if they have a tough stem. So, *Brassicaceae* family and *Solanaceae* family varieties can be pulled and placed lying down on the bed. I have noticed when the cold comes that if the stems and roots are left in the ground, they freeze in place and do not always compost. But by pulling them out, little creatures can shred the fibrous roots for their personal pleasure. Ground beetles can find solace in the stems. Any plant that is in flower or has gone to seed is left for as long as possible. Many bird species enjoy gleaning the last kernels, including many migrating sparrow species before their long journey south.

If there are still some patches or rows of lettuces, mustards, kale, or spinach, they can be protected for a while longer. Deep into the fall, when the nighttime lows reach 14F (-10C), we can keep many of these varieties alive by applying a double Agribon-17 or 19 row cover. In 2020, I harvested my last field greens the first week of December, extending the harvest as long as possible. Additionally, the following spring, the kale and spinach will grow back for extra early field greens. The biennial kale plants will go to seed for saving and create years of volunteer kale patches.

Closing Down the Gardens

In gardens where there are irrigation lines, we will drain out all the excess water out of the main lines, detach them from the pond pump, and leave it all in the field for ease of the following year's installation. If there is no more water left in the lines the risk of bursting is almost none. If preferred, hoses and drip tapes can be wrapped, coiled, and stored.

All other materials are taken out of the soil. All wooden stakes used for climbing beans, peas, and tomatoes are stacked on recycled pallets close to the gardens and covered with a tarp to extend their life. The plastic from the caterpillar tunnels is taken off and folded onto another pallet, tarped, and corded. The metal frame is left in place, as it can withstand all the winter abuse. Recycled pallets can be found at the dumpsters of most hardware stores and garden centers. All sand and rock bags for holding down covers and screens are stacked. The insect screens and Agribon row covers are pulled out, allowed to air dry, rolled up, and stored in marked recycled bags in the barn. All tools are wiped clean of dirt. Rolling carts and wheelbarrows are stored inside. The more careful we are in cleaning, marking, and organizing at the end of the season, the less expensive the following year's supply bill will be.

Reflections

The fields are closed. The fall garlic has been planted. As the nights rest into 20 degrees Fahrenheit (-7 Celsius) and below, the fields go dormant. The hibernation time begins for the plants and us growers.

We have gotten into the habit of closing down the season with an end of the year reunion, while the past growing year is still fresh in our memory. We detail what were positive developments and improved upon from the year prior. The activity/observation log that was kept daily during the year comes into play. The shorthand phrases are deciphered. The revealing notes discuss what plants performed well, what new flowers the bees were preferring, and what harvests were extraordinary. We will also discuss what can be improved upon for the following year, for there will always be something. This reunion takes place to make the following year's ordering, seeding, planting, maintaining, harvesting, and storing more efficient. This allows us to effectively remember our mistakes and not make the same ones. Every year, the gardens at La Ferme de l'Aube are more vibrant and produce higher yields because of this reflective process.

Growing our own food is challenging. In these days of rapidly changing, extreme climates, giving us record heats and colds, droughts, and rains, being able to adapt quickly is a necessity. No matter where in the world, there will always be failures, whether the plot is a thirty-two square foot urban garden or one-acre rural farmyard. But, along with the failures, there will be many successes. It is humbling and inspiring, devastating and ecstatic; thus is the growing of fruits, vegetables, and herbs, all emotions are fulfilled. Over my quarter of a century journey, I have made all mistakes possible, and more I have not even thought of are certainly on the way. Yet, every year the pantry, freezer, refrigerator, cold room, and root cellar have had my own home-grown goodness.

From the Intergovernmental Panel on Climate Change (IPCC), "Climate Change 2021: The Physical Science Basis: Summary for Policy Makers"[2], which was contributed to by over one hundred authors, the following has been concluded:

It is unequivocal that human influence has warmed the atmosphere, ocean, and land. Widespread and rapid changes in the atmosphere, ocean, cryosphere, and biosphere have occurred. Human influence has warmed the climate at a rate that is unprecedented in the last two thousand years and is affecting every inhabited region across the globe. Global warming of 1.5 to 2 degrees Celsius will be exceeded in the 21st century unless deep reductions in CO_2 and other greenhouse gas emissions occur in the coming decades. Continued global warming is projected to further intensify the global water cycle, including its variability, global monsoon precipitation and the severity of wet and dry events." "From a physical science perspective, limiting human-induced global warming to a specific level requires limiting cumulative CO_2 emissions, reaching at least net-zero CO_2 emissions, along with strong reductions in other greenhouse gas emissions. Strong, rapid, and sustained reductions in CH_4 (methane) emissions would also limit the warming effect resulting from declining aerosol pollution and would improve air quality.

Reflecting upon these statements, I wonder why, on a global scale, we appear to be the only species on the planet that actively destroys the very ecosystem we require to survive. Along that ruminating line of thought, according to Ceballos, Ehrlich, and Dirzo in "Biological annihilation via the ongoing sixth mass extinction signaled by vertebrate population losses and declines," back in 2017,

The loss of biological diversity is one of the most severe human-caused global environmental problems. Hundreds of species and myriad populations are being driven to extinction every year. From the perspective of geological time, Earth's richest biota ever is already well into a sixth mass extinction episode. Future losses easily may amount to a further rapid defaunation of the globe and comparable losses in the diversity of plants, including the local (and eventually global) defaunation-driven coextinction of plants.

The likelihood of this rapid defaunation lies in the proximate causes of population extinctions: habitat conversion, climate disruption, overexploitation, toxification, species invasions, disease, and (potentially) large-scale nuclear war—all tied to one another in complex patterns and usually reinforcing each other's impacts. Much less frequently mentioned are, however, the ultimate drivers of those immediate causes of biotic destruction, namely, human overpopulation and continued population growth, and overconsumption, especially by the rich. These drivers, all of which trace to the fiction that perpetual growth can occur on a finite planet, are themselves increasing rapidly. Thus, we emphasize that the sixth mass extinction is already here and the window for effective action is very short, probably two or three decades at most. All signs point to ever more powerful assaults on biodiversity in the next two decades, painting a dismal picture of the future of life, including human life.[3]

Dwelling on these morbid, yet very lucid ideas, my thoughts instantly turn to a bumper sticker that graced the rear of my 1973 Volkswagen Bus: "Think Global, Act Local." On a small-scale, local growing level, we can attempt to heal that anthropogenic razing of the landscape by restoring our efforts towards the very earth that breathes life into all her inhabitants.

Within these pages is the culmination of my experiences. They hold a wealth of growing advice, tips, and techniques for the budding beginner to professional farmer. It is my hope that you, the reader, will become the best possible gardener to nourish yourself and your family. By growing veganically, you are also creating the best possible environment for all native creatures who wish to inhabit where you reside.

Throughout my path there were many who told me, "You can't do it," "nothing grows here," "the soil is no good," and "you need manure to be successful." In time, I have proven all of these naive statements incorrect. I believe that you can grow no matter what commentary has floated past your ears. As small-scale urban backyard to rural farmyard growers, we have the flexibility to adapt more quickly to the coming intensifying climate challenges and strive for some semblance of food-security and independence. This comprehensive handbook will help you, like it has me, persuade others, unequivocally, that veganic growing is the new direction for us all.

End of the season colors are always a marvel, taking time to witness the magic is an imperative.

Annex A: Crop Profiles

Annex A:
Crop Profiles

Each crop and subsequent variety is unique in its characteristics. They all require specific care in seeding, transplanting, and maintenance throughout their lives. Each variety has definitive harvest practices and post-harvest handling requirements. Between this annex and Annex B: Crop Spacing and Yields, they should give all the information you will need to increase your growing success.

Legend:

Crop name/common name and *Latin genus and species*

Characteristics/growing habits: Will give the larger *Latin family name.* Characteristics of plant growth and habit in leafing, heading, flowering, and fruiting are described.

Favorite varieties: My personal favorite open-pollinated (OP) and heirloom (HL) varieties for flavor and performance (yields) are listed. I have only included F-1 (F1) hybrids if I believe they will benefit the veganic grower.

Seeding information: Recommends whether to start inside in cell plug trays (one seed per cell, unless noted differently) or direct seed, with depths and distances apart, and whether open-pollinated (OP), heirloom (HL), or F-1 hybrid (F1) types are recommended.

For most crops the veganic grower should seek out open-pollinated (OP) or heirloom (which are also open-pollinated) seed. F-1 hybrids are extremely expensive for the qualities they purport to have. However, for crops in the *Brassicaceae* family like broccoli, brussels sprouts, cabbage, and cauliflower, I would recommend F-1 hybrids, as OP and heirloom varieties seem to require higher levels of fertility and *perfect* conditions to come to fruition. For early varieties of carrots and beets, F1 hybrids can be beneficial to award the grower with an extra early crop. For growers in the colder parts of North America, hybrid sweet corn can ensure germination in our soils. When choosing, choose for days to harvest, color, and flavor. Grab an extra cup of your favorite beverage in early winter after the seed catalogs arrive, or are posted online, and peruse to your heart's desire.

Days to germination at temperature range: Expected time to germinate either inside or from direct seeding, and range of soil temperatures recommended in Fahrenheit (Celsius).

When to start inside: Number of weeks before transplanting outside at: as soon as soil can be worked (open soil), last frost, or warm and settled dates. If n/a is written, this means they do not need to be started inside for the specific crop.

Necessary to pot-up to three-inch (7.5cm) pots: Yes, no, or n/a. If yes, I will describe when. Use three to four-inch (7.5-10cm) pots.

When to transplant or direct seed outside: Whether at soil open, last frost, or warm and settled dates, for transplants and direct seeding alike, and how far apart to plant. I will mention if succession planting is recommended. Information on protection from cold nights and insect pressures will be discussed.

If in your particular growing system, you do not have a set-up for seeding inside, there is a plethora of crops that can be direct seeded outside when the seasonal time is right.

Maintenance required during growing period: Included are weeding of native flora, watering information and tolerance to drought, staking and trellising requirements, and dry straw mulching. Also included are specific fertilization requirements, if necessary, and optimal pH ranges.

No matter how infertile your soil, as long as the pH (power of hydrogen) is between 5.7 and 7.2, you will yield a harvestable crop. The only soil amendments (brought in or created onsite) I recommend is veganic compost (see Chapter 7: The Compost Piles) and dolomitic lime or wood ash, to increase soil pH. If there is a need for specific fertilization it will be listed in each individual crop profile. Having read this book, it should be obvious to understand that over the subsequent years of composting, dry mulching, cover crops, and plant residue incorporation, the garden beds will become more fertile and harvest yields will increase. So, don't be afraid to go for it even if you have never had a garden before, just ensure the proper pH range through a simple soil test and you will be reaping your own harvests very soon.

Insects to observe: The most common insect pressures I have observed in Northern Arizona and Southern Quebec, as well as the beneficial insects that the plants attract. A valuable source is the 1021-page compendium "Diseases and Pests of Vegetable Crops in Canada," available as a free pdf download.[1] If in the United States, you should also check if your regional university has a cooperative extension program.

Diseases to watch for: The most common diseases that I have experienced in Northern Arizona and Southern Quebec and best ways to control or mitigate. As above a valuable source is page 1021, "Diseases and Pests of Vegetable Crops in Canada," available as a free pdf download.[1] Like insects above, also check your regional university cooperative extension websites.

Days to harvest: The range of days that harvest can be expected as well as duration.

Harvest advice: Best methods to harvest flower buds, fruits, leaves, stems, and roots. As well as the best time of day to do so. The general rule is that if the fruit, vegetable, or herb wants to be stored cold, harvest as early in the morning as possible.

Post-harvest handling/terms of storage (best way to preserve flavor): Details the best way to store fresh, whether in plastic bags or bins (without holes) and the best way to preserve for the long term. When needed to be stored at 33-40F (1-4.5C) it is assumed to be either refrigerator, cold room, root cellar or unheated basement. This section also details whether the fruit, vegetable, or herb would be best preserved frozen, dried, pickled (fermented), or canned (hot water, pressure, or hot pack).

Health benefits: A specific peer-reviewed and/or evidence-based journal article has been located that explains the health benefits associated with each fruit, vegetable and herb profiled. The journal articles are open sourced and free to access, written by experts from around the world. Inside each one is a wealth of information for further study, with many alternative references harbored in each.

Observational field notes: Space has been provided for the grower to make notation directly in their handbook if desired. Items to be noted could be varieties trialed and the results, insects and diseases observed, days to harvest and harvest yields, or whatever else the veganic gardener may want to record. Remember: the more observational data, the better the following year will be.

Heirloom Rattlesnake Beans

Artichoke
Cynara scolymus

Characteristics/growing habits: Artichoke, a member of the family Compositae, can reach five feet (1.5m) tall and a robust three feet (90cm) in diameter. From the central crown, the main flower stem will rise and branch out. Anywhere from four to eight artichoke buds (the part eaten) will form. Perennial above zone seven, otherwise grown as an annual.

Favorite varieties: "Tavor" (OP)

Seeding information: One seed of (OP) per cell in plug trays. Seed an extra 50% for the plants you wish to have as artichokes are notoriously low in germination.

Days to germination at temperature range: Five to seven days at 70-80F (21-26.5C).

When to start inside: Eight to ten weeks before last spring frost date.

Necessary to pot-up to three-inch pots: Yes, as soon as plants have two true leaves.

When to transplant or direct seed outside: Transplant when the nights are still cold but not freezing every night, 18 to 24 inches (45-60cm) apart in a zig-zag pattern. Artichoke plants require vernalization, needing seven to ten days of nights 45-50F (7-10C) to induce budding. Protect with Agribon-19 row cover if night temperatures are forecast below freezing.

Maintenance required during growing period: Keep invasive natives like couch grass at bay. Can be under-seeded with an annual clover as desired. Optimum soil pH range is 6.0 to 7.5.

Insects to observe: Weevils, superfamily Curculionidae, make their homes in the crowns of artichoke plants but cause minimal damage from what I have seen.

Diseases to watch for: There are none of consequence from my observations.

Days to harvest: Eighty to ninety days from transplants, then continually until first hard fall frost.

Harvest advice: Cut mature buds with a one inch (2.5cm) stem before excessive flaring (which makes buds tough).

Post-harvest handling/terms of storage (best way to preserve flavor): Put dry in a plastic bag at 33-40F (1-4.5C) and will keep fourteen to twenty-one days. Best way to enjoy is to boil or steam artichokes until the outer leaves pull off easily.

Health benefits: Artichokes are rich in phenolics and rich in antioxidant activity. It has been reported that phenolic and flavonoid compounds act as antioxidants to exert antiallergic, anti-inflammatory, antidiabetic, antimicrobial, antipathogenic, antiviral, antithrombotic, and vasodilatory effects and prevent diseases such as cancer, heart problems, cataracts, eye disorders, and Alzheimer's.

Field notes:

Arugula (Roquette)
Eruca sativa

Characteristics/growing habits: Arugula, a member of the family *Brassicaceae*, is a cold hardy annual. Characterized by rounded or serrated leaves, the pungency of arugula is its most distinctive quality, being peppery and spicy.

Favorite varieties: "Astro" (OP)

Seeding information: Direct seed (OP), heirloom) ½-inch (1.25cm) deep, 2 inches (5cm) apart, rows at 6 inches (15cm).

Days to germination at temperature range: Three to six days at 50-75F (10-24C).

When to start inside: n/a

Necessary to pot-up to three-inch pots: n/a

When to transplant or direct seed outside: As soon as soil can be worked, and successively planted every three weeks thereafter to ensure a constant harvest throughout the season.

Maintenance required during growing period: Keep well weeded of native flora throughout the seedling stage. Once fully formed arugula will create a canopy that deters native flora growth. Cover immediately after planting with an insect screen. Optimum soil pH range is 6.0 to 7.5.

Insects to observe: Flea beetles are a common early spring problem creating small holes in young leaves. Best control is immediately after seeding to install insect screens. Keep greens well weeded of common plantain, the flea beetle's preferred host. Green peach aphids can become abundant in times of warm nights and humid conditions. Letting the earliest plantings go to flower will attract a whole host of native bees, syrphid flies and wasps.

Diseases to watch for: There are none of consequence in any stage.

Days to harvest: Twenty-one to thirty days from direct seeding for baby arugula, forty to fifty days for full-size leaves.

Harvest advice: Cut greens with a heavy-duty pocketknife, or pull off the oldest, largest outside leaves as soon as the desired size is reached. Cut above the central crown to allow for regrowth. Cut as early as possible in the morning before the heat of the day.

Post-harvest handling/terms of storage (best way to preserve flavor): Baby greens are highly perishable, will store for a maximum of fourteen days in plastic bags in the fridge. After harvest, immerse greens in cold water and salad-spin greens before storage. Best enjoyed fresh but can be made into a spicy pesto or tapenade and frozen for up to six months.

Health benefits: Rocket (arugula) salad is usually consumed fresh and has been described as containing several health promoting agents including fibers, proteins, calcium, iron, magnesium, vitamin A and C, carotenoids and flavonoids, some of these agents are known as powerful antioxidants.[4]

Field notes:

Asparagus
Asparagus officinalis

Characteristics/growing habits: Asparagus, a member of the family *Asparagaceae*, is one of the earliest crops to break ground in the spring. The spears, which are the flower stalks, grow back every year from the roots (crowns). Perennial to zone three through eight, asparagus can continue to produce for almost twenty years.

Favorite varieties: "Mary Washington" (HL), "Millennium" F-1

Seeding information: n/a, they can be started from seed, but I have never participated in this method for asparagus.

Days to germination at temperature range: n/a

When to start inside: Not recommended from seed, as it is easier to order crowns (F-1 hybrids tend to be more vigorous) from a reputable, organic seed company, when and if possible.

Necessary to pot-up to three-inch pots: n/a

When to transplant or direct seed outside: As soon as the soil can be worked 12 inches (30cm) apart, ensuring the entirety of the crowns are buried under the earth three to four inches.

Maintenance required during growing period: Remove all dried seed stalks in the early spring cutting them at the base of the plant. Apply a one-inch (2.5cm) compost layer over the entire asparagus growing area. Keep well weeded during the entire frost-free season as all native flora will steal nutrients from the crowns and decrease harvest and girth of spears. Optimum soil pH range is 6.0 to 7.5.

Insects to observe: Spotted asparagus beetles *Crioceris duodecimpunctata* have been noticed when spears go to multiple flower branches, but damage is minimal from my observations.

Diseases to watch for: From my monitoring, there are none of major consequence.

Days to harvest: In the first year, let spears go to full maturity without harvesting. In the second year, harvest for two weeks, the third year four weeks, the fourth year six weeks. Harvest eight weeks thereafter, any and all spears larger than the girth of a pencil.

Harvest advice: Cut at base with a pocketknife when spears reach four inches (10cm) before flower buds open.

Post-harvest handling/terms of storage (best way to preserve flavor): Store unwashed in a plastic bag at 33-40F (1-4.5C) for fourteen to twenty-one days. Best enjoyed fresh; however, asparagus can also be blanched and frozen, or pickled with a salt water and apple cider vinegar brine.

Health benefits: Asparagus spears contain steroidal saponins and possess a variety of biological properties, such as being antioxidants, immunostimulants, anti-inflammatory, antihepatotoxic, antibacterial, antioxytocic, and reproductive agents.[5]

Field notes:

Basil
Ocimum basilicum, africanum, tenuiflorum

Characteristics/growing habits: Basil, members of the family *Labiatae*, are tall (up to two feet (60cm), warm season annual plants. Their highly aromatic leaves can be small or large, rounded, pointed and/or serrated. Colors can vary from light to dark green, striped, or dark purple. It is the aromas that distinguish the varieties, ranging from lemony to spicy, sweet, or minty depending on the variety chosen.

Favorite varieties: "Genovese" (OP-green), "Rosie" (OP-purple), "Sweet Thai" (HL), "Sacred" or "Holy" (HL)

Seeding information: One seed of (OP, heirloom) per cell in plug trays.

Days to germination at temperature range: Four to seven days at 70-90F (21-32C).

When to start inside: Six weeks before warm and settled date.

Necessary to pot-up to three-inch (7.5-10cm) pots: Yes; as soon as plants have two true leaves. Basil plants will not hold in larger pots for very long before turning yellow, pot up no more than three weeks before transplanting outside. Can transplant two to three plug seedlings into each pot if desired.

When to transplant or direct seed outside: Transplant after warm and settled date. Basil does not like cold nights; protect with Agribon 17-19 row cover if night temperatures are forecast below 55F (13C). Plant at 6 inches (15cm) apart.

Maintenance required during growing period: Keep weeded of native flora throughout growing period. Very drought tolerant once established. When first flower buds form on the central stem, cut off with garden cutters just below to encourage branching. Continue to do so every time a flower forms, for a multi-branched basil plant. Optimum soil pH range is 6.0 to 7.5.

Insects to observe: None of major consequence attack the plants. If too warm and humid, aphids can infest the crowns of the plants. Letting basil go to flower, especially purple, spicy (like Thai and cinnamon), and sacred varieties will invite many native pollinating bees, flies, wasps, butterflies, and moths.

Diseases to watch for: Basil downy mildew is caused by the fungus-like organism *Peronospora belbaharii,* which will curl, yellow, and then blacken the leaves. Bacterial leaf spot caused by a bacterium called *Pseudomonas cichorii,* will blacken the leaves and stem. Both of these diseases become most prevalent in cold, humid conditions with lack of airflow. Control by limiting irrigation and not planting when nights are below 55F (13C). Cutting out infected stems is also a beneficial deterrent.

Days to harvest: Forty to sixty days from transplant, then continually until first fall frost.

Harvest advice: Harvest full sprigs of basil by cutting whole stems just above the closest leaves to the ground. Alternatively, can cut anywhere around a leaf-to-stem joint to encourage branching. Harvest in the morning but when the plants are dry to limit fungal/bacterial disease spread.

Post-harvest handling/terms of storage (best way to preserve flavor): Basil is highly perishable, holding for a maximum of five to seven days at 50F (10C). Store fresh, dry basil in plastic bags in the warmest part of the fridge or the coolest part of the house. Flavor is best preserved when blended into a pesto and frozen (up to six months), or dried (will store for a year and longer).

Health benefits: Traditionally, *Occinum basilicum* has been used to treat kidney problems, earache, menstrual irregularities, arthritis, anorexia, as a hemostyptic in childbirth, and for the treatment of colds and malaria. Basil has been shown to have positive effects against viral, fungal, and bacterial infections. Basil leaves have been used in treatment of fevers, coughs, flu, asthma, bronchitis, influenza, and diarrhea.[6]

Field notes:

Beets
Beta vulgaris

Characteristics/growing habits: Beets, members of the family *Amaranthaceae,* are a hardy biennial root crop that commences their growing with red or orange-veined green leaves, before forming round or cylindrical roots in vibrant reds, oranges, and pink candy stripes.

Favorite varieties: "Detroit Dark Red" (HL), "Cylindra" (HL), "Red Ace" F-1, "Touchstone Gold" (OP)

Seeding information: Direct seed (OP, heirloom, and F-1 for extra early) at ½-inch (1.25cm) deep, 2 inches (5cm) apart (thinning to 3 inches, 7.5cm), rows 12 inches (30cm) apart.

Days to germination at temperature range: Three to six days at 55-80F (13-26.5C).

When to start inside: Not recommended to start in plug trays

Necessary to pot-up to three-inch pots: n/a

Atlas des Plantes de France. A.Masclef 1891

Pl.276. Bette vulgaire.(Betterave). Beta vulgaris L.

When to transplant or direct seed outside: Direct seed first sowing a week before last frost date, and plant in three-four-week intervals for successions.

Maintenance required during growing period: Beets like boron to make full and healthy roots, work one-quarter teaspoon per bed foot into the soil before planting. Keep well weeded as beets like space to grow. Make sure to thin the roots to three inches (7.5cm) apart to maximize beetroot girth. Very drought tolerant once established. Optimum soil pH range is 6.0 to 7.5.

Insects to observe: Many spider species make residence under the canopy of foliage; green aphids can arrive but rarely cause major damage.

Diseases to watch for: Beets are prone to root rot and damping off most likely caused by the fungus *fusarium spp,* during leaf growth. Cercospora leaf spot caused by the fungus *Cercospora hydrangea* occurs during wet and humid conditions blackening the leaves and outright wilting them. Control both by limiting irrigation and letting it go completely dry before doing so.

Days to harvest: Fifty to sixty days and continually until all are harvested.

Harvest advice: Always harvest the biggest beets in the patch, giving time for the smaller ones to grow to potential with increased space.

Post-harvest handling/terms of storage (best way to preserve flavor): Store dry, left dirty with tops removed, in bags or bins at 33-40F (1-4.5C). Will store for six months and longer. Can also be canned or fermented as pickled beets.

Health benefits: As a rich and nutritious source, beetroot is believed to hold health-promotional characteristics, antioxidant and anti-inflammatory effects, anti-carcinogenic and anti-diabetic activities, and hepato-protective, hypotensive, and wound-healing properties.[7]

Field notes:

Broccoli
Brassica oleracea var. Italica (Cruciferae)

Characteristics/growing habits: Broccoli, a member of the family *Brassicaceae*, is a hardy biennial that grows on upright thick-stemmed plants. The flower buds (part eaten) form from the central crown and from the joint of the branch to stem.

Favorite varieties: "Belstar" F-1, "DeCicco" (HL)

Seeding information: Seed F-1 varieties (preferred for ease of growing) in cell plug trays, being aware that broccoli is prone to damping off in the small seedling stage; water cells only when dry after emergence.

Days to germination at temperature range: Three to six days at 60-85F (15.5-29.5C)

When to start inside: Four to five weeks before transplanting outside

Necessary to pot-up to three-inch pots: No.

Brocoli branchu violet.
Réd. au huitième : pousse détachée, demi-grandeur.

When to transplant or direct seed outside: Transplant as soon as soil can be worked or anytime during the growing season at 16 inches (40cm) apart.

Maintenance required during growing period: Broccoli requires boron to make full heads, work one-quarter teaspoon per bed foot (one-eighth teaspoon per plant) into the soil before planting. Immediately after transplanting, cover with insect screen and row cover if nights drop below 31F (-1C). Give consistent water throughout the growing season. Weed out native flora while plants are small. When plants reach twelve inches (30cm) in height, undersow with an annual clover (like crimson clover). Keep covered with insect screens for the duration of budding. Pull off suckers that develop, trying to form side shoots, as this will diminish greatly the size of the central head, if this is the goal. Optimum soil pH range is 6.0 to 7.0.

Insects to observe: Cutworms are the larvae of several species of night-flying moths that live in the soil and can defoliate and/or chew off the stem of newly transplanted seedlings. Control by checking the soil around the base of the plant early in the morning and removing them. White cabbage moths lay eggs and hatch as green cabbage worms. They will defoliate a crop and eat the central crown, control by keeping covered with insect screens until harvest.

Diseases to watch for: None of major consequence from my monitoring.

Days to harvest: Sixty to seventy-five days from transplant and then continually harvest small side shoots throughout the season. Broccoli plants, when fully mature, can survive frosts to 25F (-4C)

Harvest advice: Cut early in the morning with a heavy-duty pocketknife as far down on the stem as desired as the stems are quite delicious when tender. Harvest before flower buds begin to explode, but when the dome is fully formed.

Post-harvest handling/terms of storage (best way to preserve flavor): Broccoli is perishable and will begin to yellow within ten to fourteen days. Store in plastic bags or bins at 33-40F (1C-4.5C). Best eaten fresh, but can also be blanched and frozen for up to six months.

Health benefits: Cohort and case control studies conducted between 1980 and 1990 suggested an inverse relation between the consumption of cruciferous vegetables, like broccoli, and incidences of colorectal, pancreatic, lung, breast, gastrointestinal and ovarian cancer. Among many research findings published during 1990–2000 on the health benefits of cruciferous vegetables, research from the Johns Hopkins University is a milestone in the area of cancer chemoprevention.[9]

Field notes:

Broccoli Raab (Rapini)
Brassica rapa var. ruvo

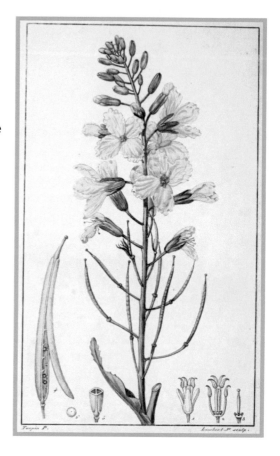

Characteristics/growing habits: Broccoli Raab (rapini), a member of the family *Brassicaceae,* is a fast-growing annual vegetable that grows on a thinner central stalk than broccoli but produces broccoli-like florets with a distinctive mustardy, peppery somewhat spicy flavor.

Favorite varieties: "Sorrento" (HL)

Seeding information: Direct seed (OP, HL) at ½-inch (1.25cm) deep, thinned to 3 inches (7.5cm) apart, rows to 6 inches (15cm).

Days to germination at temperature range: Three to six days at 50-75F (10-24C).

When to start inside: n/a

Necessary to pot-up to three-inch pots: n/a

When to transplant or direct seed outside: As soon as soil can be worked and late summer as broccoli raab prefers a cooler growing season.

Maintenance required during growing period: Cover with insect screen immediately after direct seeding. Thinning to 3-inch (7.5cm) spacing is important to give the stems room to mature. Keep well weeded of native flora when seedlings emerge. Optimum soil pH range is 6.0 to 7.5.

Insects to observe: Green peach aphids can be a problem; if they are observed under insect screens, remove at night to allow green lacewings, lady beetles, and spiders to move in.

Diseases to watch for: Damping off can occur if seedlings stay too wet after emergence. Control by limiting irrigation after germination.

Days to harvest: Forty-five to fifty-five days

Harvest advice: Cut stems with garden cutters at soil level early in the morning when first florets appear.

Post-harvest handling/terms of storage (best way to preserve flavor): Tie a hand-sized bunch with a rubber band, immerse in cold water and let mostly air dry, store in plastic bags up to fourteen days. Can also be blanched and frozen for up to six months.

Health benefits: Around the world, people are not consuming enough Green Leafy Vegetables (GLV), like rapini, on a daily basis. In several studies, many nutrients in GLV, such as dietary fiber, potassium, and antioxidants, have been associated with reduced risk for cardiovascular disease (CVD).[8]

Field notes:

Brussels Sprouts
Brassica oleracea var. gemmifera

Characteristics/growing habits: Brussels sprouts, members of the family *Brassicaceae*, are a long, cool season biennial plant that can grow to three feet (90cm) in height. The sprouts grow in the inverted armpit of the where the branch meets the trunk.

Favorite varieties: We have yet to be highly successful at La Ferme de l'Aube, but I would recommend F-1 varieties for all growers. In 2021, we were mildly fruitful with "Dagan" F-1 and harvested small sprouts.

Seeding information: Seed F-1 varieties (preferred for ease of growing) in cell plug trays being aware that brussels sprouts are prone to damping off in the small seedling stage, water cells only when dry after seeds have sprouted.

Chou de Bruxelles demi-nain de la Halle.
Réd. au dixième; pomme à demi-grandeur.

Days to germination at temperature range: Three to six days at 60-85F (15.5-28.5C).

When to start inside: Four to five weeks before transplanting outside.

Necessary to pot-up to three-inch pots: Not necessary, but could help in allowing this very long season vegetable to yield a harvest.

When to transplant or direct seed outside: As soon as soil can be worked at 20 inches (50cm) apart. Brussels sprouts are a long season crop requiring up to 120 days to mature.

Maintenance required during growing period: Brussels sprouts crave boron to make full sprouts; work one-quarter teaspoon per bed foot into the soil before planting. Immediately after transplanting, cover with insect screen and add a row cover if nights drop below 31F (-1C). Give consistent water throughout the growing season and weed out native flora while the plants are small. When plants reach twelve inches (30cm) in height, undersow with an annual clover (like crimson clover) and side-dress with veganic compost. Keep covered with insect screens for the duration of budding. As sprouts start to form, remove the bottom leaves to allow in light, which encourages larger sprout development. Optimum soil pH range is 6.0 to 7.5.

Insects to observe: White cabbage moths lay eggs and hatch as green cabbage worms. They will defoliate a crop and eat the central crown limiting growth of the plant. Control by keeping covered with insect screens and checking periodically and removing any green worms discovered.

Diseases to watch for: Powdery mildew can infect the plant during times of drought followed by a cold night. Control by keeping moisture level constant.

Days to harvest: 100-120 days from transplant

Harvest advice: Remove leaves and stems hiding sprouts by gently pulling downward. Can cut the whole stalk or pop off brussels sprouts with fingers in the field.

Post-harvest handling/terms of storage (best way to preserve flavor): Can store whole stalks in plastic bags or bins at 33-40F (1-4.5C) from four to six weeks. Sprouts can be stored loose in plastic bags or bins at 33-40F for up to eight weeks.

Health benefits: The consumption of a typical serving of vegetables such as cabbage, broccoli, brussels sprouts, and many others of cruciferin nature, may significantly decrease and lessen the incidence of carcinogenic fatality. In fact, evidence shows that individuals who consume a diet rich in cruciferous vegetables (CV) have lower risks of developing cancer.[10]

Field notes:

Bush Beans/Climbing Beans
Phaseolus vulgaris

Characteristics/growing habits: Bush beans, members of the family *Fabaceae*, materialize on robust plants that grow eighteen to twenty-four inches (45-60cm). Colors can be green, yellow, purple, or mottled. Climbing beans can be yellow, green, or mottled, flat or round, and climb up to ten feet (three meters). They are all extremely productive during the growing season.

Favorite varieties: Bush: "Provider" (OP), "Maxibel" (OP), "Gold Rush" (OP), "Dragon Langerie" (HL). Climbing: "Rattlesnake" (HL), "Kentucky Wonder" (HL)

Seeding information: Direct seed (OP, heirloom) 1-inch (2.5cm) deep, 2 inches (5cm) apart, rows at 12 inches (30cm).

Days to germination at temperature range: Four to seven days at 60-85 degrees (15.5-29.5C).

When to start inside: n/a

Necessary to pot-up to three-inch pots: n/a

PHASEOLUS COMPRESSUS LUCASIANUS *Martens.*
Haricot Beurre à écosses bleues.

When to transplant or direct seed outside: Plant after last frost. Beans are sensitive to cold soil temperatures and are preferably planted when soil temperatures reach 55F (13C).

Maintenance required during growing period: Bush and pole beans grow very fast, so normally only one good weeding of native flora is necessary, after which plants outcompete and crowd the space. Pole beans require a trellis, three-to-four pole teepees, or stake/twine system reaching a minimum six-feet (180cm) tall. The climbing beans can be "trained" to descend as well. Optimum soil pH range is 6.0 to 7.5.

Insects to observe: Mexican bean beetles *Epilachna varivestis* along with their larvae will defoliate bean plants. If the populations become intense, remove them by hand for best results. Bumblebees and Great Northern bees like to work the abundant flowers.

Diseases to watch for: White mold is a fungus that can live in the soil up to eight years and infects over four hundred different varieties of plants. It will decimate a plant and rot the beans. It is particularly prevalent during wet, semi-warm conditions. Keeping the bean plantings as dry as possible will curtail the mold. Pulling the worst infected plants can aid in limiting plant to plant infection.

Days to harvest: Fifty to sixty days and then continually throughout the growing season.

Harvest advice: Once pods begin to form to your liking in length and girth, pick every two to three days to encourage more flower and pod production. Pick when plants and beans are dew and moisture free for increased conservation time.

Post-harvest handling/terms of storage (best way to preserve flavor): Store dry in plastic bags at 33-40F (1-4.5C), will keep up to fourteen days. Can be fresh pickled and stored for one year. Larger ones can be blanched and frozen for up to six months.

Health benefits: Green beans belong to the exact same genus/species of plant—*Phaseolus vulgaris*— as black beans, navy beans, pinto beans, and kidney beans. As a leguminous vegetable, green beans are sometimes included alongside other legumes when analyzing potential health benefits. In this legume-based context, they are often linked to risk reduction for chronic disease. Specifically, there is a decreased risk of type two diabetes, high blood pressure, coronary heart disease, and metabolic syndrome.[11]

Field notes:

Cabbage
Brassica oleracea var. capitata

Characteristics/growing habits: Cabbages, members of the family *Brassicaceae*, develop from the central crown of the plant. As they mature, they become bigger and increasingly tough. Cabbages can be green or red, round or cone shaped, and even sometimes savoyed.

Favorite varieties: "Early Jersey Wakefield" (HL), "Caraflex" F-1, "Passat" F-1, "Red Express" (OP)

Seeding information: One seed (OP, heirloom or F1 varieties, which are preferred for ease of growing for some varieties) per cell in plug trays being aware that cabbages are prone to damping off in the small seedling stage. Water cells only when dry after emergence.

Brassica capitata alba, et viridis.
Ital. Cauolo Bolognese. Gall. Chou

Days to germination at temperature range: Three to six days at 60-85F (15.5-29.5C).

When to start inside: Four to five weeks before transplanting outside.

Necessary to pot-up to three-inch pots: No.

When to transplant or direct seed outside: As soon as soil can be worked at 12 inches (30cm) apart for small cone varieties, 18 inches (45cm) apart for larger ones with successions three weeks apart to stagger harvest.

Maintenance required during growing period: Cabbages appreciate boron to make full heads; work one-quarter teaspoon per bed foot (one-eighth teaspoon per plant) into the soil before planting. Immediately after transplanting, cover with insect screens and row covers if nights drop below 31F (-1C). Give consistent water throughout the growing season. Weed out native flora while plants are small. When plants reach twelve inches (30cm) in height, undersow with an annual clover (like crimson clover). Keep covered with insect screens for the duration of head forming. Remove leaves touching the soil to allow air flow and discourage disease pressures. Pull off all side shoots (suckers) as they will limit the size of the central crown. Optimum soil pH range is 6.0 to 7.0.

Insects to observe: Cutworms live in the soil and upon emergence, can defoliate and/or chew off the stem of newly transplanted seedlings. Control by checking the soil around the base of the plant early in the morning and removing them. White cabbage moths lay eggs and hatch as green cabbage worms. They will defoliate a crop and eat the central crown, limiting the growth of the cabbage plants. Control by keeping covered with insect screens and checking periodically for and removing green worms.

Diseases to watch for: Cabbages can be prone to black rot, which is caused by the bacterium, *Xanthomonas campestris* var. *campestris*, which arrives during very wet and humid times alike. Control with irrigating only when soil is drying out and removing bottom leaves to encourage air flow.

Days to harvest: Sixty to seventy days for early and 85-110 days for late varieties from transplant.

Harvest advice: As soon as cabbages are tightly wrapped, cut with heavy duty field or pocketknife half an inch (1.25cm) down stem. Be vigilant, for if left outside too long or during heavy rain, the heads may split or become sunburnt (with full sun exposure).

Post-harvest handling/terms of storage (best way to preserve flavor): Can store for six months at 33-40F (1-4.5C), ensuring to keep humidity moderate, like in plastic bags or bins. Can be fermented into sauerkraut or kimchi for storage up to one year.

Health benefits: Cabbage has been widely used in traditional medicine to treat various diseases. Specifically, it is used to alleviate symptoms associated with gastrointestinal disorders (gastritis, peptic ulcers, and irritable bowel syndrome) and idiopathic cephalalgia, as well as treat injuries. Growing evidence indicates that cabbage has pharmacological activities against various diseases, including liver cirrhosis, hepatitis, cancer, and hypocholesterolemia.[12]

Field notes:

Carrots
Daucus carota

Characteristics/growing habits: Carrots, members of the family *Umbelliferae*, are a hardy biennial root crop that form long orange, yellow, white, or red roots underground. Above ground is a showy green, fern-like leaf system.

Favorite varieties: "Scarlet Nantes" (HL), "Dolciva" (OP), "Cosmic Purple" (OP), "Napoli" F-1

Seeding information: Direct seed "Nantes" type (OP, heirloom and F1 for extra early) at ½ inch (1.25cm) deep, 1 inch (2.5cm) apart, rows at 6 inches (15cm).

Days to germination at temperature range: Ten to twenty-one days at 50-80F (10-26.5C), keeping soil well moist until germination.

When to start inside: n/a

Necessary to pot-up to three-inch pots: n/a

When to transplant or direct seed outside: Direct seed first sowing as soon as soil can be worked and every three weeks for succession harvests.

Maintenance required during growing period: Keep well weeded as carrots like space to grow, making sure seedlings are thinned to one inch (2.5cm) apart. Carrots, when given too little space, will produce only very thin roots; given too much space they will become too large and lose their flavor. Optimum soil pH range is 5.5 to 7.5.

Insects to observe: Many spider and beetle species make residence under the canopy of foliage. Wireworms, which are the larvae of click beetles (family *Elateridae*) can cause mining (many tunnels and holes) in the carrot. Carrot fly (*Chamaepsila rosae*) lay their eggs at the base of the carrots. When hatched, the larvae burrow down and cause damage similar to wireworms. From my experience with these crops, they are most damaging when carrots are left in the ground too long after fully developed size has been realized. It is wise to practice a three-to-four-year rotation to discourage an abundance of these insects.

Diseases to watch for: None of major consequence. At the end of the season, greens could exhibit signs of powdery mildew, a fungal disease, when there is sudden high humidity among the patch, but the weather has been dry.

Days to harvest: Fifty (early) to ninety-five (late) days and continually until all are harvested.

Harvest advice: Harvest in the morning when the weather is still cool, pulling the size you prefer. If the weather has been dry, a four-pronged spading fork is helpful to loosen the soil.

Post-harvest handling/terms of storage (best way to preserve flavor): Store dry with tops removed and dirty in bags or bins at 33-40F (1-4.5C). Will store for eight months and longer.

Health benefits: Like many other colored vegetables, carrots are a gold mine of antioxidants. carotenoids, and polyphenols. Vitamins present in carrots act as antioxidants, anticarcinogens, and immunoenhancers. Carotenoids widely distributed in orange carrots are potent antioxidants which can neutralize the effect of free radicals. They have been shown to have inhibition mutagenesis activity contributing to decrease risk of some cancers.[13]

Field notes:

Cauliflower
Brassica oleracea var. botrytis

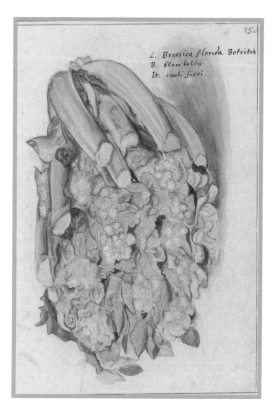

Characteristics/growing habits: Cauliflower, a member of the family *Brassicaceae*, grows on upright thick stemmed plants. The flower buds (part eaten) or curds form from the central crown. Cauliflower is usually white, but other hybrid varieties can be purple, orange, or spiky pointed green (Romanesco).

Favorite varieties: "Adona" F-1, "Veronica Romanesco" F-1

Seeding information: Seed F-1 varieties (preferred for ease of growing) in cell plug trays, knowing that cauliflower is prone to damping off in the small seedling stage. Water cells only when dry after emergence.

Days to germination at temperature range: Three to six days at 60-85F (15.5-29.5C).

When to start inside: Four to five weeks before transplanting outside.

Necessary to pot-up to three-inch pots: No.

When to transplant or direct seed outside: Best transplanted 18 inches (45cm) apart in mid-summer for fall crops, as cauliflower likes warm days and cool nights.

Maintenance required during growing period: Cauliflower cherishes boron to make full heads, work one quarter teaspoon per bed foot into the soil before planting. Give consistent water throughout the growing season. Weed out native flora while plants are small. When plants reach twelve inches (30cm) in height, undersow with an annual clover (like crimson clover). Keep covered with insect screens for the duration of budding. Pull off any side shoots that develop, as this will diminish greatly the size of the central head. When curds form, tie or band outside leaves to cover cauliflower from light (a process called blanching), otherwise buds will turn tough and yellow. Optimal soil pH range is 5.8 to 7.5.

Insects to observe: White cabbage moths lay prolific amounts of eggs and hatch as green cabbage worms. They will defoliate a crop and eat the central crown. Their excrement will blacken curds. Control by keeping the plant covered with an insect screen.

Diseases to watch for: None of major consequence from my observations.

Days to harvest: Sixty to seventy-five days from transplant. Cauliflower plants when fully mature can survive frosts to 25F (-4C)

Harvest advice: Cut early in the morning with a heavy-duty pocketknife at the base of the cauliflower, leaving a few leaves as protection in storage. Harvest before flower buds begin to explode. Cauliflowers can be cut immature and are quite tasty and gourmet.

Post-harvest handling/terms of storage (best way to preserve flavor): Cauliflower is highly perishable, and crowns will begin to yellow within ten to fourteen days. Before storage, wipe away any dirt as that will immediately begin to rot the crown. Store in plastic bags or bins at 33-40F (1-4.5C). Best to enjoy fresh, but can be blanched and frozen for up to six months.

Health benefits: Cauliflower, like broccoli and cabbage, belongs to the *cruciferous* (*Brassicaceae*) family of vegetables, which has been shown to be effective in fighting certain forms of cancer. Cauliflower is so closely related to broccoli that both are designated as the same variety of the *cruciferous* family, which not only share the wonderful phytochemicals, but also contain nutritive value of vitamin A, thiamine, riboflavin, niacin, vitamin C, calcium, iron, phosphorus, and fat (Omega-3) to help fight diseases.[14]

Field notes:

Celery & Celery Root (Celeriac)
Apium graveolens

Characteristics/growing habits: Celery and celery root are members of the family *Apiaceae*. Celery grows upright in a tall, light to dark green, loose bunch with a nice leaf head. Celery roots form knobby, off-white bulbs underground and also produce a loose-leaf head. Both plants are biennial.

Favorite varieties: Celery: "Tall Utah" (OP), "Tango" (OP); Celery Root: "Diamant" (OP)

Seeding information: Seed (OP, heirloom) in cell plug trays one to two seeds each, thinning to one after emergence.

Days to germination at temperature range: Seven to fourteen days at 60-75F (15.5-24C).

When to start inside: Eight to ten weeks before transplanting outside.

Necessary to pot-up to three-inch pots: Recommended, as potting-up will help increase the chances of these sometimes fussy crops to reach full maturity.

Apium graveolens. 266.

When to transplant or direct seed outside: Transplant after last frost and when nights are consistently above 50F (10C), otherwise celery will have a tendency to bolt. Space 12 inches (30cm) apart.

Maintenance required during growing period: Celery and celery root appreciate boron and granulated seaweed to realize full heads and roots, work one-quarter teaspoon per bed foot of each into the soil prior to planting. Celery and celery root are long to establish and require continuous moisture. Ensure they are free of native flora. Optimum soil pH range is 5.8 to 7.0.

Insects to observe: None of major consequence attack the plants, if too warm and humid, aphids can infest the crowns of the plants. Beetles and spiders will make homes under the humid canopy.

Diseases to watch for: Celery mosaic virus is a plant pathogenic virus that appears to be carried by aphids when the weather turns warm and humid. Cutting out infected stems is a beneficial way of disrupting the problem, however the plants do seem to grow out of it.

Days to harvest: 80-90 days for celery and 105-115 days for celery root from transplant.

Harvest advice: Cut early in the morning with a heavy-duty pocketknife at the base of celery plant. Harvest celeriac roots before first fall frost when bulbs have reached full potential.

Post-harvest handling/terms of storage (best way to preserve flavor): Celery can be stored dry up to one month at 33-40F (1-4.5C). Celery root stored dry and dirty will keep for more than six months. Celery stalks can be cut and fresh frozen for storage up to one year. Celery and celeriac's small stems and leaves can be chopped and fresh frozen to be used in bouillons, soups, and stews and will also store for up to a year.

Health benefits: Celery can prevent cardiovascular diseases, jaundice, liver and lien diseases, urinary tract obstruction, gout, and rheumatic disorders. Celery reduces glucose, blood lipids, and blood pressure, which can strengthen the heart. Experimental studies show that celery has antifungal and anti-inflammatory properties. Moreover, its essential oils have antibacterial effects. Its seeds are useful in the treatment of bronchitis, asthenopia, asthma, chronic skin disorders (including psoriasis), vomiting, fever, and tumors.[15] It is known that celeriac contains compounds called polyacetylenes, which have been researched largely in carrots and show promising anti-cancer effects. A few studies have also shown anti-allergenic, anti-inflammatory, anti-platelet aggregating and immune-stimulating properties in celeriac.[16]

Field notes:

Chamomile
Matricaria recutita

Characteristics/growing habits: Chamomile, a member of the family *Asteraceae*, is a tall, bushy, and spreading hardy annual plant that can reach up to three feet (75cm). The dark green plants produce a plethora of daisy-like flowers with delicate white petals surrounding a spherical yellow center. They are self-seeding annuals producing prolific seedlings the following spring.

Favorite varieties: "German Chamomile" (OP)

Seeding information: Sprinkle tiny seeds on soil surface of 1020 flats. Need light to germinate. Can be direct seeded after last frost if preferred, keep very moist until germination.

Days to germination at temperature range: Seven to ten days at 55-70F (13-21C).

When to start inside: Five weeks before last frost date.

Necessary to pot-up to three-inch pots: Yes, as soon as seedlings have two true leaves. Can transplant two to three seedlings into each pot if desired.

When to transplant or direct seed outside: Transplant after last frost date. Plant at 10-12 inches (25-30cm) apart. Well suited for companion planting with all other types of flowers.

Maintenance required during growing period: Keep weeded of native flora throughout growing period as chamomile plants are slow to root in. Very drought-tolerant once established. Once established, they will grow into their bushy habit and outcompete native flora. Optimum soil pH range is 5.5 to 7.5.

Insects to observe: None of major consequence attack the plants, if too warm and humid, aphids can infest the crowns of the plants, but rarely do more than just live there. Showy and prolific chamomile flowers are inviting to the smallest native bees, flies, wasps, moths, and butterflies.

Diseases to watch for: None of consequence.

Days to harvest: Sixty days from transplants, seventy-five days from direct seeding then continually until first fall hard frost.

Harvest advice: Harvest flowers when petals and central core are firm to the touch with small type garden cutters when plants are dry.

Post-harvest handling/terms of storage (best way to preserve flavor): Can be stored in plastic bags in the fridge for ten to fourteen days. Best method of preservation is to dry flowers and pack into glass jars once cooled, which will keep for one year.

Health benefits: Chamomile is one of the most ancient medicinal herbs known to mankind. The dried flowers of chamomile contain many terpenoids and flavonoids contributing to its medicinal properties. Chamomile preparations are commonly used for many human ailments such as hay fever, inflammation, muscle spasms, menstrual disorders, insomnia, ulcers, wounds, gastrointestinal disorders, rheumatic pain, and hemorrhoids. Chamomile tea is frequently used as a mild sedative to calm nerves and reduce anxiety.[17]

Field notes:

Chicory
Cichorium endivia, intybus

Characteristics/growing habits: Chicories are members of the family *Asteraceae*, whether frisée, endive or escarole (*endivia*) or radicchio (*intybus*); and are all low growing head-type vegetables. *Endivias* are green and frilly, serrated or savoyed, while radicchios are red or green, round or pointed. Their distinctive bitter flavor diminishes when cooked.

Favorite varieties: Endive: "Frissé" (OP); Escarole: "Eros" (OP); Radicchio: "Leonardo" F-1, "Virtus" F-1

Seeding information: One seed (OP, heirloom, F-1 for some radicchios) per cell in plug trays.

Days to germination at temperature range: Three to six days at 60-85F (15.5-29.5C).

When to start inside: Three to four weeks before transplanting outside

Necessary to pot-up to three-inch pots: No.

When to transplant or direct seed outside: After last frost, transplant 12 inches (30cm) apart.

Maintenance required during growing period: Cover with insect screen after transplanting and keep well-weeded of native flora until plants touch each other. Keep well-watered throughout growing period, pulling back the irrigation when heads form. Optimum soil pH range is 6.0 to 7.5.

Insects to observe: Green peach aphids can become abundant in times of warm nights and humid conditions but are usually not a major problem.

Diseases to watch for: Tip burn can occur where calcium has been leached out from over irrigation. Head rot caused by the pathogen *Erwinia carotovora* occurs after heads are formed and then exposed to too much water sometimes by over irrigation.

Days to harvest: Fifty to sixty days from transplant for full-size heads.

Harvest advice: Harvest full heads with biggest first allowing smaller ones time to size up. Cut all as early as possible in the morning before the heat of the day.

Post-harvest handling/terms of storage (best way to preserve flavor): Chicories can store two-to-three months in plastic bags or bins at 33-40F (1-4.5C). After harvest, immerse heads in cold water and let air dry before storage.

Health benefits: One of the most important and obvious characteristics of chicory is its antioxidant activity. Chicory can provide neuro-protectivity and also can prohibit the harms of neurons induced by oxygen free radicals. In recent years, chicory's anti-microbial activity has been revealed on some microbial strains such as Agrobacter, Radiobacterium pseudomonas, Florecens and Pseudomonas aeroginoas.[18]

Field notes:

Chinese Cabbage (Nappa)
Brassica rapa var. pekinensis

Characteristics/growing habits: Chinese cabbage, a member of the family *Brassicaceae*, form tight, tall oblong heads in green or red. They are distinctive from other cabbages as their leaves contain a higher level of water.

Favorite Varieties: "Bilko" F-1, "Merlot" F-1

Seeding Information: Seed F-1 varieties (preferred for ease of growing) in cell plug trays, remembering that Chinese cabbages are prone to damping off in the small seedling stage. Water cells only when dry after emergence. Timing of planting is crucial as they will bolt if the temperatures drop below 50F (10C) in spring. Best for a late summer to early fall crop.

Days to germination at temperature range: Three to six days at 60-85F (15.5-29.5C).

When to start inside: Four weeks before transplanting outside.

Necessary to pot-up to three-inch pots: No.

When to transplant or direct seed outside: Plant at mid-summer 12 inches (30cm) apart.

Maintenance required during growing period: Chinese cabbage need boron to make healthy heads, work one-quarter teaspoon per bed foot (one-eighth teaspoon per plant) into the soil before planting. Immediately after transplanting, cover with insect screens, and keep covered for the duration of the head forming. Give consistent water throughout the growing season. Weed out native flora while plants are small. Remove leaves touching the soil to allow air flow and discourage disease pressures. Optimum soil pH range is 6.0 to 7.5.

Insects to observe: White cabbage moths lay eggs in the forming head and hatch as green cabbage worms. They will defoliate a crop and eat the central crown, limiting growth of the plant. Control by keeping covered with insect screens and checking periodically for and removing green worms. Green peach aphids can also be a nuisance, managing insect screens by removing them at night will allow ants, green lacewings, lady beetles and spiders to move in. Leaving a couple of plants out all the time, may work as a trap crop for both cabbage moths and aphids.

Diseases to watch for: Cabbages can be prone to black rot, which is caused by the bacterium *Xanthomonas campestris* var. *campestris*, which arrives during very wet and humid times. Control with irrigating only when dry. Chinese cabbage is also prone to powdery mildew when too dry preceding a temperature drop. Pull infected plants if any.

Days to harvest: Sixty to sixty-five days from transplant.

Harvest advice: As soon as cabbages are firm, cut with a heavy-duty field or pocketknife one-quarter inch (0.63cm) below cabbage base. Be vigilant, for if left too long, heads will split and/or rot.

Post-harvest handling/terms of storage (best way to preserve flavor): Can store for two months and more in plastic bags and bins at 33-40F (1-4.5C). Chinese cabbage can be fermented into kimchi to be preserved for up to one year.

Health benefits: Chinese cabbage is a natural source of nutrients and phytochemicals. Among phytochemicals, flavonoids, glucosinolate and their hydrolytic products are associated with many biological effects such as antibacterial and antifungal actions.[19]

Field notes:

_____

_____

_____

_____

_____

_____

_____

_____

_____

_____

_____

_____

_____

_____

Chives & Garlic Chives
Allium schoenoprasum & tuberosum

Characteristics/growing habits: Chives (both types), members of the family *Amaryllidaceae*, are hardy perennial plants that can reach two feet (60cm) tall. The dark green spear-like leaves of chives have the characteristic onion smell and flavor, while garlic chives plants smell and taste like garlic. Both produce prolific, showy purple flowers on tall flower stalks. As well as being perennial, they will also self-seed the following spring.

PUR-LØG, ALLIUM SCHOENOPRASUM.

Favorite varieties: "Chives" (OP), "Garlic Chives" (HL)

Seeding information: Seed two to three seeds per cell in plug trays. Can also be direct seeded if desired.

Days to germination at temperature range: Six to ten days at 60-80F (15.5-26.5C).

When to start inside: Eight weeks before last frost date.

Necessary to pot-up to three-inch pots: Yes, transplant two to six seedlings into each pot if desired.

When to transplant or direct seed outside: Direct seed one week after "as soon as soil can be worked" date. Transplant after last frost. Space transplants at 6 inches (15cm) apart. Thin direct-seeded seedlings to the same distance when growing robustly.

Maintenance required during growing period: Keep weeded of native flora throughout growing period as compact plants can become overcrowded limiting leaf production. Very drought tolerant once established. Can cut off first flowers (which are also edible) to encourage more leaf growth, however since they are some of the first perennial flowers to form it is recommended to let the flowers open to invite a whole host of pollinating insects (see below.) Optimum soil pH range is 5.5 to 7.5.

Insects to observe: None of major significance attack the plants. Beautiful purple chive flowers are highly attractive to bumblebees, small and large native bees, syrphid flies and wasps, as well as larger butterflies, including Swallowtail and Monarch.

Diseases to watch for: None of major consequence from my investigations.

Days to harvest: Seventy-five days from transplants, ninety days from direct seeding then continually until first fall hard frost. Perennial plants will begin to put up edible leaf spears about two weeks before last frost date, making it one of the earliest edibles to grow back in the garden.

Harvest advice: Harvest leaves by cutting above the base of the plant with garden cutters when the desired size is reached.

Post-harvest handling/terms of Storage (best way to preserve flavor): Can be stored in plastic bags at 33-40F (1-4.5C) for ten to fourteen days. Best enjoyed for fresh eating.

Health benefits: The chive plant was used in traditional folk medicine to stimulate digestion, treat anemia, enhance the immune system and to cleanse the blood. Recent studies investigated the antioxidant properties of the bulb, leaf, and stalk of *Allium schoenoprasum L.* All the *Allium* species may help to prevent tumor promotion, cardiovascular diseases and aging due to their high concentrations of total flavonoids, carotenoids and chlorophylls, and very low concentrations of toxic oxygen radicals.[20]

Field notes:

_____
_____
_____
_____
_____
_____
_____
_____
_____
_____
_____
_____
_____
_____
_____

Cilantro (Coriander)
Coriandrum sativum

Characteristics/growing habits: Cilantro, a member of the family *Umbelliferae*, is a tall, (can reach four feet (120cm), hardy annual plant. The dark green leaves create a low growing rosette at first. Flower stalks develop, yielding a profuse amount of delicate white flowers that will form green seeds (edible), which then dry brown (coriander seeds). Cilantro is self-seeding the following spring.

Favorite varieties: "Santo" (OP)

Seeding information: Direct seed (OP, heirloom) ½-inch (1.25cm) deep, thinning to 4 inches (10cm) apart.

Days to germination at temperature range: Seven to ten days at 50-80F (10-26.5C).

When to start inside: n/a

Necessary to pot-up to three-inch pots: n/a

When to transplant or direct seed outside: Direct seed as soon as soil can be worked. Succession plant every three weeks for continual harvest throughout the season, as cilantro is quick to bolt to flower when weather turns warm and dry.

Maintenance required during growing period: Keep weeded of native flora throughout growing period. Cilantro grows quickly and will create a canopy limiting native growth. Can cut off first flowers to encourage more leaf growth, however since they are some of the first annual or self-seeding flowers to form it is recommended to let the flowers open to invite a whole host of pollinating insects (see below). Optimum soil pH range is 5.5 to 7.5.

Insects to observe: None of great magnitude attack the plants. Delicate white cilantro flowers are highly attractive to small native bees, flies, wasps, butterflies, and moths.

Diseases to watch for: None of major consequence from my cognizance.

Days to harvest: Fifty to sixty days from direct seeding then continually until first fall hard frost. Self-seeding plants will begin to put out edible leaves about a week before last spring frost.

Harvest advice: Harvest leaves by cutting above the base of the plant with garden cutters when desired size is reached, or alternatively can cut the entire plant at the base to give room for others to grow. When coriander seeds are brown, pop off with fingers and allow to fully cure in a dry place, away from direct sunlight.

Post-harvest handling/terms of storage (best way to preserve flavor): Cilantro is highly perishable. Can be stored in plastic bags at 33-40F (1-4.5C) for ten to fourteen days. Best enjoyed for fresh eating, but can be fresh frozen (whole sprigs and leaves) if desired—however, flavor is somewhat compromised. Alternatively, can be made into a rich pesto that can be frozen and stored for six months.

Health benefits: In traditional remedies, coriander (cilantro), both fresh and dry were used for relief of gastrointestinal maladies, although other historical uses included as an aphrodisiac, antibiotic, a remedy for respiratory ailments and pain, and a treatment for loss of appetite and memory. Current uses being investigated include its antioxidant, antimicrobial, diabetes-modulating and neurological benefits.[21]

Field notes:

Collards
Brassica oleracea

Characteristics/growing habits: Collards, a member of the family *Brassicaceae*, are a hardy biennial, closely related to broccoli and cabbage. As the leaves mature, they become quite large, green with a slight bluish tint. The leaves are succulent and can be sometimes slightly savoyed.

Favorite varieties: "Georgia Southern" (HL)

Seeding information: One seed (OP, heirloom) per cell in plug trays acknowledging that collards are prone to damping off in the small seedling stage. Water cells only when dry after emergence.

Days to germination at temperature range: Three to six days at 60-85F (15.5-29.5C).

When to start inside: Four to five weeks before transplanting outside.

Necessary to pot-up to three-inch pots: No.

When to transplant or direct seed outside: As soon as soil can be worked at 12 inches (30cm) apart.

Brassica Oleracea. — Wild Cabbage.

Maintenance required during growing period: Collards appreciate boron to reach full potential, work one-quarter teaspoon per bed foot into the soil before planting. Immediately after transplanting cover with insect screen and row cover if nights drop below 31F (-1C). Give consistent water throughout the growing season. Weed out native flora while plants are small. When plants reach twelve inches (30cm) in height undersow with an annual clover, like crimson clover. Keep covered with insect screens up until harvest window begins. Optimum soil pH range is 6.0 to 7.5.

Insects to observe: Cutworms live in the soil and can defoliate and/or chew off the stem of newly transplanted seedlings. Control by checking the soil around the base of the plant early in the morning and removing them. White cabbage moths lay eggs and hatch as green cabbage worms. They will defoliate a crop and eat the central crown, limiting the growth of the plant. Control by keeping covered with insect screens until harvest and checking periodically for green worms, removing them if found.

Diseases to watch for: Collards can be prone to powdery mildew. Control by never letting soil completely dry out.

Days to harvest: Fifty-five to sixty-five days from transplant and continually throughout the harvest season.

Harvest advice: As soon as collard leaves reach desired size, harvest by pulling off oldest leaves first, always leaving the central crown untouched as this is where growths spur from.

Post-harvest handling/terms of storage (best way to preserve flavor): Can store for fourteen to twenty-one days at 33-40C (1-4.5C) in plastic bags. Collards can also be blanched and frozen and stored for six months.

Health benefits: Collard Greens like the other *Brassicaceae* vegetables prevent oxidative stress, induce detoxification enzymes, stimulate immune system, decrease the risk of cancers, inhibit malignant transformation and carcinogenic mutations, as well as reduce proliferation of cancer cells.[22, 23]

Field notes:

Corn (Sweet)
Zea Mays

Characteristics/growing habits: Sweet corn, a member of the family *Poaceae*, is a tender annual, whole grain, related to grass that grows on six to eight-foot (1.8-2.4m) tall, thick-stemmed stalks. The corn ears develop at a rate of one to two per plant in the nooks of the stem and large elongated leaves.

Favorite varieties: "Allure" F-1, "Enchanted" F-1, "Peaches & Cream" F-1

Seeding information: One seed of (OP, F-1, organic and/or non-treated only) per cell in plug trays. Although not required to seed inside, I find it a recommended practice as corn can sometimes be difficult to germinate in the field if soil temperatures are too cold.

Days to germination at temperature range: Four to seven days at 70-90F (21-32C).

When to start inside: Ten days before warm and settled date.

Necessary to pot-up to three-inch pots: No.

When to transplant or direct seed outside: Transplant when seedlings have first true leaves, being diligent as the long taproot of corn seedlings develop rapidly. Plant 10-12 inches (25-30cm) apart in rows at 18 inches (45cm). Can also be direct seeded at the same distance. Plant at least six row blocks of varieties with similar days to harvest, to encourage wind-driven pollination. Pollen from the tassels will fall onto the emerging silks.

Maintenance required during growing period: Keep well weeded of native flora. Once plants are eighteen inches (45cm) tall undersow with clover, like crimson clover. Very drought tolerant once established. Optimum soil pH range is 5.8 to 7.5.

Insects to observe: European corn borer *Ostrinia nubilalis* can become a problem in developing ears damaging the kernels themselves. However, in well diversified gardens they are rarely a huge problem as many native insects feed on the larvae. In addition, wild-established honeybees and many wasp species collect the pollen off the corn tassels.

Diseases to watch for: Powdery mildew and common smut, caused by the fungus *Ustilago maydis* are not common but can be a concern in corn ears when there has been a prolonged period of dry weather, followed by a temperature plummet, during ear formation. Control by irrigating bi-weekly during droughts.

Days to harvest: Seventy to ninety days from transplants, then continually until all ears are harvested.

Harvest advice: Corn ears are ready when kernels are fully formed, and when punctured with a fingernail are milky. Pull off ears with a downward motion from the plant, removing some of the husk but leaving a good wrapper. Harvest readily, as corn will turn starchy in the field if pulled late but will retain sweetness in storage when harvested at the correct time. A general rule is that ears are ready twenty-one days after reddish silks appear.

Post-harvest handling/terms of storage (best way to preserve flavor): Will store in bags or bins at 33-40F (1-4.5C) for fourteen days. Can be cooked, kernels cut off the cob and frozen to store for six months and more.

Health benefits: Whole grain corn is rich in nutrients and bioactive compounds including fiber, vitamins, minerals, and phytochemicals. More and more scientific evidence suggests the regular consumption of whole grains reduces the risk of developing chronic diseases, including cardiovascular disease, type 2 diabetes, overweight and obesity, and digestive disorders.[24]

Field notes:

Cucumbers
Cucumis sativus

Characteristics/growing habits: Cucumbers, members of the family *Cucurbitaceae*, are tender annuals that prefer a warm to hot growing season. They will vine and run, flowering profusely and forming fruits which can be round or long, yellow or green, under the canopy of the sprawling plants. Cucumbers require pollinators to set fruit, unless parthenocarpic (seedless).

Favorite varieties: "Marketmore 76" (OP), "H-19 Little Leaf" (OP)

Seeding information: One seed of (OP, heirloom) per cell in three to four-inch pots. Although not required and direct seeding is a viable method, starting inside can give a ten-to-fourteen-day jump on the harvest.

Days to germination at temperature range: Four to seven days at 65-90F (18-32C).

When to start inside: Three weeks before warm and settled date.

Necessary to pot-up to three-inch pots: Not necessary to pot up, sow seed directly into a three to four-inch pot.

When to transplant or direct seed outside: Transplant or direct seed at warm and settled date as cucumber seeds are difficult to germinate in cold soils (below 55F (13C) and roots of the transplants do not react well to the same. Plant 12 inches (30cm) apart, rows at 18 inches (45cm).

Maintenance required during growing period: Keep well weeded of native flora. Cover with Agribon-type 17 or 19 row covers until every plant has a flower or two. Upon removal, applying a dry straw mulch under plants and vines will trap soil humidity and keep cucumbers from rotting on wet soil. Where space is an issue, cucumbers can be trellised and trained to climb. Optimum soil pH range is 5.8 to 7.5.

Insects to observe: Striped and spotted cucumber beetles are migrating insects that can become quite numerous in the early season. Control by planting later and keep the plants covered with row covers. The larvae are predated on by spined soldier bugs and assassin beetles. Usually the density of cucumber beetles, both types, subside by mid-summer.

Diseases to watch for: Powdery mildew can become a major problem when there has been a prolonged period of dry weather, followed by a cold snap. Anthracnose of cucurbits, caused by *Colletotrichum orbiculare*, can arrive in rainy summers, presented by brown lesions on the leaves and fruits. Control by irrigating regularly during the drought times and limiting during the rainy ones.

Days to harvest: Thirty-five to forty-five days from transplants, fifty to sixty days from direct seeding then continually until first fall frost.

Harvest advice: Harvest cucumbers regularly, even every day, as cucumbers are easily overlooked and bulk up very fast. Can be harvested immature for a gourmet, next to seedless treat. Harvest when the plants are dry to avoid passing fungal disease when searching under the vines.

Post-harvest handling/terms of storage (best way to preserve flavor): Cucumbers are highly perishable, due to high water content and will store for a maximum of seven to ten days. Store in plastic bags or bins at 33-40F (1-4.5C). Can be made into fresh pickles or canned as dill or "bread and butter" pickles and stored for up to one year.

Health benefits: Consisting mostly of water, and containing important electrolytes, cucumbers can help prevent dehydration during the hot summer months or during and after a workout. As a member of the *Cucurbitaceae* family of plants, cucumbers contain high levels of nutrients known as cucurbitacins, which may help prevent cancer by stopping cancer cells from proliferating and surviving.[25]

Field notes:

_____
_____
_____
_____
_____
_____
_____
_____
_____
_____

Dill
Anethum graveolens

Characteristics/growing habits: Dill, a member of the family *Umbelliferae*, is a huge, (can reach six feet (180cm), bushy, hardy annual plant. Dill creates a low growing bush at first. The dark green aromatic fern-like leaves will produce thick flower stalks, yielding a rosette of dainty yellow flowers. Seeds eventually appear, first green (edible) then brown when dry. Dill is self-seeding the following spring.

Favorite varieties: "Bouquet" (OP)

Seeding information: Direct seed (OP, heirloom) ¼-inch (.7cm) deep, thinning to 4 inches (10cm) apart.

Days to germination at temperature range: Six to ten days at 50-75F (10-24C).

When to start inside: n/a

Necessary to pot-up to three-inch pots: n/a

When to transplant or direct seed outside: Direct seed as soon as soil can be worked. Succession plant every three weeks for continual harvest throughout the season as dills' edible leaves dry up when flower stalks produce flowers.

Maintenance required during growing period: Keep weeded of native flora throughout growing period, but dill grows quickly and will cohabit with all types of low-growing native flora creating a bountiful insect habitat. It is recommended to let the flowers open to invite a whole host of pollinating insects (see below.) Optimum soil pH range is 5.5 to 7.5.

Insects to observe: None of major consequence attack the plants. Delicate yellow dill flowers are highly attractive to small native bees, flies, wasps, butterflies, and moths. Chickadees, goldfinches, juncos, and sparrows will eat the dried seeds of late summer.

Diseases to watch for: None of great significance from my monitoring.

Days to harvest: Forty-five to fifty-five days from direct seeding then continually until first fall frost. Self-seeding plants will begin to put out edible leaves about a week before last spring frost.

Harvest advice: Harvest leaves by cutting above the base of the plant with garden cutters when desired size is reached, or alternatively, cut the entire plant at base to give room for others to grow. When some seeds begin to dry, cut the entire rosette and put it in a well-ventilated place, out of direct sunlight, to dry thoroughly.

Post-harvest handling/terms of storage (best way to preserve flavor): Dill is highly perishable and can be stored in plastic bags in the fridge for seven to ten days. Best enjoyed for fresh eating, but can be used to make herbal vinegars and oils. Dill ferns can be dried to store for up to one year. Dill seeds can also be dried for the same length of time.

Health benefits: There is evidence that *Anethum graveolens* (AG) has been used for centuries in Asian traditional medicine, and its constituents have useful effects on the control and management of diabetes and cardiovascular disorders. Dill has many useful effects, including hypolipidemic and hypoglycemic effects, and it has been reported to reduce the incidence of diabetic complications.[26]

Field notes:

Dry Beans
Phaseolus vulgaris

Characteristics/growing habits: Like bush beans, drying bean varieties, members of the family *Fabaceae,* grow on robust plants, with the intention of letting the pods go dry on the plants. When dried they will reveal a vast assortment of colors from black to white, red to yellow, mottled to yin/yang swirls.

Favorite varieties: "Black Turtle" (HL), "Calypso" (HL), "Cannellini" (HL), "Jacob's Cattle" (HL), "Pinto" (HL), "Vermont Cranberry" (HL)

Seeding information: Direct seed (OP, heirloom) 1-inch (2.5cm) deep, 2 inches (5cm) apart, rows at 12 inches (30cm).

Days to germination at temperature range: Four to seven days at 60-80F (15.5-26.5C).

When to start inside: n/a

Necessary to pot-up to three-inch pots: n/a

When to transplant or direct seed outside:

L'ILLUSTRATION HORTICOLE

HARICOT FLAGEOLET BEURRE SANGUIN A RAMES

Direct seed about one week after last frost date. Most beans, to reach full dry pod potential, require a long growing season (90+ days).

Maintenance required during growing period: Dry bush beans grow very fast, so normally only one good weeding of native flora is necessary, after which plants outcompete and crowd the space. Dry beans are exceptionally drought resistant due to their extensive and deep root systems. Optimum soil pH range is 5.5 to 7.5.

Insects to observe: Mexican bean beetles *Epilachna varivestis* along with their larvae will defoliate bean plants, but seem to be less prevalent on dry bean varieties. Hand-pick for best results if the populations become intense. Bumblebees and Great Northern bees like to work the flowers.

Diseases to watch for: White mold is a fungus that can live in the soil up to eight years and infects over four hundred different varieties of plants. It will decimate a plant and rot the beans. It is particularly prevalent during wet, semi warm conditions. Keeping the bean plantings as dry as possible will curtail the mold. Pulling the worst infected plants will limit plant to plant infection.

Days to harvest: 90-105 days and continually until first fall frost.

Harvest advice: Start harvesting pods as soon as dry after the dew and rain has dried off the plants. Let pods sit in a tray or bin in a well-ventilated sunny location to continue curing.

Post-harvest handling/terms of storage (best way to preserve flavor): Shuck beans and store in glass containers in a dark place no warmer than 70F (21C). Will store for many years.

Health benefits: Along with being a highly nutritious food, evidence shows that legumes can play an important role in the prevention and management of a number of health conditions, including type 2 diabetes, hypertension, hyperlipidemia, and weight management. A high intake of fruits, vegetables, whole grains, legumes (beans), nuts, and seeds is linked to significantly lower risks of heart disease, high blood pressure, stroke, and the above-mentioned type 2 diabetes.[27]

Field notes:

Eggplant
Solanum melongena

Characteristics/growing habits: Eggplant, members of the family *Solanaceae*, are grown as tender annuals, but are actually perennial in places where it does not freeze. Many plants together can become a prolific hedge. As annuals they reach about twenty-four to thirty-six inches (60-90cm) tall and come in a dazzling variety of shapes; long, oblong, egg-size to large classic bell shapes. The amazing color array can be every shade of purple as well as red, white, streaked, orange, yellow and even green. Eggplants have perfect flowers; will set fruit by vibration from natural (wind, insects) or human (brushing by, or "tripping") causes.

Favorite varieties: "Diamond" (OP), "Edirne" (HL), "Ping Tung Long" (HL), "Turkish Orange" (HL)

Seeding information: One seed (OP, heirloom, or F-1, for large classic Italian types) per cell in plug trays.

Days to germination at temperature range: Five to eight days at 70-90F (21-32C).

When to start inside: Eight weeks before last spring frost date.

Necessary to pot-up to three-inch pots: Yes, as soon as plants have two true leaves. Eggplants will not hold in larger pots for very long before turning yellow, pot up no more than three weeks before transplanting outside.

When to transplant or direct seed outside: Transplant after last frost date. Eggplants can tolerate nights down to 40F (4.5C) but prolonged exposure to these temperatures will stunt growth and limit flower production. Protect with Agribon-type 17 or 19 row covers if night temperatures forecast below 40F. Plant at 18 inches (45cm) apart.

Maintenance required during growing period: Keep well-weeded of native flora throughout growing period. Once the soil temperatures are consistently warm, above 60F (15.5C), side-dress with veganic compost and dry straw mulch if desired. Keep well-watered during the growing season. Optimum soil pH range is 5.8 to 7.5.

Insects to observe: Colorado potato beetles will invade plants in early summer, lay eggs, and the larvae will defoliate the plant quickly. Control by pulling adult beetles and letting spined soldier bugs and assassin beetles proliferate. Cutworms live in the soil, emerge at night, and can chew off the stem of newly transplanted seedlings. Control by checking the soil around the base of the plant early in the morning and removing them.

Diseases to watch for: White mold is a fungus that can live in the soil up to eight years and infects over four hundred different varieties of plants. It will decimate a plant and rot the eggplants. It is particularly prevalent during wet, semi warm conditions. Pulling the worst infected plants will limit plant to plant infection. Eggplant fruits can be subject to blossom end rot which is caused by a calcium deficiency, correct by side-dressing with wood ash or powdered dolomitic lime if detected.

Days to harvest: Sixty to eighty days from transplants, then continually until first fall frost

Harvest advice: Cut eggplants with about one inch (2.5cm) of stem with garden cutters when the eggplant is slippery to the touch, not tacky, but before it has turned matte (this is overripe). Harvesting them smaller will encourage the production of smaller gourmet fruits. Harvest after the morning dew has burned off or plants have dried from the rain.

Post-harvest handling/terms of storage (best way to preserve flavor): Eggplants are perishable and will last ten to fourteen days in plastic bags or bins at 33-40F (1-4.5C). Best enjoyed fresh.

Health benefits: Eggplants are a rich source of magnesium, manganese, potassium, and copper that are important for healthy bones. Eggplant is also known as an Fe (iron) chelator that is suggested particularly for pregnant women, lactating mothers, and teenage girls specifically. The fruits are important in the treatment of various disorders like asthma, dysuria, dysentery, high blood pressure, as well as osteoporosis, arthritis, diabetes and bronchitis, heart diseases and strokes.[28]

Field notes:

Fennel
Foeniculum vulgare

Characteristics/growing habits: Fennel, a member of the family *Apiaceae*, has a bushy fern-like set of fronds that grow off a creamy white bulb. The characteristic flavor is that of black licorice and anise. Can be grown for the bulb, the leaves, or the seeds.

Favorite varieties: "Finale" (OP), "Florence" (OP)

Seeding information: One seed of (OP, heirloom) per cell in plug trays.

Days to germination at temperature range: Seven to ten days at 60-75F (15.5-21C).

When to start inside: Four to five weeks before last spring frost date.

Necessary to pot-up to three-inch pots: No.

When to transplant or direct seed outside: Transplant after last frost date at 12 inches (30cm) apart.

Maintenance required during growing period: Keep weeded of native flora throughout growing period. Fennel requires constant moisture throughout the growing season. Optimum soil pH range is 6.0 to 7.5.

Insects to observe: Monarch and swallowtail caterpillars readily march along the mature fronds.

Diseases to watch for: None of major consequence from my surveillance.

Days to harvest: Fifty-five to eighty days from transplants, then continually until first fall frost.

Harvest advice: Cut with garden cutters below the bulb when bulbs reach a girth of at least one inch (2.5cm), before browning and before bolting of the main stem to seed head. Harvest in the morning when still cool.

Post-harvest handling/terms of storage (best way to preserve flavor): Fennel with the fronds trimmed to three inches (7.5cm) can store in plastic bags or bins at 33-40F (1-4.5C) for up to one month. Best enjoyed fresh.

Health benefits: Fennel is an effective remedy for visual acuity, cataract, catarrh, stomachache, chronic diarrhea, nausea, vomiting, chronic fever, kidney stones, internal obstructions, and urinary diseases. Fennel is also a valuable plant in management of women's health issues especially premenstrual syndrome.[29]

Field notes:

Flax
Linum usitatissimum

Characteristics/growing habits: Flax, a member of the family *Linaceae*, is a delicate, tall (reaching four feet (120cm) grass-like annual. Flax stalks are many-stemmed and green, that produce a prolific amount of delicate, blue to lavender flowers. The flowers then set a bulb in which is housed the flax seeds. The consumable seeds can either be brown or golden.

Favorite varieties: "Golden Flax" (HL)

Seeding information: Direct seed by broadcasting many seeds per bed foot.

Days to germination at temperature range: Seven to ten days at 60-80F (15.5-26.5C).

When to start inside: n/a

Necessary to pot-up to three-inch pots: n/a

When to transplant or direct seed outside: Direct seed after last frost date.

Maintenance required during growing period: Keep well-weeded of native flora when seedlings are emerging, and well-watered. Flax is very drought tolerant once established, after which she can be companion planted with low growing flowers, like nasturtium or green crops like clover. Optimum soil pH range is 5.5 to 7.5.

Insects to observe: None of major consequence attack the plants. Native bees, bumblebees, syrphid flies and wasps are highly attracted to the showy blue and lavender flowers.

Diseases to watch for: None of great significance has been perceived.

Days to harvest: Flax seeds develop at about one hundred days, once in this stage can survive a hard frost 25F (-4C).

Harvest Advice: In early fall, harvest seed bulbs with fingers when plants and seed pods are completely dry.

Post-harvest handling/terms of storage (best way to preserve flavor): Let seed pods continue to dry in a well-ventilated location until seeds are fully dry (when they can no longer be pierced with the fingernail). Seeds can be stored in glass jars for multiple years.

Health benefits: Flaxseed is a rich source of the omega-3 fatty acid, alpha linolenic acid, the lignan, secoisolariciresinol diglucoside, and fiber. These compounds provide bioactivity of value to the health of animals and humans through their anti-inflammatory action, anti-oxidative capacity and lipid modulating properties. The current evidence on the benefits or limitations of dietary flaxseed in a variety of cardiovascular diseases, cancer, gastro-intestinal health and brain development and function, as well as hormonal status in menopausal women, are comprehensive topics for discussion.[30]

Field notes:

Garlic
Allium sativum

Characteristics/growing habits: Garlic (hardneck or softneck), members of the family *Amaryllidaceae,* are perennial roots that are grown from the clove or left in the ground year after year to divide. Normally one clove is planted in the fall for each bulb wished to harvest. In spring, emergence begins with the first garlic leaves. Garlic can reach a height of four feet (120cm) and produces a beautifully curled scape in hardneck varieties.

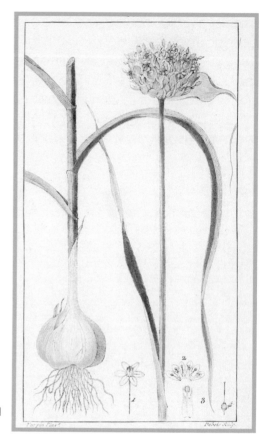

Favorite varieties: Hardneck: "Chesnok Red" (HL), "German Red" (HL), "Metechi" (HL), "Spanish Roja" (HL). Softneck: "California White" (HL)

Seeding information: Direct seed (OP, heirloom) at 2 inches (5cm) deep, 4 inches (10cm) apart, rows at 12 inches (30cm).

Days to germination at temperature range: n/a

When to start inside: n/a

Necessary to pot-up to three-inch pots: n/a

When to transplant or direct seed outside: Direct seed outside two weeks before the soil freezes hard. Garlic requires a dormant period to reproduce the bulb. We like to mulch with dry straw, but can be left without, as is individual preference.

Maintenance required during growing period: Keep well weeded of native flora as garlic bulb size is limited when crowded. Upon emergence in the spring fertilize with a liquid nettle/comfrey tea or even a 20:1 dilution of human pee. In hardneck varieties, when scapes form, let them make a first or second turn, and then snap off to let bulb increase girth. Optimum soil pH range is 5.5 to 7.5.

Insects to observe: Wireworm the larvae of the click beetle (*Alaus oculatus*) will pockmark garlic wrappers but are not a huge problem. Leek moth, or onion leafminer, *Acrolepiopsis assectella* shows in late spring and deposits eggs into the central growing stem, observed in garlic by holes in the leaves and scape. If left unchecked, they will burrow all the way down to the garlic bulb. Control by checking the neck every few days and squeezing out larvae.

Diseases to watch for: Because of their long growing season and widely varied temperature growing conditions, garlic is susceptible to many fungal diseases. White Rot (*Sclerotium cepivorum*) attacks the stem and yellows the leaves prematurely. Fusarium bulb rot, *F. proliferatum*, and fusarium basal rot, *F. culmorum* & *F. oxysporum*, damage cloves by attacking the bulb. Botrytis neck rot of garlic (*Botrytis porri*) will display as neck damage caused by too much water in the stem and will proceed down to the plant. All diseases can be mitigated by keeping well weeded and pulling mulch (if using) back from stems when the days and nights begin to warm in late spring.

Days to harvest: For hardneck varieties about fifteen to twenty-one days after scapes are pulled and desired bulb size is achieved. Depending on your region, usually from mid-June to late July.

Harvest advice: When the majority, of all types of garlic, has five to six green leaves left on the plant pull straight up and out of the soil on a sunny day. Let garlic sit in the garden for a few hours in the sun. Bring into a dry environment with good air circulation out of direct sunlight, like an airy barn or garden shed. Caterpillar tunnels or in a greenhouse, with 70-80% shade cloth, are excellent options for curing locations. Cure for two to four weeks depending on humidity.

Post-harvest handling/terms of storage (best way to preserve flavor): For hardneck varieties, after curing cut with 1-1.5-inch (2.5-4cm) stems, peel off the dirtiest outer wrappers and keep in a cool, dry, out of sunlight place. If when cut, the stem is still green and oozing with juice, she requires more curing time. Soft neck varieties can also be cut as above, or can be braided when leaves are dry and hung in the same conditions. Garlic can store for up to one-year in a dark location in paper bags; the best temperature is between 50-60F (10-15.5 C).

Health benefits: Several experimental and clinical investigations suggest many favorable effects of garlic and its preparations. These effects have been largely attributed to reduction of risk factors for cardiovascular diseases, reduction of cancer risk, antioxidant effect, antimicrobial effect, and enhancement of detoxification foreign compound and hepatoprotection.[31]

Field notes:

_____
_____
_____
_____
_____
_____

Greek Oregano
Origanum heracleoticum

Characteristics/growing habits: Oregano, a member of the family *Lamiaceae*, is a low, bushy, sprawling hardy perennial (to zone four). Greek oregano has a distinctive pungent aroma with a slightly sweet, spicy flavor nestled in fuzzy dark green leaves. The delicate white flowers that bolt in mid-summer are highly attractive to native bees.

Favorite varieties: "Greek Oregano" (HL)

Seeding information: Sprinkle tiny seeds (OP, heirloom) on soil surface of 1020 flats. Need light to germinate. Can also be direct seeded as soon as soil can be worked. Keep moist until sprouting.

Days to germination at temperature range: Seven to fourteen days at 55-70F (13-21C).

When to start inside: Eight weeks before last frost date.

Necessary to pot-up to three-inch pots: Yes, as soon as seedlings have two true leaves. Can transplant two to three seedlings into each pot if desired.

When to transplant or direct seed outside: Direct seed as soon as soil can be worked. Transplant after last frost date. Plant at 12 inches (30cm) apart.

Maintenance required during growing period: Keep weeded of native flora throughout growing period as oregano plants are slow to root in and create their low sprawling canopy. Very drought tolerant once established. Once installed, they will spread in their bushy habit and outcompete native flora. Optimum soil pH range is 5.5 to 7.5.

Insects to observe: None of major consequence attack the plants. Delicate white flowers are inviting to the smallest native bees, flies, and wasps.

Diseases to watch for: None of great significance have been discovered.

Days to harvest: Fifty to sixty days from transplants, eighty days from direct seeding then continually until first fall hard frost.

Harvest Advice: Harvest sprigs (stems and leaves) with garden cutters when desired size is reached, leaving central crown untouched.

Post-harvest handling/terms of storage (best way to preserve flavor): Can be stored in plastic bags at 33-40F (1-4.5C) for fourteen to twenty-one days. Best method of long-term preservation is to dry leaves and pack into glass jars once cooled, which will keep for one year.

Health benefits: Medicinal uses for oregano date back to the ancient Greek and Roman empires where applications of the leaves were used to treat such maladies as skin sores and relieve aching muscles and as an antiseptic. Oregano also has been used in traditional medicines for such ailments as asthma, cramping, diarrhea, and indigestion. In Greece, an oregano infusion is still used as a folk remedy against colds and upset stomach and to maintain general health.[32]

Field notes:

Greens (Asian)
Brassica rapa

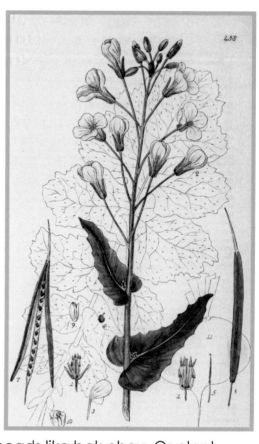

Characteristics/growing habits: Asian greens, members of the family *Brassicaceae*, are cold hardy annuals. They are characterized by being long-stemmed, large-leafed, with an open habit style of growing. Asian greens come in purple and green, serrated or smooth, depending on variety.

Favorite varieties: "Mizuna" (OP), "Tat Soi" (OP), "Prize Choy" Bok Choy (OP)

Seeding Information: Seed (OP, heirloom) in cell plug trays to extend the season. Can also be direct seeded.

Days to germination at temperature range: Three to six days at 60-85F (15.5-29.5C).

When to start inside: Three to four weeks before transplanting outside

Necessary to pot-up to three-inch pots: No.

When to transplant or direct seed outside: As soon as soil can be worked at 12 inches (30cm) apart for transplants desiring full-sized heads like bok choy. Or plant ½-inch (1.25cm) deep, 2 inches (5cm) apart rows at 6 inches (15cm) for baby greens. Can be succession planted in spring and early fall as befitting.

Maintenance required during growing period: Asian greens appreciate boron to reach full potential, work one-quarter teaspoon per bed foot into the soil before planting. Immediately after transplanting cover with insect screen and row cover if nights drop below 31F (-1C). Give consistent water throughout the growing season. Weed out native flora while plants are small. Optimum soil pH range is 5.8 to 7.5.

Insects to observe: White cabbage moths lay eggs and hatch as green cabbage worms. They will defoliate a crop and eat the central crown limiting growth of the plant. Flea beetles are a common early spring problem creating small holes in young leaves. Keep greens well weeded of common plantain, the flea beetle's preferred host. Control both by keeping plants covered with insect screens until harvest. Green peach aphids can become abundant in times of warm nights and humid conditions. Bok choy specifically can be used as a trap crop for all insects, but especially, white cabbage moths. Allowing some of the first spring sowings of Asian greens to flower will invite a whole host of native bees, flies, wasps, butterflies, and moths.

Diseases to watch for: None of major consequence have been viewed.

Days to harvest: Twenty-one to thirty days from direct seeding for baby greens, twenty-eight to forty days from transplant for full-size heads.

Harvest advice: Cut baby greens with a heavy-duty pocketknife as soon as desired size is reached, cutting above the central crown to allow for regrowth. Harvest full heads starting with the biggest, allowing smaller ones to size up. Cut all as early as possible in the morning, before the heat of the day.

Post-harvest handling/terms of storage (best way to preserve flavor): Baby greens are highly perishable, will store a maximum of ten days in plastic bags at 33-40F (1-4.5C). Full heads can store up to two weeks at the same temperature range. After harvest, immerse greens and heads in cold water and let air dry or salad-spin greens before storage. Larger leaves can be blanched and frozen, to be stored for six months.

Health benefits: The beneficial effects of Brassica vegetables (including all *Brassica rapa sp.*) on human health have been linked to phytochemicals. They prevent oxidative stress, induce detoxification enzymes, stimulate immune system, decrease the risk of cancers, inhibit malignant transformation and carcinogenic mutations, as well as reduce proliferation of cancer cells.[33]

Field notes:

Greens (Mustard)
Brassica juncea

Characteristics/growing habits:
Mustard greens, members of the family *Brassicaceae*, are cold hardy annuals. They are characterized by being long-stemmed, large-leafed, with an open habit style of growing. Specifically grown for mesclun-type salad mixes that add the mustard flavor component. They make their presence in purple and green, serrated or savoyed depending on variety.

Favorite varieties: "Ruby Streaks" (OP), "Golden Frills" (OP)

Seeding information: Direct seed (OP, heirloom) ½-inch (1.25cm) deep, thinned to 2 inches (5cm) apart, rows at 6 inches (15cm).

Days to germination at temperature range: Three to six days at 55-85F (13-29.5C).

When to start inside: n/a

Necessary to pot-up to three-inch pots: n/a

When to transplant or direct seed outside: As soon as soil can be worked, and succession planted every three weeks thereafter to ensure a constant harvest throughout the season.

Maintenance required during growing period: Keep well-weeded of native flora throughout the seedling stage. Once fully formed, mustard greens will create a canopy that deters native flora growth. Cover immediately after planting with insect screens. Optimum soil pH range is 5.5 to 7.5.

Insects to observe: Flea beetles are a common early spring problem creating small holes in young leaves. Best control is to install insect screens immediately after seeding. Keep greens well weeded of common plantain, the flea beetle's preferred host. Green peach aphids can become abundant in times of warm nights and humid conditions. Letting the earliest plantings go to flower will attract a whole host of native bees, syrphid flies and wasps.

Diseases to watch for: None of consequence have been detected.

Days to harvest: Twenty-one to thirty days from direct seeding.

Harvest advice: Cut baby greens with a heavy-duty pocketknife as soon as desired size is reached, cutting above the central crown to allow for regrowth. Cut all as early as possible in the morning, before the heat of the day.

Post-harvest handling/terms of storage (best way to preserve flavor): Baby greens are highly perishable, will store for a maximum of ten days in plastic bags or bins at 33-40F (1-4.5C). After harvest, immerse greens in cold water and salad-spin greens before storage.

Health benefits: Mustard (*Brassica juncea* L.) is a *Brassicaceae* vegetable that contains various health-promoting phytochemicals including carotenoids, phenolic compounds, and glucosinolates. These compounds are often associated with their ability to act as detoxifiers against oxidative stress. This is of particular interest for human health, considering that an imbalance of oxidants and antioxidants in the body can lead to the development of certain chronic diseases, such as cancer, diabetes, and cardiovascular disease.[34]

Field notes:

Ground Cherry
Physalis pruinosa

Characteristics/growing habits: Ground Cherries, members of the family *Solanaceae*, also known as husk cherry, are tall (can reach three feet (90cm) tall), bushy, warm season annual plants that yield a bounty of fruits. They have perfect flowers, which means they do not require pollinators to set fruit; simply needing vibration of the plants. Husked fruits turn from unripe green in light green wrappers to bright yellow wrappers housing golden sweet, tropical tasting morsels.

Favorite varieties: "Goldie" (OP)

Seeding information: One to two seeds of (OP, heirloom) per cell in plug trays, thinning to one seedling after emergence. They require light to germinate.

Days to germination at temperature range: Four to seven days at 65-90F (18-32C).

When to start inside: Six to seven weeks before last spring frost date.

Necessary to pot-up to three-inch pots: Yes, as soon as plants have two true leaves. Ground cherries will not hold in larger pots for very long before turning yellow, pot up no more than three weeks before transplanting outside.

When to transplant or direct seed outside: Transplant after last frost date. Ground cherries can tolerate nights down to 35F (2C). Protect with Agribon-type 17 or 19 row covers if night temperatures are forecast below 35F. Transplant at 12 inches (30cm) apart.

Maintenance required during growing period: Keep weeded of native flora throughout growing period. Very drought tolerant once established. Dry straw mulch when soil temperatures reach 60F (16C) if desired, to keep dropped fruits from rotting. Yields are increased when planted in low tunnels. Prefer drip irrigation to overhead watering. Ground cherries are self-seeding annuals, they will make many volunteers, fruits that drop over winter and sprout the following spring. Usually, those can be allowed to grow up to full plants. Optimum soil pH range is 5.8 to 7.5.

Insects to observe: Cutworms live in the soil, emerge at night, and can chew off the stem of newly transplanted seedlings. Control by checking the soil around the base of the plant early in the morning and removing them. Striped and spotted cucumber beetles are migrating insects that can become quite numerous in the early season. The larvae are predated on by spined soldier bugs and assassin beetles. Usually the density of cucumber beetles, both types, subsides by mid-summer.

Diseases to watch for: White mold can live in the soil up to eight years and infects over four hundred different varieties of plants. It will decimate a plant and rot the fruits. It is particularly prevalent during wet, semi warm conditions. Pulling the worst infected plants will limit plant to plant infection.

Days to harvest: Fifty-five to sixty days from transplants, then continually until first fall frost.

Harvest Advice: Harvest all ground cherries that have dropped from plants, regardless of color, regularly as there are many insects and small mammal creatures that will feed on the dropped gems. Harvest when fruit wrappers are as dry as possible.

Post-harvest handling/terms of storage (best way to preserve flavor): Ground cherries will ripen to golden orange at room temperature five to seven days after harvesting. Will keep for fresh eating from fourteen to twenty-one days. Can be made into fresh or canned preserves and even dried whole, to be used like raisins and stored for up to one year.

Health benefits: Results showed that *physalis* crops (of which ground cherry is one) contain many essential minerals and vitamins, notably potassium and the immune system-supporting Vitamin C, also known for its antioxidant activity. Beyond nutritional properties, these crops also contain a class of steroidal lactones called withanolides, which have been recognized for their antitumor, and anti-inflammatory properties. In some studies, withanolide extract from Physalis species have exhibited cytotoxicity towards cancers cells.[35]

Field notes:

Kale
Brassica napus, oleracea

Characteristics/growing habits: Kale, a member of the family *Brassicaceae*, is a hardy biennial that grows on upright thick stemmed plants. The leaves can be dark green to light green, red-veined, and purple. The shape can be smooth, serrated or deeply frilled.

Favorite varieties: "Curly Roja" (HL), "Darkibor" (F1), "Lacinato" (HL), "Red Russian" (HL), "Siberian" (OP)

Seeding information: Seed (OP, heirloom, or F1 varieties for long-harvest season varieties) in cell plug trays taking note that kale is prone to damping off, in the small seedling stage. Water cells only when dry after emergence.

Days to germination at temperature range: Three to six days at 60-85F (15.5-29.5C).

When to start inside: Three to four weeks before transplanting outside.

Necessary to pot-up to three-inch pots: No.

When to transplant or direct seed outside: Transplant as soon as soil can be worked or anytime during the growing season at 12 inches (30cm) apart. Can also be direct seeded ½ inch (1.25cm) deep, 1 inch (2.5cm) apart, rows at 6 inches (15cm) for baby greens and succession sow every three weeks as desired.

Maintenance required during growing period: Kale favors boron to make full leaves, work one-quarter teaspoon per bed foot into the soil before planting. Immediately after transplanting cover with insect screen and row cover if nights drop below 31F (-1C). Give consistent water throughout the growing season. Weed out native flora while plants are small. Keep covered with insect screens up until leaves are full-sized and throughout the harvest window if cutting for baby greens. When harvesting large-leaved varieties, pull off any yellow leaves and use as mulch around the plants. Optimum soil pH range is 5.8 to 7.5.

Insects to observe: Cutworms, which live in the soil, can defoliate and/or chew off the stem of newly transplanted seedlings (less of a problem in direct-seeded plantings). Control by checking the soil around the base of the plant early in the morning and removing them. White cabbage moths lay eggs and hatch as green cabbage worms. They will defoliate a crop and eat the central crown, deforming the newest growing leaves. Control by keeping covered with insect screens as long as possible and check periodically when uncovered. Cabbage aphids can become a nuisance in late summer plantings when the weather is warm and humid.

Diseases to watch for: Powdery mildew can affect older plants when conditions have been too dry followed by a cold snap. Towards the end of the season Alternaria leaf spot, caused by the fungus *Alternaria brassicicola* may appear on the oldest leaves, but it rarely causes mortality.

Days to harvest: Twenty-one to thirty days from direct seeding for baby greens, fifty to sixty days for full-size leaves and then continually throughout the season. Kale plants when fully mature can survive frosts to 25F (-4C)

Harvest advice: Cut early in the morning with a heavy-duty pocketknife leaving the central crown to grow back for baby greens. Pull the oldest outside leaves of full-sized kale plants, straight down to harvest.

Post-harvest handling/terms of storage (best way to preserve flavor): Large-leaved kale can be stored for fourteen to twenty-one days in plastic bags at 33-40F (1-4.5C). Baby kale last up to ten days in plastic bags at the same temperature. Immediately after harvest, immerse in cold water. Let large leaves air dry, salad-spin dry baby leaves.

Health benefits: Kale places high on the list of healthiest foods and is also known as a superfood. Kale, ranked 15th in a Centers for Disease Control study, and is strongly associated with reducing the risk of heart disease and other non-communicable diseases.[36]

Field notes:

_____

_____

_____

_____

_____

_____

_____

_____

Kohlrabi
Brassica oleracea var. gongylodes

Characteristics/growing habits: Kohlrabi, a member of the family *Brassicaceae*, is a hardy biennial that grows as a bulb, with broccoli-like leaves protruding from the central crown. Skin color can be lime-green or purple with a creamy, white, semi-sweet flesh inside. Bulbs can become quite large in long season varieties reaching 8-10 inches (20-25cm) diameter, while shorter season cultivars are typically 3-4 inches (7.5-10cm).

Favorite varieties: "Azur Star" (OP), "Superschmelz" (HL)

Seeding information: Seed (OP, heirloom varieties) in cell plug trays comprehending that kohlrabi is prone to damping off, in the small seedling stage. Water cells only when dry after emergence.

Chou-rave

Days to germination at temperature range: Three to six days at 60-85F (15.5-29C).

When to start inside: Three to four weeks before transplanting outside.

Necessary to pot-up to three-inch pots: No.

When to transplant or direct seed outside: Transplant as soon as soil can be worked or anytime during the growing season at 4 inches (10cm) apart for smaller varieties, 6 inches (15cm) for larger ones.

Maintenance required during growing period: Kohlrabi savors boron to make full healthy bulbs, work one-quarter teaspoon per bed foot into the soil before planting. Immediately after transplanting cover with insect screen and row cover if nights drop below 31F (-1C). Give consistent water throughout the growing season. Weed out native flora while plants are small. Keep covered with insect screens up until bulbs have matured. Pull off any yellow leaves and use as mulch around the plants. Optimum soil pH range is 5.8 to 7.5.

Insects to observe: Cutworms that live in the soil and emerge at night can defoliate and/or chew off the stem of newly transplanted seedlings. Control by checking the soil around the base of the plant early in the morning and removing them. Flea beetles can damage seedlings to mortality, control by keeping the plant covered with insect screens as long as possible. Cabbage aphids can become prevalent in late summer plantings when the weather is warm and humid.

Diseases to watch for: None of major consequence have been revealed.

Days to harvest: Forty-five to fifty-five days from transplant for short season, seventy to eighty days for long season and then continually until all are harvested.

Harvest advice: Cut early in the morning with garden cutters, just below the bulb, and leave the older leaves in the field. Harvest the biggest kohlrabi first to give the smallest time to grow.

Post-harvest handling/terms of storage (best way to preserve flavor): Kohlrabi can be stored for three to four months in plastic bags or bins at 33-40F (1-4.5C). Store bulbs dry and dirty without leaves and are best consumed raw. Leaves can store up to fourteen days at the same temperature. They are best cooked, used like kale. Can also be blanched and frozen for up to six months.

Health benefits: During the last two decades several epidemiological and case control studies have been published that associate the intake of cruciferous vegetables, of which Kohlrabi is one, with a decreased risk for developing cardiovascular disease and different types of cancer, particularly in the digestive tract, liver, lung, and breast.[37]

Field notes:

Leeks
Allium porrum

Characteristics/growing habits: Leeks, members of the family *Amaryllidaceae*, are a cool season biennial. The seedlings develop long flowing bluish-green leaves while the root end becomes a long, white sometimes slightly bulbed shaft.

Favorite varieties: "Alto" (OP), "Bandit" (OP)

Seeding information: Seed (OP, heirloom) in 1020 flats, 250-300 per tray maximum inside. Because of their long time resting in the same soil, it is beneficial to side-dress the trays with organic soybean meal about three-four weeks after emergence. It can be prudent to give leeks a "haircut" once they reach four inches (10cm) in their trays, once per week, to encourage further root development.

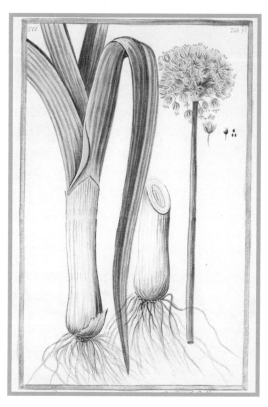

Days to germination at temperature range: Six to ten days at 60-80F (15.5-26.5C).

When to start inside: Eight to ten weeks before transplanting outside.

Necessary to pot-up to three-inch pots: n/a

When to transplant or direct seed outside: Transplant outside one week after soil can be worked. Leeks can tolerate a light freeze 31F (-1C) but prolonged frost exposure can limit growth. Upon removal from the tray, cut off roots, leaving two to three inches (5-7.5cm), and give them a "haircut," cutting the greens, which will spur root development. Transplant at 3 inches (7.5cm) apart, rows at 12 inches (30cm). Plant by poking a hole deep into soil so that the entire shaft is buried, ensuring that the entire root system is covered.

Maintenance required during growing period: Keep well-weeded of native flora as leek size is limited when overcrowded. After the growth spurt begins, hill leeks by mounding dirt up to the base of the first leaves and applying a layer of veganic compost. Leeks also enjoy a once-monthly foliar spraying of liquid fermentation (like clover/comfrey/nettle/yarrow). Keep well-watered throughout the growing season. Optimum soil pH range is 6.0 to 7.5.

Insects to observe: Wireworm, the larvae of the click beetle, will pockmark leek wrappers but are not a huge problem. Leek moth, or onion leafminer,

Acrolepiopsis assectella shows in late spring and deposits eggs into the central growing stem of allium plants observed by holes in the leaves. Cutworms emerge at night and can chew off the stem and leaves of newly transplanted seedlings (although less of a problem than in onions). Control by checking the soil around the base of the plant early in the morning and removing them. Flea beetles can also attack seedlings.

Diseases to watch for: Because of their long growing season and widely varied temperature growing conditions, leeks can be susceptible to fungal diseases. Powdery mildew can occur in times of warm, dry weather followed by a cold snap, but all usually subside on their own.

Days to harvest: Seventy-five to ninety days for summer varieties and 95-110 days for fall varieties from transplant.

Harvest advice: When summer leeks obtain a girth of a three-quarter inch (2cm), harvest bigger ones first, being diligent, as summer leeks will readily begin to put up their flower stalks, making the central core tough. Fall leeks are very hardy and can continue outside until the ground freezes hard 15F (-9.5C). Harvest by loosening soil around the leeks with a garden fork before pulling out.

Post-harvest handling/terms of storage (best way to preserve flavor): Cut off roots to one-half-inch (1.25cm) and outer yellowing leaves in the field. Store dry and dirty in plastic bags or bins at 33-40F (1-4.5C) for three to four months. If washed, leeks will store in plastic bags at the same temperature for eight weeks.

Health benefits: A. porrum is largely used as a soup ingredient and vegetable throughout Africa, and is known to possess anthelmintic, antiasthmatic, anticholesterolemic, antiseptic, antispasmodic, cholagogue, diaphoretic, diuretic, expectorant, febrifuge, stimulant, stomachic, tonic, vasodilator, antibacterial, antioxidant, cytotoxic, insecticidal, fungicidal properties.[38]

Field notes:

_____
_____
_____
_____
_____
_____
_____
_____
_____

Lettuce
Lactuca sativa

Characteristics/growing habits: Lettuce, members of the family *Asteraceae*, are hardy annuals that may be the most diverse of all the vegetable species. Colors range from light-dark green, light-dark red, and can be speckled in a combination of the two colors. Lettuce can be frilly, serrated, oak-leaved, smooth, round, tall and squat. Typical types include batavia, butterhead/bibb, iceberg, oak leaf, red and green leaf, romaine, and summer crisp.

Favorite varieties: "Cherokee" (OP), "Concept" (OP), "Freckles" (HL), "Magenta" (OP), "Muir" (OP), "Pirat" (OP), "Red Salad Bowl" (HL)

Seeding information: Seed (OP, heirloom) in cell plug trays for heading varieties noting that lettuce is prone to damping off, in the small seedling stage. Water cells only when dry after emergence.

Days to germination at temperature range: Three to six days at 55-75F (13-24C). Will germinate poorly in temperatures above this range.

When to start inside: Three to four weeks before transplanting outside.

Necessary to pot-up to three-inch pots: No.

When to transplant or direct seed outside: Transplant as soon as soil can be worked or anytime during the growing season at 10-12 inches (25-30cm) apart. Can also be direct seeded ½-inch (1.25cm) deep, 1-inch (2.5cm) apart, rows at 6 inches (15cm) for baby lettuce mix and succession planted as pertinent.

Maintenance required during growing period: Lettuce is very fast growing, covering the space quickly. Immediately after transplanting cover with insect screen and row cover if nights drop below 31F (-1C), recommended, but not required. Give consistent water throughout the growing season when small, pulling back when heads develop to induce fuller flavor and crispness. Weed out native flora while plants are small. Optimum soil pH range is 5.5 to 7.5.

Insects to observe: Green peach aphids can be a problem. If they are surveyed under insect screen, remove at night to allow lacewings, lady beetles and spiders to move in.

Diseases to watch for: Lettuce soft rot, *Pectobacterium carotovorum* subsp. *carotovorum,* can occur after a long, dry, growing season followed by hard frequent rains. Inundation can be mitigated by insect screens.

Days to harvest: Twenty-eight to thirty-five days from direct seeding for baby lettuce, thirty-five to fifty days for full-size heads from transplant. Lettuce can survive frosts to 25F (-4C).

Harvest advice: Cut early in the morning with a heavy-duty pocketknife just above the central crown for baby lettuce greens. Cut just below the base of lettuce for full-sized heads.

Post-harvest handling/terms of storage (best way to preserve flavor): Lettuce is perishable but can store up to fourteen days with good post-harvest practices. Immerse immediately after cutting in cold water. Let full heads air dry, baby leaves salad-spin dry. Pack in bins or plastic bags at 33-40F (1-4.5C).

Health benefits: Beneficial health properties of lettuce have mainly been attributed to carotenoids and other phytochemicals such as phenolic compounds. High quantities of carotenoids (i.e., β-carotene and lutein) were reported for several lettuce types including crisphead, butterhead, romaine, green and red leaf lettuces. Phenolic acids and anthocyanins were reported in red and green butterhead, crisphead (subtype Batavia), and green and red oak leaf lettuces.[39]

Field notes:

_____
_____
_____
_____
_____
_____
_____
_____
_____
_____
_____
_____

Lovage
Levisticum officinale

Characteristics/growing habits: Lovage, a member of the family *Apiaceae,* is a tall (reaching six feet (180cm), hardy, perennial plant. Thick stalks and leaves are reminiscent of celery, but more pungent and slightly minty. The tight, yellow flower rosettes arrive early in summer and are attractive to a whole host of insect species.

Favorite varieties: "Lovage" (OP)

Seeding information: One seed per cell in plug trays. Can also be direct seeded. Keep well-watered until germination.

Days to germination at temperature range: Ten to fourteen days at 55-70F (13-21C).

When to start inside: Six weeks before last frost date.

Necessary to pot-up to three-inch pots: Yes, as soon as plants have two true leaves. Can transplant in two to three plug seedlings into each pot if desired.

When to transplant or direct seed outside: Transplant or direct seed after last frost date. Plant at 12 inches (30cm) apart.

Maintenance required during growing period: Keep weeded of native flora when seedlings are small. Very drought tolerant once established. Lovage is fast growing and will companion with most native flora. Under-sowing with a native creeping clover or any other low growing variety plant will create a buoyant ecosystem. Optimum soil pH range is 5.5 to 7.5.

Insects to observe: None of great significance attack the plants. If too warm and humid, aphids can infest the crowns of the plants but do not pose a major problem to the fast-growing lovage. Insect species (many different types) flock to the yellow flowers. Goldfinches, pine siskins and sparrows enjoy the seeds.

Diseases to watch for: None of major consequence have been perceived.

Days to harvest: Seventy to seventy-five days from transplants, ninety days from direct seeding, then continually until first fall hard frost or until flowering, which makes stem over tough.

Harvest advice: Harvest full stems of lovage by cutting whole stems just above soil level when desired size is reached.

Post-harvest handling/terms of storage (best way to preserve flavor): Lovage can hold for up to one month at 33-40F (1-4.5C). Flavor is best enjoyed cooked in soups and stews, or minced finely in salads. Can also be cut and fresh frozen (with leaves) or dried for up to one year.

Health benefits: Lovage belongs to the *Apiaceae* family. *Apiaceae*, which is one of the largest plant families, comprises many culinary and medicinal plants usually characterized by a pungent or aromatic smell due to the presence of essential oil. Additionally, herbs from the *Apiaceae* family possess many compounds exerting different biological effects: they possess antioxidant, antibacterial, hepatoprotective, vaso-relaxant, cyclooxygenase inhibitory, and antitumor activities.[40]

Field notes:

Melons
Cucumis melo

Characteristics/growing habits: Melons, members of the family *Cucurbitaceae*, are warm season tender annuals that prefer a warm to hot growing season. The varied melon class of ananas, canary, cantaloupe, charentais, crenshaw, galia, and honeydew types (among others) will vine and run and set their fruits among the tangles. Melons require pollinators to set fruit.

Favorite varieties: "Charentais" (HL), "Hale's Best Jumbo" (HL), "Halona" F-1

Seeding information: One seed (OP, heirloom, or F-1, if desired) per three to four-inch (7.5-10cm) pots.

Days to germination at temperature range: Four to seven days at 65-90F (18.5-32C).

When to start inside: Three weeks before warm and settled date.

Necessary to pot-up to three-inch pots: Not necessary to pot up, sow seed directly into a three to four-inch pot.

When to transplant or direct seed outside: Transplant at warm and settled date as melon seedlings do not react well to nights below 55F (13C). Transplant 12 inches (30cm) apart.

Maintenance required during growing period: Keep well weeded of native flora. Cover with Agribon-type 17 or 19 row covers until every plant has one to two flowers. The cover will create a warm humid environment that melon plants prefer. Upon removal, applying a dry straw mulch under plants and vines will trap soil humidity and keep melons from rotting on wet soil. When melon plants have set full-size fruit, discontinue watering for the final two weeks until harvest. Too much water in the ripening stage will make melons tasteless. Optimum soil pH range is 6.0 to 7.5.

Insects to observe: Striped and spotted cucumber beetles are migrating insects that can become quite numerous in the early season. Control by planting later in the season and keeping the plants covered with row cover. The larvae are predated on by spined soldier bugs and assassin beetles. Usually the density of cucumber beetles, both types, subsides by mid-summer.

Diseases to watch for: Powdery mildew can become a major problem when there has been a prolonged period of dry weather, followed by a cold snap. Control by irrigating regularly during droughts.

Days to harvest: Seventy to eighty-five days from transplants and continually until first fall frost.

Harvest advice: Harvest melons when color begins to change (for example cantaloupes nets turn from green to tan-orange), as it is distinctive when it happens. Also, most melon varieties (excluding honeydews) are ready when a sharp tug will remove melon from the vine, called "slipping." Check every day as melons do not conserve well in the field once ripe.

Post-harvest handling/terms of storage (best way to preserve flavor): Melons are highly perishable and can store seven to ten days at 33-40F (1-4.5C).

Health benefits: Pharmacological studies conducted on *Cucumis melo* indicate its immense potential in the treatment of conditions such as pain, inflammation, cardiovascular disorders, liver diseases, cancer, coughs, and dysuria.[41]

Field notes:

Mint (all types)
Mentha sp.

Characteristics/growing habits: Mint, members of the family *Lamiaceae*, are low, bushy, sprawling hardy perennials that readily create new seedlings from their rather extensive rhizome network. Common types include chocolate, Moroccan, peppermint, and spearmint, among others. All are distinctive with the pungent spicy mint flavor varying in degree, depending on species.

Favorite varieties: "Chocolate" (F1), "Moroccan" (OP), "Peppermint" (OP)

Seeding information: Best to purchase seedlings (preferably organic) from a local grower or nursery of the preferred variety, since mint readily cross-pollinates. However, if a true source is located, she can be started inside. Sow one seed (OP, heirloom) per cell in plug trays. Keep well-watered until germination. Can also be direct seeded if preferred.

Days to germination at soil temperature range: Ten to fourteen days at 55-70F (13-21C).

When to start inside: Eight weeks before last frost date.

Necessary to pot-up to three-inch pots: Yes, as soon as seedlings have first true leaves. Can transplant two-three seedlings per pot as desired.

When to transplant or direct seed outside: Transplant or direct seed after last frost date. Plant at 6 inches (15cm) apart. Thin seedlings to the same distance if direct seeding.

Maintenance required during growing period: Keep weeded of native flora throughout growing period as mint plants are slow to root in and create their low sprawling canopy. Very drought tolerant once established. Once entrenched, plants will spread seedlings through their rhizomes (roots). If mint plantation becomes too invaded by native flora (which readily happens), one can restart the mint plot by rooting in rhizomes of the plant in potting soil medium and recreating the patch. Optimum soil pH range is 5.5 to 7.5.

Insects to observe: None of major consequence attack the plants. Delicate white to pink flowers, that cluster together in a cone shape, are inviting to the smallest native bees.

Diseases to watch for: None of great significance have been regarded.

Days to harvest: Fifty to sixty days from transplants then continually until first fall hard frost. Perennial plantings will grow back and be ready to harvest by last frost date.

Harvest advice: Harvest sprigs (stems and leaves) with garden cutters when desired size is reached, leaving central crown untouched.

Post-harvest handling/terms of storage (best way to preserve flavor): Can be stored in plastic bags at 33-40F (1-4.5C) for up to twenty-one days. Best method of long-term preservation is to dry leaves and pack into glass jars once cooled, which will keep for one year.

Health benefits: Different parts of the wild mint plant including its leaves, flower, stem, and seeds have been used widely in traditional folk medicine as antimicrobial, carminative, stimulant, antispasmodic and for the treatment of various diseases such as headaches and digestive disorders. In pharmacological research, there is enough indication for different biological effects of *M. longifolia*, and the chemical compounds present in the essential oil of the plant.[42]

Field notes:

Okra
Abelmoschus esculentus

Characteristics/growing habits: Okra, a member of the family *Malvaceae*, is a warm season, fast-growing annual that grows on tall stalks up to five feet (1.5m) high. Showy, large yellow blossoms are highly attractive to bees and wasps. The okra fruit sets off those flowers in the nook between plant stem and leaves. Okra has perfect flowers; will set fruit by vibration from natural (wind, insects) or human (brushing by, or "tripping") causes.

Favorite varieties: "Clemson Spineless 80" (OP)

Seeding information: Seed (OP, heirloom) in plug trays one per cell.

Days to germination at temperature range: Four to seven days at 70-95F (21-35C).

When to start inside: Four to five weeks before warm and settled date.

Necessary to pot-up to three-inch pots: n/a

When to transplant or direct seed outside: Transplant at warm and settled date 12 inches (30cm) apart.

Maintenance required during growing period: Give consistent water throughout the growing season, however once flowering, okra plants are quite heat and drought tolerant. Weed out native flora while plants are small. When plants reach twelve inches (30cm) in height undersow with an annual clover (like crimson clover). Optimum soil pH range is 6.0 to 7.5.

Insects to observe: Mostly pollinating insects like bees, syrphid flies and wasps.

Diseases to watch for: None of great significance have been detected.

Days to harvest: Fifty-five to sixty-five days from transplant and continually throughout the harvest season.

Harvest advice: As soon as okra pods attain a three-inch (7.5cm) length cut with garden cutters with one inch (2.5cm) of stem. Harvest regularly, as doing so promotes more flower blooms and fruit set.

Post-harvest handling/terms of storage (best way to preserve flavor): Okra is highly perishable and will keep up to ten to fourteen days in plastic bags at 33-40F (1-4.5C). Best enjoyed fresh cooked. Can also be pickled with an apple cider vinegar-water-salt brine and store for up to one year.

Health benefits: Okra seed is rich in protein and unsaturated fatty acids such as linoleic acid. Okra contains high fiber, which "helps to stabilize blood sugar by regulating the rate at which sugar is absorbed from the intestinal tract". Promoting the consumption of traditional vegetables such as okra could provide cheap sources of macro and micronutrients and mineral elements that can improve the nutritional status of resource-poor subsistence farmers of the world.[43]

Field notes:

Onions (Bunching)
Allium fistulosum x cepa

Characteristics/growing habits: Bunching onions, or Welsh onions, members of the family *Amaryllidaceae*, otherwise known as green onions and scallions, are shorter season than full-size onions and have genetically adapted to resist bulbing. They are biennial, flowering in their second year. Some varieties are perennial. Seedlings develop long straight green shoots and underground shanks, which can be red or white.

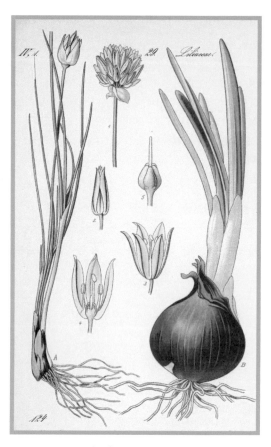

Favorite varieties: "Evergreen Hardy" (OP), "He Shi-Ko" (HL), "Parade" (OP), "Red Baron" (OP)

Seeding information: Seed (OP, heirloom) in 1020 flats, 250-300 per tray maximum inside. Because of their long time resting in the same soil, it is beneficial to side-dress the trays with organic soybean meal three-four weeks after emergence. It can be prudent to give bunching onions a "haircut" once they reach four inches (10cm) in their trays, once per week, to encourage further root development. Can also be direct seeded outside if desired.

Days to germination at temperature range: Six to ten days at 60-80F (15.5-26.5C).

When to start inside: Eight weeks before transplanting outside.

Necessary to pot-up to three-inch pots: n/a

When to transplant or direct seed outside: Transplant or direct seed outside one week after soil can be worked. If transplanting, upon removal from the tray, cut off roots to 2-3 inches (5-7.5cm) and give them a "haircut," cutting the greens which will spur root development. Transplant in bunches of two to three seedlings, 2 inches (5cm) apart, rows at 6 inches (15cm). Push onion seedlings gingerly up to the neck, with thumb and forefinger into soil ensuring that all roots are buried. Onions can tolerate a light freeze 31F (-1C) but prolonged frost exposure can hinder growth. It is advisable to cover with Agribon-type 17 or 19 row cover to minimize transplant shock associated with freezing temperatures and/or root disturbance.

Maintenance required during growing period: Keep well weeded of native flora. Bunching onions enjoy a monthly foliar spraying of liquid fermentation (like clover/comfrey/nettle/ yarrow). Keep well-watered throughout the growing season. Can tolerate heat and drought when fully formed. Optimum soil pH range is 5.8 to 7.5.

Insects to observe: Wireworm, the larvae of the click beetle, will pockmark onion wrappers but are not a huge problem. Leek moth, or onion leafminer, *Acrolepiopsis assectella* shows in late spring and deposits her eggs into the central growing stem of allium plants observed by holes in the leaves. Night marching cutworms can chew off the stem and leaves of newly transplanted seedlings. Control by checking the soil around the base of the plant early in the morning and removing them. Flea beetles can attack seedlings when small.

Diseases to watch for: Bunching onions are less disease prone than full-size onions, but if left late into the season they can be susceptible to fungal diseases like powdery mildew which can occur in times of warm, dry weather followed by a cold snap, but usually subsides on its own.

Days to harvest: Forty to fifty-five days from transplanting or sixty to seventy days from direct seeding and continually until all are harvested.

Harvest advice: When bunching onions reach harvestable size, thicker than a pencil, pull onions straight up and out. It is a good practice to cut off roots and yellowing greens directly in the garden with garden cutters.

Post-harvest handling/terms of storage (best way to preserve flavor): Green onions should be cleaned of all dirt and immersed in cold water after harvesting. Can be stored in bags or bins fourteen to twenty-one days at 33-40F (1-4.5C).

Health benefits: Welsh onion (bunching onion) has traditionally been used as an herbal medicine for many ailments such as headache, abdominal pain, diarrhea, and colds. Phytochemical study reported that organosulfur compounds and polyphenolic compounds were included in Welsh onion. Other studies have demonstrated the anti-fungal, anti-oxidative, anti-hypertensive, anti-platelet, and anti-obesity effects of Welsh onion.[44]

Field notes:

_____

_____

_____

_____

_____

Onions (bulbing)
Allium cepa

Characteristics/growing habits:
Bulbing onions, members of the family *Amaryllidaceae*, are long season biennials dependent on day length for bulb formation. Short, intermediate, and long day varieties come in white, yellow, and red in sizes ranging from flat, torpedo, round and globular. Good seed catalogs recommend onion varieties by latitudinal adaptation which can be very helpful in choosing the correct varietal for a specific region.

Favorite varieties: "Cabernet" (F-1-red), "Gladstone" (OP-white), "New York Early" (HL-yellow), "Red Long of Tropea" (HL-red)

Seeding information: Seed (OP, heirloom, F1 for long day reds) in 1020 flats, 250-300 per tray maximum inside. Because of their long time resting in the same soil, it is beneficial to side-dress the trays with organic soybean meal three-four weeks after emergence. It can also be advantageous to give onions a "haircut" once they reach four inches (10cm) in their trays, once per week, to encourage further root development.

Days to germination at temperature range: Six to ten days at 60-80F (15.5-26.5C).

When to start inside: Eight weeks before transplanting outside.

Necessary to pot-up to three-inch pots: n/a

When to transplant or direct seed outside: Transplant outside one week after soil can be worked. Upon removal from the tray cut off roots to 2-3 inches (5-7.5cm) and give them a "haircut," cutting the greens which will spur root development. Transplant at 3 inches (7.5cm) apart, rows at 10 inches (25cm). Push onion seedlings gingerly with thumb and forefinger into soil ensuring that all roots are buried, but not too deep on the bulb stem. Onions can tolerate a light freeze 31F (-1C) but prolonged frost exposure can hamper growth. It is advisable to cover with Agribon-type 17 or 19 row cover to minimize transplant shock associated with freezing temperatures and/or root disturbance.

Maintenance required during growing period: Keep well weeded of native flora. Bulbing onions appreciate a monthly foliar spraying of liquid fermentation (like clover/comfrey/ nettle/yarrow). Keep well-watered throughout the growing season. When growth spurt begins remove dirt from around the base of leaves as onions require light exposure to induce bulbing. Can tolerate heat and drought when fully formed. Optimum soil pH range is 5.8 to 7.5.

Insects to observe: Wireworm, the larvae of the click beetle, will pockmark onion wrappers but are not a huge problem. Leek moth, or onion leafminer, *Acrolepiopsis assectella* shows in late spring and deposits eggs into the central growing stem of *allium* plants observed by holes in the leaves. Night marching cutworms can chew off the stem and leaves of newly transplanted seedlings. Control by checking the soil around the base of the plant early in the morning and removing them. Flea beetles can also attack seedlings when they are small.

Diseases to watch for: Because of their long growing season and widely varied temperature growing conditions, onions can be susceptible to fungal diseases. Powdery mildew can occur in times of warm, dry weather followed by a cold snap but usually subsides on its own. Black rot caused by *Aspergillus niger* can permeate the outer leaves and invade the onion layers. All can be controlled by limiting irrigation when plants are reaching full-size.

Days to harvest: Seventy to one hundred days from transplanting and continually until all are harvested.

Harvest advice: Onion necks (base of leaves at bulb) when ready will be soft and flop over, but readiness can also be determined by pushing gently on the neck to see if it gives. At this point the onion has ceased growing and should be pulled immediately. Opposingly, they can be gathered when necks are still firm and bulbs have formed for fresh eating onions. Onions, leaves and all, need to cure in a dry and sunny location for long-term storage. When necks are cut at one-half-inch (1.25cm) up the stem and no more water is emitted when squeezed, onion is fully cured.

Post-harvest handling/terms of storage (best way to preserve flavor): Onions should be stored in cardboard boxes when fully cured at 33-40F (1-4.5C). Long storage varieties can store for nine months.

Health benefits: *Allium cepa* is highly valued for its therapeutic properties. It has been used as a food remedy from time immemorial. Research shows that onions may help guard against many chronic diseases. That's probably because onions contain generous amounts of the flavonoid quercetin. Studies have shown that quercetin protects against cataracts, cardiovascular disease, and cancer.[45]

Parsley
Petroselinum crispum

Characteristics/growing habits: Parsley, a member of the family *Umbelliferae,* is a hardy, bushy biennial plant. The most typical are curly, producing tight curled leaves and flat leaf (sometimes called Italian) with flat fingered leaves on strong stems.

Favorite varieties: "Italian Flat Leaf" (OP), "Moss Curled" (OP)

Seeding information: One to two seeds of (OP, heirloom) per cell in plug trays.

Days to germination at temperature range: Fourteen to twenty-one days at 55-70F (13-21C).

When to start inside: Eight weeks before last frost date.

Necessary to pot-up to three-inch pots: Yes, as soon as plants have two true leaves. Parsley plants will not hold in larger pots for very long before turning yellow, pot up no more than three weeks before transplanting

outside. Two to three plug seedlings can be transplanted into each pot if desired.

When to transplant or direct seed outside: Transplant after last frost date. Parsley can survive a light frost, but prolonged exposure will restrict early growth. Plant at 12 inches (30cm) apart.

Maintenance required during growing period: Keep weeded of native flora throughout growing period. Very drought tolerant once established. Optimum soil pH range is 5.5 to 7.5.

Insects to observe: None of major consequence attack the plants. If too warm and humid, aphids can infest the crowns of the plants.

Diseases to watch for: Celery mosaic virus is a plant pathogenic virus in the genus *Potyvirus* that appears to be carried by aphids when the weather turns warm and humid. Cutting out infected stems is a beneficial way of disrupting the problem and the plants do seem to grow out of it.

Days to harvest: Fifty-five to sixty days from transplants, then continually until first fall hard frost.

Harvest advice: Harvest full sprigs of parsley by cutting whole stems just above soil level when desired size is reached. Harvest in the morning while the weather is still cool.

Post-harvest handling/terms of storage (best way to preserve flavor): Parsley can hold in plastic bags or bins for fourteen to twenty-one days at 33-40F (1-4.5C). Immerse in cold water immediately after harvesting and allow to air-dry. Flavor is best enjoyed fresh but can also be fresh frozen (with sprigs or just leaves) for up to one year.

Health benefits: Parsley has been used as a carminative, gastro tonic, diuretic, antiseptic of urinary tract, anti-urolithiasis, anti-dote and anti-inflammatory and for the treatment of amenorrhea, dysmenorrhea, gastrointestinal disorder, hypertension, cardiac disease, urinary disease, otitis, sniffle, diabetes, and also various dermal diseases in traditional and folklore medicines.[46]

Field notes:

Parsnips
Pastinaca sativa

Characteristics/growing habits: Parsnips, members of the family *Apiaceae,* are a hardy biennial root crop that form long, tapered white to off-white to yellowish roots. They require a long growing season and form a beautiful canopy of twenty-four to thirty-six inch (60-90cm) tall greens.

Favorite varieties: "Lancer" (OP)

Seeding information: Direct seed (OP, heirloom) at ½-inch (1.25cm) deep, 2 inches (5cm) apart, rows at 12 inches (30cm).

Days to germination at temperature range: Fourteen to twenty-one days at 50-70F (10-21C).

When to start inside: n/a

Necessary to pot-up to three-inch pots: n/a

When to transplant or direct seed outside: Direct seed as soon as soil can be worked.

Maintenance required during growing period: Keep parsnip bed damp prior to emergence as they tend to be long to germinate. Ensure they are well weeded, as parsnips like space to grow, making sure roots are thinned to three inches (7.5cm) apart when first true leaves appear. Parsnips, when given too little space, will produce only very thin roots. For sweeter flavor allow to experience two fall freezes 31F (-1C) or below before harvesting.

Insects to observe: Many beetle and spider species make residence under the canopy of foliage. Wireworms, which are the larvae of click beetles, can cause mining (many tunnels and holes) in the parsnip. Limit wireworms in subsequent years by practicing a solid three-year rotation between *Apiaceae* family crops that wireworms prefer.

Diseases to watch for: None of significance do major damage. At the end of the season greens could exhibit signs of the fungal disease powdery mildew when there is an abrupt increase in humidity among the patch, and a cold snap, however this pathogen does not seem to limit root size development.

Days to harvest: 110-120 days.

Harvest advice: Harvest after the second good frost below 31F (-1C). With the help of a garden fork to loosen the soil, pop out the roots and pull off the greens in the field.

Post-harvest handling/terms of storage (best way to preserve flavor): Store dry with tops removed and dirty in plastic bags or bins at 33-40F (1-4.5C). Will store for six months and longer.

Health benefits: In Iranian traditional medicine (ITM), the parsnip is recognized as a stomach astringent, liver and uterine tonic and stimulates ovulation. It is named as a semen or sexual desire increaser and fertile agent. In the viewpoint of ITM, attention to the health of main or vital members of the body (including the heart, brain, and liver) in addition to the health of the urogenital system, may have led to the treatment of infertility.[47]

Field notes:

Peas
Pisum sativum

Characteristics/growing habits: Tall, climbing pea plants, members of the family *Fabaceae*, can reach up to five feet (1.5m) high and are over productive of green pods. Can be grown for English/shelling types (just shucked pea eaten), sugar snap peas (pod and plump peas eaten), and/or snow peas (pod and pea consumed in flat stage).

Favorite varieties: "Green Arrow" (OP-shelling), "Cascadia" (OP-sugar), "Oregon Sugar Pod II" (OP-snow)

Seeding information: Direct seed (OP, heirloom) 1-inch (1.25cm) deep, 2 inches (5cm) apart, double rows at 2 inches (5cm). Double rows should be 18 inches (45cm) from each other.

Days to germination at temperature range: Four to seven days at 50-75F (10-24C).

When to start inside: n/a

Necessary to pot-up to three-inch pots: n/a

When to transplant or direct seed outside: As soon as soil can be worked.

Maintenance required during growing period: Pea plants grow very fast, so normally only one good weeding of native flora is necessary, after which plants outcompete and crowd the space. Peas require a trellis at least four to five feet (1.2-1.5m) high made with wooden or metal stakes and twine or netting as the tendrils form readily and wish to grip hold somewhere. Optimum soil pH range is 5.5 to 7.5.

Insects to observe: Many native bees will buzz around the flowers. Spiders and ground beetles make homes under the humid canopy.

Diseases to watch for: Powdery mildew becomes a problem in mid-summer as the weather turns hot and dry followed by a cold snap. This fungus will render peas inedible, infecting the entire plant.

Days to harvest: Fifty to seventy days and then continually throughout the growing season.

Harvest advice: Once pods begin to form at full-size, harvest every two to three days to encourage more flower and pod production. Pick when plants are dew and moisture free to discourage potential mildew spread. For shelling peas wait until pods are completely plump, for sugar snap peas wait until peas form and pods are plump but still pliable. For snow peas wait until size is long and just beginning to see their peas increase in girth.

Post-harvest handling/terms of storage (best way to preserve flavor): Store dry in plastic bags or bins at 33-40F (1-4.5C). All will keep for ten to fourteen days. Snap and snow peas are best enjoyed fresh. English shelling pea types can be shucked and fresh frozen for up to one year storage.

Health benefits: Pisum sativum (Family: *Fabaceae*), as known as green pea or garden pea, has long been important in diet due to its content of fiber, protein, starch, trace elements, and many phytochemical substances. It has been shown to possess antibacterial, antidiabetic, antifungal, anti-inflammatory, anti-hypercholesterolemia, and antioxidant activities and also shown anticancer property.[48]

Field notes:

Peppers (hot, chili peppers)
Capsicum annuum, Capsicum chinense

Characteristics/growing habits: Hot Peppers, members of the family *Solanaceae*, are grown as a tender heat-loving annual but actually are perennial in places where it does not freeze. The hotter and drier the summer the hotter the chili peppers will become. Rated for heat intensity in Scofield heat units (SHU), hot peppers vary from a relatively mild 3,000 (poblano type) to 1,000,000+ (ghost chili-Bhut Jolokia). As an annual, they reach twelve to twenty-four inches (30-60cm) tall and grow and produce vastly different types and ways. All will start green or purple in the immature stage and finish either red, orange, or yellow. Peppers have perfect flowers; will set fruit by vibration from natural (wind, insects) or human (brushing by, or "tripping") causes.

Favorite varieties: "Ancho Poblano" (OP), "Bhut Jolokia" (HL), "Early Jalapeno" (OP), "Gordz Cherry Bomb" (HL), "Hungarian Hot Wax" (OP), "NuMex Joe E. Parker" (HL), "Ring-O-Fire Cayenne" (OP), "Shishito" (OP)

Seeding information: One seed (OP, heirloom) per cell in plug trays.

Days to germination at temperature range: Five to eight days at 70-90F (21-32C).

When to start inside: Seven weeks before last spring frost date, eight weeks for *chinense* types.

Necessary to pot-up to three-inch pots: Yes, as soon as plants have two true leaves. Peppers will not hold in larger pots for very long before turning yellow, pot up three weeks before transplanting outside.

When to transplant or direct seed outside: Transplant after last frost date. Hot peppers can tolerate nights down to 45F (7C) but prolonged exposure to these temperatures will stunt growth. Protect with Agribon-type 17 or 19 row covers if night temperatures forecast below 45F. Plant at 12 inches (30cm) apart.

Maintenance required during growing period: Keep weeded of native flora throughout growing period. Once the soil temperatures are consistently warm, above 60F (15.5C), mulch with dry straw if desired. Keep well-watered during the growing season, but limit water when hot pepper plants start to produce as drought conditions during fruit development will increase heat intensity. Optimum soil pH range is 6.0 to 7.5.

Insects to observe: Cutworms that live in the soil emerge at night and can chew off the stem of newly transplanted seedlings. Control by checking the soil around the base of the plant early in the morning and removing them.

Diseases to watch for: White mold is a fungus that can live in the soil up to eight years and infects over four hundred different varieties of plants. It will decimate the plants and rot the peppers. It is particularly prevalent during wet, semi warm conditions. Pulling the worst infected plants will limit plant to plant infection. However, I have observed that this condition is more prevalent in sweet, bell pepper types than chili peppers.

Days to harvest: Forty-five to sixty-five days from transplant for green, sixty to one hundred days for colored then continually until first fall frost.

Harvest advice: Pull peppers when the pepper is matte, not tacky. If coloration is desired, wait until more than 75% colored to ensure full ripeness. At this stage, it will continue to turn in storage. All peppers should be harvested (gleaned) before frost.

Post-harvest handling/terms of storage (best way to preserve flavor): Hot peppers can store for up to four weeks in plastic bags or bins at 33-40F (1-4.5C). They can be fresh pickled, canned whole or as hot sauce and store for up to one year.

Health benefits: A prospective cohort analysis in China provided the most convincing evidence to date of the clinical benefits of spices, particularly peppers. It showed an inverse relationship between chili pepper consumption and mortality from all causes of cancer, respiratory and cardiovascular disease. Chili peppers also protect against rheumatoid arthritis in all various colorations.[49]

Field notes:

Peppers (sweet)
Capsicum annuum

Characteristics/growing habits: Peppers, members of the family *Solanaceae*, are grown as a tender heat-loving annual but actually are perennial in places where it does not freeze. As an annual they reach about twenty-four to thirty inches (60-75cm) tall and come in a few different shapes including the classic four-lobed bell and the long-tapered type. Most peppers start as green (a few start purple) and when ripe can be yellow, orange, red, mauve, and many other color variants along the spectrum. Peppers have perfect flowers; will set fruit by vibration from natural (wind, insects) or human (brushing by, or "tripping") causes.

Favorite varieties: "Corno di Toro" (HL), "Jupiter" (OP), "Lipstick" (OP), "Sweet Chocolate" (OP)

Seeding information: One seed (OP, heirloom) per cell in plug trays.

CAPSICUM TETRAGONUM.—Mill.—DC.—Miq.

Days to germination at temperature range: Five to eight days at 70-90F (21-32C).

When to start inside: Seven weeks before last spring frost date.

Necessary to pot-up to three-inch pots: Yes, as soon as plants have two true leaves. Peppers will not hold in larger pots for very long before turning yellow, pot up three weeks before transplanting outside.

When to transplant or direct seed outside: Transplant after last frost date. Peppers can tolerate nights down to 45F (7C) but prolonged exposure to these temperatures will stunt growth. Protect with Agribon-type 17 or 19 row covers if night temperatures forecast below 45F. Plant at 12 inches (30cm) apart.

Maintenance required during growing period: Keep weeded of native flora throughout growing period. Once the soil temperatures are consistently warm above 60F (15.5C), mulch with dry straw. Pop off the first flower to encourage increased flower production in larger bell types. Keep well-watered during the growing season, but limit water when sweet peppers start to turn red as they are prone to cracking and rotting. Optimum soil pH range is 6.0 to 7.5.

Insects to observe: Cutworms that live in the soil, materializing at night, can chew off the stem of newly transplanted seedlings. Control by checking the soil around the base of the plant early in the morning and removing them.

Diseases to watch for: White mold is a fungus that can live in the soil up to eight years and infects over four hundred different varieties of plants. It will decimate the plants and rot the peppers. It is particularly prevalent during wet, semi warm conditions. Pulling the worst infected plants will limit plant to plant infection. Bacterial leaf spot, caused by *Xanthomonas campestris,* presents as brown lesions on the foliage and eventually the fruits. This pathogen is encouraged by humid conditions when an unexpected cold snap arrives. Control by limiting irrigation and pulling most infected leaves. Pepper fruits can be subject to blossom end rot, which is caused by a calcium deficiency, correct by side-dressing with wood ash or powdered dolomite lime. Blossom drop can occur when temperatures become consistently hot, over 85F (29.5C), for a long duration of the day.

Days to harvest: Fifty-five to sixty-five days from transplants for green, sixty-five to ninety-five days for colored then continually until first fall frost.

Harvest advice: Cut peppers with about one-half-inch (1.25cm) of stem with garden cutters when the pepper is matte, not tacky. If colored is desired, wait until more than 75% colored to ensure full sweetness. Peppers are notorious for becoming over ripe and soft if left on plants too long. All peppers should be harvested (gleaned) before frost.

Post-harvest handling/terms of storage (best way to preserve flavor): Green peppers can store for up to three weeks in plastic bags or bins at 33-40F (1-4.5C), colored peppers a little less. Peppers can be cut and frozen fresh and will keep for six months and longer.

Health benefits: Bell pepper have many health benefits, they protect us against free radicals, reduce risk of cardiovascular disease, promote optimal health, promote lung health, and protect us against rheumatoid arthritis in all various colorations.[50]

Field notes:

_____
_____
_____
_____
_____

Potatoes
Solanum tuberosum

Characteristics/growing habits: Potatoes, members of the family *Solanaceae*, are a semi-hardy perennial root crop, although grown as an annual. This staple comes in many different colors inside and out. Yellow and tan, pink and red, even blue on the outside hides flesh of reds, blues, yellows, and whites. Potato plants are low growing bushes but can reach thirty inches (75cm) tall in good growing conditions. Potatoes are classified as early (70-80 days), mid (75-85 days), or late (80-90 days) season.

Favorite varieties: "Caribe" (HL) (purple skin, white flesh), "Milva" (OP) (white skin, white flesh), "Norland" (OP) (red skin, white flesh), "Yukon Gold" (OP) (yellow skin, yellow flesh)

Seeding information: Direct seed (OP, heirloom) in furrows 6 inches (15cm) deep, 8-10 inches (20-25cm) apart. Seed potatoes can be planted whole if 3-inch x 3-inch (7.5cm x 7.5cm). They should be cut in half if larger, planting cut-side down.

Pl.234. *Morelle tubéreuse (Pomme de terre)*.
Solanum tuberosum L.

Days to germination at temperature range: Seven to fourteen days at 50-75F (10-24C).

When to start inside: n/a

Necessary to pot-up to three-inch pots: n/a

When to transplant or direct seed outside: Two weeks before last frost date.

Maintenance required during growing period: Keep potato patch well weeded as invasive native flora will limit tuber development. When potato seedlings emerge, "hill" the potatoes by bringing soil up in a mound up to the central crown. This may want to be done a second time during the season as the bulk of the potato tuber production resides just under the soil surface. Potatoes require regular watering throughout the season, not too wet and not too dry. Dry straw mulch will guard humidity after the soil has warmed greater than 60F (15.5C). Optimum soil pH range is 5.4 to 7.5.

Insects to observe: Colorado potato beetles will invade plants in early summer. They lay eggs and the larvae will defoliate the plant quickly. Control by pulling adult beetles and letting spined soldier bugs and assassin beetles proliferate. Wireworms can cause mining (many tunnels and holes) in the potato. Control by practicing a solid three-year rotation with other crops wireworms prefer.

Diseases to watch for: Due to potatoes' long underground season a variety of fungi can be present. White mold can live in the soil up to eight years and infects over four hundred different varieties of plants. It will decimate a plant and rot the potatoes. It is particularly prevalent during wet, semi warm conditions. Pulling the worst infected plants will limit plant to plant infection. Aerial stem rot usually occurs when there is some damage to the stem (mechanical or late-spring frost), causing wilting, yellowing leaves. Tuber soft rot displays as a mushy, watery, and rotten tuber, caused by too much water or not enough drainage. Scab is a condition that makes the skin of the potato tough but still edible.

Days to harvest: Seventy to ninety days until all are harvested.

Harvest advice: With the aid of a spade shovel loosen the soil and pull the plants straight up out of the ground. Harvest all potatoes (even the small ones) in slatted bins to allow dirt to escape. Best to pull when the soil has been drying for a few days.

Post-harvest handling/terms of storage (best way to preserve flavor): Store dry and dirty in cardboard boxes, separating out those with damage in a cool (50-60F, 10-15.5C) dark place to cure. Once cured (about three weeks) can be stored in the same boxes at 33-40F (1-4.5C) for up to nine months. Important to keep in the dark, as light will cause potato skins to turn green, which should not be consumed.

Health benefits: The potato has been a dietary staple for centuries and remains a popular and frequently consumed vegetable today. Potatoes contribute important nutrients to the diet including potassium, vitamin C and dietary fiber. Observational data indicate that potato consumption is associated with an increase in overall vegetable consumption and dietary nutrient density among children, teens, and adults in the United States. Research suggests that potato nutrients and components may have favorable impacts on blood pressure, satiety and 412 gut health.[51]

Field notes:

_____
_____
_____
_____
_____

Radishes
Raphanus sativus

Imp.Lemercier, r. de Seine 57 Paris.

Characteristics/growing habits: Radishes, members of the family *Brassicaceae*, are fast growing cold hardy annuals. They are well-known as globe shaped in colors that range from red, pink, purple and white; but can also be long and a mix of white and pink. Winter radish types like black and daikon are planted later in the season for long term storage. All radishes form round or tapered bulbs and have a nice head of mustard tasting greens.

Favorite varieties: "Cherry Belle" (OP), "D'Avignon" (HL), "Miyashige Daikon" (OP), "Pink Beauty" (OP), "Schwarzer Runder" (OP), "Watermelon" (OP)

Seeding information: Direct seed (OP, heirloom) ½-inch (1.25cm) deep, 2 inches (5cm) apart, rows at 6 inches (15cm) for globe types; 4 inches (10cm) apart, rows at 12 inches (30cm) for winter types.

Days to germination at temperature range: Three to six days at 55-85F (13-29.5C).

When to start inside: n/a

Necessary to pot-up to three-inch pots: n/a

When to transplant or direct seed outside: As soon as soil can be worked. Radishes can be succession planted every three weeks thereafter to ensure a constant harvest throughout the season. Winter radish should be well timed to be harvested before first fall frost.

Maintenance required during growing period: Keep well-weeded of native flora throughout the seedling stage. Once fully formed, it will create a canopy that deters native flora growth. Cover immediately after planting with insect screens. Optimum soil pH range is 6.0 to 7.5.

Insects to observe: Flea beetles are a common early spring problem creating small holes in young leaves. Best control is to install insect screens immediately after seeding. Keep greens well weeded of common plantain, the flea beetle's preferred host. Green peach aphids and gray turnip aphids *Hydaphis pseudobrassicae* can become abundant in times of warm nights and humid conditions, especially in winter types. Letting some of the earliest radish plantings go to flower will attract a whole host of native bees, syrphid flies and wasps.

Diseases to watch for: None of major consequence have been noticed.

Days to harvest: Twenty-one to thirty days from direct seeding, fifty to sixty days for winter types.

Harvest advice: Pull radishes by removing them by the root early in the morning as the leaves will wilt readily. Start by harvesting larger ones first and letting smaller ones size up. Keep all greens for eating, as they are highly nutritional. Before fall frost and when fully formed, extract all winter types.

Post-harvest handling/terms of storage (best way to preserve flavor): Globe types should be immersed in cold water and washed, can store up to three weeks in plastic bags or bins 33-40F (1-4.5C). Winter types should be stored dry and dirty in bags or bins at the same temperature and can store four to five months. Greens should be removed before storage and eaten like mustard greens if desired.

Health benefits: The roots and leaves of radishes consist of vital nutritional values and diverse secondary metabolites with antioxidant properties. When compared with roots, leaves possessed higher levels of proteins, calcium, and ascorbic acid whereas the total phenol contents were two-fold higher in leaves than roots which corresponded with the free radical scavenging ability.[52]

Field notes:

Rhubarb
Rheum rhabarbarum

Rheum rhabarbarum.

Characteristics/growing habits: Rhubarb, a member of the family *Polygonaceae*, is a tall, hardy perennial reaching four feet (120cm). Rhubarb has an open growing habit which sees thick fibrous stems growing from a central crown with large fan-like leaves. The edible stalks can be dark red, reddish-green and/or green, with the redder being sweeter, along with the classic tasty tart rhubarb flavor.

Favorite varieties: "Canada Red" (HL), "Victoria" (F1)

Seeding information: Best to purchase rhubarb crowns (preferably organic) from a local grower, nursery, or seed company as this method is easiest to establish.

Days to germination at temperature range: n/a

When to start inside: n/a

Necessary to pot-up to three-inch pots: n/a

When to transplant or direct seed outside: Transplant after last frost date. Plant at 24 inches (60cm) apart.

Maintenance required during growing period: Keep well-watered during the entire season. Rhubarb likes compost that is still very active (new compost or hot), applied prior to planting. When first flower stalks form, remove them from the central crown to encourage more leaf and root development. Will companion well with many different species of native flora. Optimum soil pH range is 6.0 to 7.0

Insects to observe: Many species of spiders and ground beetles make their homes under the humid canopies.

Diseases to watch for: In areas where the spring is very wet and rhubarb seedlings are re-emerging, crown rot can occur, stunting growth and impeding shoot development for the entirety of the year. Control by increasing drainage around rhubarb plants.

Days to harvest: Rhubarb will begin to emerge as soon as the soil warms. Harvest when desired stalk length and girth are realized.

Harvest advice: Harvest stalks at the base of the plant with garden cutters, removing the large fan-like leaves in the field. Take care to leave the central crown and cut no more than 50% of the stalks on each plant.

Post-harvest handling/terms of storage (best way to preserve flavor): Can be stored for two months in plastic bags or bins at 33-40F (1-4.5C). Best method of long-term preservation is to freeze freshly chopped stalks, as they will keep for one to two years to be made into breads, jams, pies, and preserves.

Health benefits: In the past decade, pharmacological research revealed rhubarb's potential to be applied to infectious disease for its numerous pharmacological activities such as anti-inflammatory, antimicrobial, antifungal, antivirus, and immuno-enhancing. Recent studies have further researched rhubarb as a treatment for sepsis in humans.[53]

Field notes:

Rutabaga
Brassica napus

Characteristics/growing habits: Rutabaga, a member of the family *Brassicaceae,* is a cold hardy biennial and close cousin to the turnip. Rutabagas are grown to full-size where roots can reach six inches (15cm) in diameter. Purple skins conceal yellowish-whitish interiors.

Favorite varieties: "Joan" (OP)

Seeding information: Recommended to seed (OP, heirloom) in plug trays, one seed per cell. Or can be direct seeded ½-inch (1.25cm) deep, 6 inches (15cm) apart, rows at 12 inches (30cm).

Days to germination at temperature range: Three to six days at 55-85F (13-29.5C).

When to start inside: Two to three weeks before transplanting as specified below.

Necessary to pot-up to three-inch pots: No.

When to transplant or direct seed outside: Rutabagas require two good freezes, below 31F (-1C) to reach sweetness potential, so timed planting is crucial. Plan to plant seventy-five days before fall frost. Transplant 6 inches (15cm) apart, rows at 12 inches (30cm). From direct seed, make sure to thin to 6 inches (15cm) when seedlings put on first leaves, planting around ninety days before fall frost.

Maintenance required during growing period: Keep well-weeded of native flora throughout the seedling stage. Once fully formed, it will create a canopy that deters native flora growth. Cover immediately after planting with insect screens. Optimum soil pH range is 6.0 to 7.5.

Insects to observe: Flea beetles (many different families and species) are a common early spring problem creating small holes in young leaves. Best control is to install insect screens immediately after seeding. Keep greens well-weeded of common plantain, the flea beetle's preferred host. Green peach aphids and gray turnip aphids *Hydaphis pseudobrassicae* can become abundant in times of warm nights and humid conditions, but seem to be less prevalent than on turnips.

Diseases to watch for: Brown heart of rutabaga is caused by a boron deficiency and will make the rutabaga hollow and in extreme cases rot the whole root. Work in one-quarter teaspoon of boron per bed foot before planting.

Days to harvest: Seventy-five to eighty-five days from transplant, ninety to one hundred days from direct seeding.

Harvest advice: Pull rutabagas by pulling from the root. Cut off large leaf systems and trim roots with garden cutters in the field after the second good frost.

Post-harvest handling/terms of storage (best way to preserve flavor): Rutabagas should be stored in bins or plastic bags dry and dirty at 33-40F (1-4.5C). Can store for nine months and longer.

Health benefits: Findings strongly suggest that one of the biological activities of rutabaga is antiproliferative and proapoptotic potential specific to tumor cells. The obtained results demonstrate the antioxidant property of rutabaga and its potential as a nutritional supplement in cancer prevention. These findings also strongly advocate the application of rutabaga sprouts in functional food.[54]

Field notes:

Sage (Common)
Salvia officinalis

Characteristics/growing habits: Sage, a member of the family *Lamiaceae*, is a low, bushy, sprawling hardy perennial (to zone four). Sage has a distinctive pungent aroma in fuzzy gray-green, long, wide-to-pointed leaves. Beautiful purple flowers on woody stems are prolific in mid-summer and are highly attractive to native bees.

Favorite varieties: Any OP or heirloom.

Seeding information: One to two seeds (OP, heirloom) per cell in plug flats. Need light to germinate. Can be direct seeded as soon as soil can be worked, keeping well moist until germination.

Days to germination at temperature range: Seven to fourteen days at 55-70F (13-21C).

When to start inside: Six weeks before last frost date.

Necessary to pot-up to three-inch pots: Yes, as soon as seedlings have two true leaves. Can transplant two to three seedlings into each pot if desired.

When to transplant or direct seed outside: Transplant or direct seed after last frost date. Plant at 10 inches (25cm) apart.

Maintenance required during growing period: Keep weeded of native flora throughout growing period as sage plants are slow to root in and create a low bush. Very drought tolerant once established. Once settled, they will spread in their bushy habit. Well suited to companion planting with other, taller, perennial herbs and flowers. Optimal soil pH range is 5.5 to 7.5.

Insects to observe: None of major consequence attack the plants. Prolific purple flowers are inviting to a whole host of native bees, flies, and wasps, especially bumblebees.

Diseases to watch for: Sage can be prone to damping off in the seedling stage, control by keeping seedlings a little warmer and a little drier.

Days to harvest: Sixty-five to seventy-five days from transplants, eighty to ninety days from direct seeding then continually until first fall hard frost. Perennial plants will begin to emerge after last spring frost.

Harvest advice: Harvest sprigs (stems and leaves) with garden cutters when desired size is reached at soil base, leaving central crown untouched.

Post-harvest handling/terms of storage (best way to preserve flavor): Can be stored in plastic bags at 33-40F (1-4.5C) for fourteen to twenty-one days. Best method of long-term preservation is to dry leaves and pack into glass jars once cooled, which will keep for one year.

Health benefits: For a long time, sage (*Salvia*) species have been used in traditional medicine for the relief of pain, protecting the body against oxidative stress, free radical damages, angiogenesis, inflammation, bacterial and virus infection. Several studies suggest that sage species can be considered for drug development because of their reported pharmacology and therapeutic activities in many countries of Asia and Middle East, especially China and India. These studies suggest that *Salvia* species, in addition to treating minor common illnesses, might potentially provide novel natural treatments for the relief or treatment of many serious and life-threatening diseases such as depression, dementia, obesity, diabetes, lupus, heart disease, and cancer.[55]

Field notes:

Savory (summer and winter)
Satureja hortensis, montana

Characteristics/growing habits: Savory, members of the family *Lamiaceae*, are low, bushy, open-habit, hardy plants. Winter savory is perennial (to zone four), while summer savory is an annual. Both have distinctive light to dark green needle-like leaves, with a flavor crossing thyme, marjoram, and oregano. Delicate pinkish-whitish flowers arrive in mid-summer and are attractive to the smallest native bees, flies, and wasps.

Favorite varieties: "Summer Savory" (HL), "Winter Savory" (HL)

Seeding information: One to two seeds per cell in plug flats. Can be direct seeded at last frost, keeping moist until germination.

Days to germination at temperature range: Seven to fourteen days at 55-70F (13-21C).

When to start inside: Six weeks before last frost date.

Winter Savory.
Elizt. Blackwell delin. sculp. et Pinx.
1. Flower
2. Flower separate
3. Calix
4. Seed.
Satureia durior.

Necessary to pot-up to three-inch pots: Yes, as soon as seedlings have two true leaves. Can transplant two to three seedlings into each pot if desired.

When to transplant or direct seed outside: Transplant after last frost date. Plant at 8 inches (20cm) apart. Direct seed at ½-inch (1.25cm) deep, thinning to 8 inches (20cm) apart upon emergence.

Maintenance required during growing period: Keep weeded of native flora throughout growing period as savory plants are slow to root in and create a low, open bush. Drought tolerant once established. Can be companion planted with taller annual or perennial herbs and flowers. Optimal soil pH range is 5.5 to 7.5.

Insects to observe: None of great significance attack the plants. Delicate pinkish-whitish flowers are inviting to the smallest native bees, flies, and wasps.

Diseases to watch for: None of major consequence have been observed.

Days to harvest: Thirty-five to forty-five days from transplants for summer savory, fifty to sixty days from direct seeding. Eighty days for winter savory, one hundred days from direct seeding. Perennial winter savory will emerge prevalently after last frost.

Harvest advice: Harvest sprigs (stems and leaves) with garden cutters when desired size is reached at soil base, leaving central crown untouched.

Post-harvest handling/terms of storage (best way to preserve flavor): Can be stored in plastic bags at 33-40F (1-4.5C) for up to one month. Best method of long-term preservation is to dry leaves and pack into glass jars once cooled, which will keep for one year.

Health benefits: Savory (*Satureja* L.) plant species have been used for centuries as culinary herbs and spices, as well as traditional remedies for the treatment or relief of various common health symptoms in many parts of the world. Recent studies suggest that the use of some *Satureja* species is effective in protecting the body against oxidative stress, free radical damage, inflammation, and microbial infections. A review of many studies suggests that savory species, in addition to treating minor ordinary ailments, can potentially provide a novel natural prevention or treatment for some chronic and serious illnesses such as diabetes, cardiovascular diseases, cancer, and Alzheimer's.[56]

Field notes:

Sorrel
Rumex acetosa

Characteristics/growing habits: Sorrel, a member of the family *Polygonaceae*, is a low growing perennial green among one of the first to regrow in the spring. Sorrel's somewhat serrated light green, lemony-flavored leaves are a welcome early addition to the spring salad.

Favorite varieties: "Garden Sorrel" (HL)

Seeding information: Direct seed one-half-inch (1.25cm) deep, 6 inches (15cm) apart.

Days to germination at temperature range: Seven to fourteen days at 50-80F (10-26.5C).

When to start inside: n/a

Necessary to pot-up to three-inch pots: n/a

When to transplant or direct seed outside: Direct seed in late summer/early fall giving enough time for seedlings' root systems to develop to survive the winter.

Maintenance required during growing period:
Keep weeded of native flora throughout growing period but since planted in the fall native flora pressures should be light. Keep well-watered until germination. Optimal soil pH range is 5.5 to 7.0.

Diseases to watch for: None of major consequence have been observed.

Insects to observe: None of significance attack the plants.

Days to harvest: Will begin to send up shoots as soon as soil warms in the spring and should be at harvestable size a week or two before last frost date.

Harvest advice: Harvest leaves by pulling older leaves first, but do not wait too long as the warm days of late spring/early summer can turn the leaves quite tough.

Post-harvest handling/terms of storage (best way to preserve flavor): Sorrel can be stored in plastic bags at 33-40F (1-4.5C) for up to three weeks. Best enjoyed for fresh eating.

Health benefits: Primarily roots but also other tissues of many species belonging to the genus *Rumex* have been reported to have various biological activities. They have been used in folk remedies from ancient times as anti-inflammatory, antioxidant, diuretic, antimicrobial, antihypersensitive, diuretic, analgesic, antiviral, and antifungal agents to treat various health disorders, such as diabetes, constipation, infections, diarrhea, oedema, jaundice, scurvy, and liver and gallbladder disorders. The antioxidant capacity of sorrel is reported to be approximately the same as in Japanese green tea. The flowers and rhizomes contain compounds that are suggested to have tumor arresting effects. Traditionally, water from boiled sorrel has been used to wash chicken pox sores, boils, shingles-afflicted skin, poison ivy rashes, blisters, acne, and other skin sores. It is supposed to ease pain, relieve itches, and speed up the healing process.[57]

Field notes:

Soybeans (Edamame)
Glycine max

Characteristics/growing habits: Soybean plants, members of the family *Fabaceae*, are tall twenty-four to thirty-inch (60-75cm) plants, with an upright, open growing habit. They are fuzzy-haired on stems, branches, and pods. Pods set in productive clusters.

Favorite varieties: "Black Jet" (HL), "Chiba Green" (OP)

Seeding information: Direct seed (OP, heirloom) 1-inch (2.5cm) deep, 2 inches (5cm) apart, rows at 12 inches (30cm).

Days to germination at temperature range: Four to seven days at 65-90F (18.5-32C).

When to start inside: n/a

Necessary to pot-up to three-inch pots: n/a

When to transplant or direct seed outside: Direct seed around one week after last frost, soybeans germinate poorly in cold soil conditions below 55F (13C).

Maintenance required during growing period: Weed native flora throughout the duration of the growing season. The soybean plants' tall, upright habit creates lots of light, space, and air circulation. Optimal soil pH range is 5.8 to 7.5.

Diseases to watch for: None have been revealed of consequence.

Insects to observe: Assassin beetles *Reduviidae spp.* and spined soldier bugs *Podisus maculiventris* will feed on Mexican bean beetle larvae, but in my twenty years of growing soybeans in both Arizona and Québec I have yet to see major insect damage from Mexican bean beetles or any other insect species to the soybean crop.

Days to harvest: Seventy-five to ninety-five days.

Harvest advice: Start picking when the soybean pods plump and just begin to lose some of their vibrant green color. Usually, soybeans are ready to picked all at once, as they are considered to have a determinate production habit.

Post-harvest handling/terms of storage (best way to preserve flavor): Store fresh up to fourteen days in plastic bags at 33-40F (1-4.5C). Can be blanched and frozen for up to twelve months.

Health benefits: The health benefits associated with consumption of edamame include increased bone density, reduction of cholesterol levels, prevention of cardiovascular disease, and reduction in mammary and prostate cancers.[58] *Author note*-There is contradictory medical research into the health benefits of soy, when researching the information, it is important to confirm the source and the potential funder of the related article.

Field notes:

Spinach
Spinacia oleracea

Characteristics/growing habits: Spinach, a member of the family *Amaranthaceae*, is a cool season biennial characterized by round, savoyed or slightly savoyed green leaves. Spinach grows from a central crown with deep root systems and many leaf shoots developing. Can be planted early in the spring and again in late summer for fall/winter and over-wintering harvest.

Favorite varieties: "Renegade" (F1), "Space" (F1), "New Zealand" (OP-*tetragonia tetragonioides)*

Seeding information: Direct seed (OP, heirloom, F-1 for ease of growing) ½-inch (1.25cm) deep, 2 inches (5cm) apart, rows at 10 inches (25cm).

Days to germination at temperature range: Four to eight days at 50-70F (10-21C).

When to start inside: n/a

Necessary to pot-up to three-inch pots: n/a

When to transplant or direct seed outside: As soon as soil can be worked and successively planted in spring as well as in late summer/early fall.

Maintenance required during growing period: Keep well-weeded of native flora throughout the seedling stage. Once fully formed, it will create a canopy that will crowd out native flora growth. Cover immediately after planting with insect screens to guard humidity. Optimal soil pH range is 6.5 to 7.5.

Insects to observe: Flea beetles are a common early spring problem creating small holes in young leaves. Best control is to install insect screens immediately after seeding. Keep greens well weeded of common plantain, the flea beetle's preferred host. Green peach aphids can become abundant in times of warm nights and humid conditions.

Diseases to watch for: Damping off can be a problem in baby seedlings. Control by watering generously upon emergence and then backing off as spinach (with her deep root system complex) can handle drought conditions.

Days to harvest: Forty to fifty days for baby, fifty to sixty days for full-size leaves from direct seeding.

Harvest advice: Pull leaves off by hand, leaving the central crown untouched for regrowth.

Post-harvest handling/terms of storage (best way to preserve flavor): Spinach is perishable, will store up to fourteen days in plastic bags at 33-40F (1-4.5C). After harvest, immerse greens in cold water and salad-spin greens before storage. Can be blanched and frozen to be stored for six months.

Health benefits: Spinach is rich with iron; its use can prevent some diseases like osteoporosis, anemia resulting from iron deficiency. In addition to its food value, spinach has numerous therapeutic uses. Use of spinach for gastrointestinal disorder, blood-generating therapy, growth stimulation in children, appetite stimulation, convalescent support, and fatigue. It has been also suggested to be used as an anticancer agent, antioxidant, and cancer preventative. Spinach may also reduce age-related eyesight worsening from macular deterioration and cataract.[59]

Field notes:

Strawberry
Fragaria x ananassa

Characteristics/growing habits: Garden strawberry, a member of the family *Rosaceae*, is a low growing, vining, sprawling, hardy perennial. They readily create new seedlings from their rather extensive runners, which root in, creating new seedlings. Fruits are classic dark red, round to tapered, delectable early summer jewels.

Favorite varieties: "Albion" (F1), "Jewel" (F1), "Kent" (F1)

Seeding information: Best to purchase bare root plants (preferably organic) from a local grower, nursery, or seed company as this method is easiest to establish.

Days to germination at temperature range: n/a

When to start inside: n/a

Necessary to pot-up to three-inch pots: Not applicable, however, in subsequent years, the strawberry patch can be restarted by rooting in potting soil medium the small runner seedlings that grow back in the spring and replanting them.

When to transplant or direct seed outside: Transplant after last frost date. Plant at 12 inches (30cm) apart.

Maintenance required during growing period: Keep weeded of native flora throughout growing period as strawberry plants are slow to root in and create their low sprawling canopy. Keep well- watered during the entire season. When flowers form on first year seedlings, pop them off, not allowing any fruits to form as this will encourage further root development. Before late fall dormancy cut off all runners leaving the bushy main plant, as this is where the following spring's flower and fruit set will be concentrated. Dry straw mulch to protect over winter. Make sure spring emergent growth is well watered. After fruit set and strawberries begin to blush, discontinue irrigation as drier times yield sweeter berries. Strawberries will produce well for their first two to three full-fruiting years. Optimal soil pH range is 5.8 to 7.5.

Insects to observe: Rose chafers *Macrodactylus subspinosus* are a mostly tan scarab beetle who feed on the flowers and fruits. Control by picking off when they become too abundant. They usually disperse by mid-summer. Ants will also seek out ripe fruits. American robins and cedar waxwings like to patrol the patch especially where there are wild strawberries in proximity. Control by harvesting before they do.

Diseases to watch for: The most discouraging of all are deformed strawberries which are not caused by disease but other factors. A late frost can damage part of the flowers. A lack of calcium and boron can cause misshapen fruit. Lack of pollinating insects in the early season can lead to poor fruit set and deformities.

Days to harvest: Early strawberries will ripen in late spring to early summer; midseason varieties, early to mid-summer and late season varieties, mid to late summer.

Harvest advice: Harvest berries when they are fully colored and as red as possible. Pull by pinching the stem off the plant. Harvest strawberries every day as they will not hold well in the field once ripe. Can also be pulled a little unripe, as long as the entire berry is colored, they will ripen at room temperature. Only harvest when plants and berries are dry to increase shelf life.

Post-harvest handling/terms of storage (best way to preserve flavor): Should be stored at room temperature to preserve sweetness. Strawberries are highly perishable and will last at most seven days. Best method of long-term preservation is to freeze whole berries fresh; they will keep for one year, after which they can be made into cakes, cobblers, preserves, and smoothies.

Health benefits: Strawberries have been reported to be potent antioxidants and reduce cardiovascular risk factors, such as elevated blood pressure, hyperglycemia, dyslipidemia, and inflammation in limited studies. Benefits of strawberries have also been supported by observational data from the Iowa Women's Health Study and Women's Health Study, in which strawberry intake was inversely associated with cardiovascular mortality, and C-reactive protein, a biomarker of inflammation, respectively.[60]

Field notes:

_____
_____
_____
_____
_____

Summer Squash (Zucchini)
Cucurbita pepo

Characteristics/growing habits: Summer Squash (zucchini), members of the family *Cucurbitaceae,* are tender annuals that prefer a warm to hot season. Plants can become very large and bushy, reaching three feet (90cm) high and in diameter. A wide array of shapes and colors exist from dark to light green, green-white striped and yellow. They can be long, crook-necked, round, or flying saucer shaped. Summer squashes and zucchinis require pollinators to set fruit.

Favorite varieties: "Cocozelle" (OP), "Costata Romanesco" (HL), "Dark Green" (OP), "Lebanese White Bush" (HL), "Ronde de Nice" (HL)

Seeding information: One seed (OP, heirloom) per three to four-inch (7.5-10cm) pot. Can also be direct seeded if preferred.

Days to germination at temperature range: Three to six days at 65-90F (18.5-32C).

When to start inside: Two weeks before last frost date.

Necessary to pot-up to three-inch pots: Not necessary to pot up, sow seed directly into a three to four-inch pot.

When to transplant or direct seed outside: Transplant or direct seed at last frost date. Summer squash can tolerate nights at 45F (7C). Transplant or direct seed at 18 inches (45cm) apart.

Maintenance required during growing period: Keep well weeded of native flora. Cover with Agribon-type 17 or 19 row covers until every plant has a flower or two. Upon removal, applying a dry straw mulch under plants will trap soil humidity and keep squashes from rotting on wet soil. They prefer drip irrigation to sprinkler type or overhead watering. Optimal soil pH range is 6.0 to 7.5.

Insects to observe: Striped and spotted cucumber beetles are migrating insects that can become quite numerous in the early season. The larvae are predated on by spined soldier bugs and assassin beetles. Usually the density of cucumber beetles, both types, subsides by mid-summer. Squash bug (*Anasa tristis*) is a greyish-brownish sap-sucking insect that are prolific breeders, laying dozens of eggs. The larger larvae and adults have toxic saliva, like the cucumber beetles, and once bitten, the leaves will wilt. Plants will cease growing and eventually die. Control all by planting later in the season, keeping the plants covered with row cover and picking off the adults if observed when possible.

Diseases to watch for: Powdery mildew can become a major problem when there has been a prolonged period of dry weather, followed by a cold snap. Control by irrigating regularly during droughts.

Days to harvest: Thirty-five to forty-five days from transplants, fifty to sixty days from direct seeding and then continually until first fall frost.

Harvest advice: Harvest summer squash often to encourage more production, even every day is not too much, as they can become quite large, quite fast. Can be harvested immature when length reaches six inches for a gourmet, hard to find treat. Harvest early in the day to keep fruits cool.

Post-harvest handling/terms of storage (best way to preserve flavor): Summer squash is quite perishable and will store ten to fourteen days in plastic bags or bins at 33-40F (1-4.5C) Store dry and wipe clean. Can be grated and frozen for up to six months. Can also be sliced and dried and, when cool, packed into glass jars, which will keep for one year and longer.

Health benefits: Summer squash (*Cucurbita pepo* subsp. *pepo*) is a seasonal vegetable that contains a number of beneficial micronutrients such as minerals, carotenoids, vitamin C and phenolic compounds. It has been used in traditional folk medicine to treat colds and alleviate aches, due to its antioxidant/anti-radical, anti-carcinogenic, anti-inflammatory, antiviral, antimicrobial, and analgesic activities.[61]

Field notes:

_____
_____
_____
_____
_____
_____
_____
_____
_____

Sweet Potatoes
Ipomoea batatas

Characteristics/growing habits: Sweet potatoes, members of the family *Convolvulaceae*, are a tender annual root crop, but are perennial where the nights do not freeze. The profuse vining plants will become a dense mat of foliage, while the tubers underneath develop. Sweet potatoes can have skins in shades of red, orange, white, or blue and with flesh in white, cream, orange, yellow, red, or purple.

Favorite varieties: "Beauregard" (OP), "Covington" (OP), "Georgia Jet" (OP), "Jewel" (OP), "Molokai" (HL)

Seeding information: Plant from slips, which are the vine cuttings that can be ordered from some seed companies. Or sprout your own by buying organic sweet potatoes and letting the plant grow to a few inches. Pinch off the slip and place in water until roots develop.

Days to germination at temperature range: n/a

When to start inside: Root slips in soil medium, in three to four-inch pots, three weeks before transplanting outside, keeping them above 65F (18.5C)

Necessary to pot-up to three-inch pots: Yes, plant directly into three to four-inch pots once slips have roots.

When to transplant or direct seed outside: Transplant at warm & settled date at 12 inches (30cm) apart.

Maintenance required during growing period: Keep sweet potato patch well weeded as invasive native flora will limit tuber development. Sweet potatoes require regular watering throughout the season, ensuring to not let the patch go over-dry. After planting, cover with Agribon-type 17 or 19 row covers until the vines are running profusely, as the plants prefer warm and humid environments. Optimum soil pH range is 6.0 to 7.0.

Insects to observe: Green peach aphids and melon aphids *Aphis gossypii* can become abundant in times of warm nights and humid conditions under row covers. Remove during warm days and evenings to let in ants, green lacewings, lady beetles and spiders to control populations.

Diseases to watch for: Fusarium root rot, caused by the fungus *Fusarium solani*, creates circular brown lesions on sweet potatoes. It can become problematic in late-stage development of the potatoes, when the weather turns cold and damp. It will also present itself in storage if the sweet potatoes are too cold.

Days to harvest: 90-105 days until all are harvested.

Harvest advice: With the aid of a spade shovel, loosen the soil in a widecircle around the plant. Sweet potatoes are very fragile and being bruised or damaged will greatly limit storage life. Excavate potatoes carefully with the aid of a trowel. Harvest all before first fall frost. Leaves can also be eaten, cooked like spinach.

Post-harvest handling/terms of storage (best way to preserve flavor): Let cure dry and dirty in cardboard boxes at 70-85F (21-29.5C) for four to seven days, separating out those with damage. Once cured, store in covered cardboard boxes at no less than 60F (15.5C). Will store two to three months if cured properly. Greens can be eaten fresh or blanched and frozen to keep for six months and more.

Health benefits: Sweet potato's tubers have anti-diabetic, antioxidant and antiproliferative properties due to the presence of valuable nutritional and mineral components. Furthermore, *Ipomoea batatas* tubers, which are a steady item in the Americans' diet, appear to be very beneficial in the diet of diabetics and consumers with an insulin resistance, because they have a low glycemic index.[62]

Field notes:

Swiss Chard
Beta vulgaris

Characteristics/growing habits: Swiss chard, a member of the family *Amaranthaceae*, is a tender biennial that grows on upright thick stemmed plants. The succulent, lustrous leaves are savoyed and come in a rainbow of colors. From white to yellow, orange to pink and brilliant rubies throughout the foliage, stems, and veins.

Favorite varieties: "Fordhook Giant" (HL), "Oriole" (OP), "Ruby/Rhubarb Red" (HL)

Seeding information: Seed (OP, heirloom) in plug trays one per cell being aware that Swiss chard is prone to damping off in the small seedling stage. Water cells only when dry after emergence.

Days to germination at temperature range: Four to seven days at 65-85F (18.5-29.5C).

When to start inside: Four to five weeks before transplanting outside.

Necessary to pot-up to three-inch pots: No.

When to transplant or direct seed outside: Transplant after last frost or anytime during the growing season at 12 inches (30cm) apart. Can also be direct seeded 1-inch (2.5cm) deep, 2 inches (5cm) apart, rows at 6 inches (15cm) for baby greens.

Maintenance required during growing period: Swiss chard favors boron to make full and healthy leaves, work one-quarter teaspoon per bed foot into the soil before planting. Keep well-weeded of all native flora throughout the growing period. When harvesting, pull off any yellow leaves and use as mulch around the plants. Very drought tolerant once established. Optimum soil pH range is 5.8 to 7.5.

Insects to observe: Many spider species make residence under the canopy of foliage. Green aphids can arrive but rarely cause major damage.

Diseases to watch for: Swiss chard is prone to root rot and damping off during initial leaf growth. Cercospora leaf spot caused by the fungus *Cercospora hydrangea* occurs during wet and humid conditions blackening the leaves and outright wilting them. Control both by limiting irrigation and letting it go completely dry before watering. Powdery mildew can affect older plants when conditions have been too dry followed by a cold snap.

Days to harvest: Twenty-five to thirty days from direct seeding for baby greens, thirty-five to forty-five days for full-size leaves from transplant, and then continually throughout the season.

Harvest advice: Cut early in the morning with garden cutters far down on the plant at the base. Harvest the oldest outside leaves first. Harvest all eatables before frost.

Post-harvest handling/terms of storage (best way to preserve flavor): Swiss chard can be stored for fourteen days in plastic bags at 33-40F (1-4.5C). Baby chard up to ten days in plastic bags at the same temperature. Immerse in cold water immediately after harvest. Let large leaves air dry, baby leaves salad-spin dry. Swiss chard can also be blanched and frozen for up to one year storage.

Health benefits: Swiss chard, as one of the GLVs (Green Leafy Vegetables), is rich in phytopigments such as chlorophyll and carotenoids. Phytopigments improve immune, detoxification and antioxidant systems of the human body, thus indirectly helping the prevention of disease.[63]

Field notes:

Thyme
Thymus vulgaris, serpyllum

Characteristics/growing habits: Thyme, a member of the family *Lamiaceae,* is a low, bushy, sprawling, hardy perennial (to zone four). She has a distinctive pungent aroma and spicy flavor harbored in small, needle-like leaves. Varieties can be planted for small bushes or as a ground cover which emits a delightful aroma when gently walked upon. Beautiful and delicate purple flowers are prolific in mid-summer and are highly attractive to native bees and syrphid flies.

Favorite varieties: "German Winter" (OP)

Seeding information: Sprinkle tiny seeds (OP, heirloom) on soil surface of 1020 flats. They will need light to germinate.

Days to germination at temperature range: Seven to fourteen days at 55-70F (13-21C).

When to start inside: Eight weeks before last frost date.

Necessary to pot-up to three-inch pots: Yes, as soon as seedlings have two true leaves. Can transplant two to three seedlings into each pot if desired.

When to transplant or direct seed outside: Transplant after last frost date. Plant at 8 inches (20cm) apart. Can be also direct seeded as soon as soil can be worked. Keep moist until germination.

Maintenance required during growing period: Keep weeded of native flora throughout growing period as thyme plants are slow to root in and create their low sprawling canopy. Very drought tolerant once established. Once installed, they will spread in their bushy habit and outcompete native flora. Can be companion planted with taller annual and perennial flowers and herbs. Optimal soil pH range is 5.8 to 7.5.

Insects to observe: None of great significance attack the plants. Prolific purple flowers are inviting to a whole host of native bees, flies and wasps, especially smaller size bumblebees.

Diseases to watch for: In the seedling stage thyme can be prone to damping off. Pay strict attention to soil moisture, not too wet and not too dry.

Days to harvest: Seventy-five to eighty days from transplants, ninety to ninety-five days from direct seeding then continually until first fall hard frost.

Harvest advice: Harvest sprigs (stems and leaves) at soil base with garden cutters when the desired size is reached, leaving central crown untouched.

Post-harvest handling/terms of storage (best way to preserve flavor): Can be stored in plastic bags at 33-40F (1-4.5C) for up to one month. Best method of long-term preservation is to dry leaves and pack into glass jars once cooled, which will keep for one year.

Health benefits: *Thymus* species are considered as medicinal plants due to their pharmacological and biological properties. Its properties are due to its main components, thymol and carvacrol. Fresh thyme has the highest level of antioxidants among all herbs. *Thymus vulgaris L.* is widely used in folk medicine in the treatments of a variety of diseases such as gastroenteric and bronchopulmonary disorders. The essential oil of thyme and the compound thymol have antimicrobial activity in vitro against E. coli strains. The essential oil of thyme has been found to possess the strongest antimicrobial properties.[64]

Field notes:

Tomatillo
Physalis philadelphica

Characteristics/growing habits: Tomatillos (husk tomato), members of the family *Solanaceae*, are tall, bushy and vining, warm season annual (can be self-seeding) plants that yield a bounty. They have perfect flowers, which means they do not require pollinators to set. Husked fruits will turn from light green to dark green or purple becoming yellow-green, purple tinged and/or completely purple when fully ripe. An optimal mix of tartness and sweetness is attained at this stage. Classic for making salsa verde.

Favorite varieties: "Purple" (OP), "Toma Verde" (OP)

Seeding information: One seed (OP, heirloom) per cell in plug trays.

Days to germination at temperature range: Four to seven days at 65-90F (18.5-32C).

When to start inside: Four to five weeks before last spring frost date.

Necessary to pot-up to three-inch pots: Yes, as soon as plants have two true leaves. Tomatillos will not hold in larger pots for very long before turning yellow, pot up no more than three weeks before transplanting outside.

When to transplant or direct seed outside: Transplant after last frost date. Tomatillos can tolerate nights down to 35F (1.5C). Protect with Agribon-type 17 or 19 row covers if night temperatures are forecasted below 35F. Plant at 12 inches (30cm) apart.

Maintenance required during growing period: Keep weeded of native flora throughout growing period. My preferred staking method is six-foot wooden stakes (one-inch x two-inch) pounded in the ground. Tie with strips of old cotton clothes that have become rags. Once the soil temperatures are consistently warm above 60F (15.5C), dry straw mulch if desired. Very drought tolerant once established. Tomatillos make many volunteers, fruits that drop over winter, sprouting the following spring. Usually, they can be left to grow to full plants. Optimal soil pH range is 5.5 to 7.5.

Insects to observe: Cutworms live in the soil, emerge at night, and can chew off the stem of newly transplanted seedlings. Control by checking the soil around the base of the plant early in the morning and removing them. Striped and spotted cucumber beetles are migrating insects that can become quite numerous in the early season. Control by planting later in the season and keeping the plants covered with row cover. The larvae are predated on by spined soldier bugs and assassin beetles. Usually the density of cucumber beetles, both types, subsides by mid-summer.

Diseases to watch for: White mold is a fungus that can live in the soil up to eight years and infects over four hundred different varieties of plants. It will decimate a plant and rot the tomatillos. It is particularly prevalent during wet, semi warm conditions. Pulling the worst infected plants will limit plant to plant infection.

Days to harvest: Sixty days from transplants, then continually until first fall frost

Harvest advice: Harvest vine-ripened tomatillos when they pull easily from the vines and their wrappers have pulled away from the fruits. Also, harvest those that have fallen to the ground. Harvest when plants are dry to maximize storage life of fruits.

Post-harvest handling/terms of storage (best way to preserve flavor): Tomatillos should be stored at room temperature for best flavor. They can hold for fourteen to twenty-one days. Preferred method of storage is to make into salsa verde, fresh or canned.

Health benefits: Results showed these *physalis* crops (of which Tomatillo is one) contain many essential minerals and vitamins, notably potassium and immune system supporting vitamin C, also known for its antioxidant activity. Beyond nutritional properties, these crops also contain a class of steroidal lactones called withanolides, which have been recognized for their antitumor, and anti-inflammatory properties. In some studies, withanolide extract from Physalis species have exhibited cytotoxicity towards cancer cells.[35]

Field notes:

Tomatoes (Cherry types)
Solanum lycopersicum

Characteristics/growing habits: Cherry tomatoes, members of the family *Solanaceae*, are warm season perennials, grown as an annual crop. They include cherry, saladettes, and plum types that come in a dazzling array of shapes and colors. Pear, plum, round, oval and oblong shapes can be black, bluish, brown, green, orange, pink, red, yellow, and striped in many combinations from the colors listed. Plants are either determinate (classified as short, reaching three feet (one meter) with production during a determined period), semi-determinate (classified as mid-size reaching five feet (1.5m), producing many fruits over the whole frost-free season) or indeterminate (classified as tall and vining reaching eight feet (2.4m) and producing abundantly over the whole frost-free season). Cherry tomatoes have perfect flowers; will set fruit by vibration from natural (wind, insects) or human (brushing by, or "tripping") causes.

Favorite varieties: "Black Cherry" (OP), "Gold Nugget" (OP), "Green Frosted Doctor's" (HL), "Jaune Flamme" (HL), "Peacevine" (OP), "Pink Bumblebee" (OP), "Sundrop" (OP), "Yellow Pear" (HL)

Seeding information: One seed (OP, heirloom) per cell in plug trays.

Days to germination at soil temperature range: Four to seven days at 65-90F (18.5-32C).

When to start inside: No more than four to five weeks before last spring frost date.

Necessary to pot-up to three-inch pots: Yes, as soon as plants have two true leaves after a minimium of fourteen days. Tomatoes will not hold in larger pots for very long before turning yellow, pot up no more than three weeks before transplanting outside.

When to transplant or direct seed outside: Transplant after last frost date. Tomatoes can tolerate nights down to 35F (1.5C). Protect with Agribon-type 17 or 19 row covers if night temperatures are forecasted below 35F. Plant at

12 inches (30cm) apart. Cherry tomatoes grow and produce much better in a small tunnel or greenhouse environment to control environmental factors.

Maintenance required during growing period: Keep weeded of native flora throughout growing period. My preference for staking is eight-foot wooden stakes (one-inch x two-inch) pounded in the ground for indeterminate varieties, six-foot for semi-determinate and four-foot stakes for determinate varieties. We tie-up stems with strips of old cotton clothes that have become rags. Once the soil temperatures are consistently warm, above 60F (15.5C), dry straw mulch if desired. Keep well-watered during the growing season. They prefer a drip-type irrigation method. Optimal soil pH range is 5.8 to 7.5.

Insects to observe: Cutworms that live in the soil, emerging at night, can chew off the stem of newly transplanted seedlings. Control by checking the soil around the base of the plant early in the morning and removing them. Tomato/ tobacco hornworm *Manduca quinquemaculata* (Five-spotted hawk moth) can defoliate a large tomato plant in a matter of days. Control by checking daily. They are best found by locating piles of fresh caterpillar poop on the tops of leaves, usually the camouflaged worms are right above, underneath a leaf.

Diseases to watch for: White mold is a fungus that can live in the soil up to eight years and infects over four hundred different varieties of plants. It will decimate a plant and rot the tomatoes. It is particularly prevalent during wet, semi warm conditions. Pulling the worst infected plants will limit plant to plant infection. Tomato fruits can be subject to blossom end rot (less of a problem in cherry types) which is caused by a calcium deficiency; correct by side-dressing with wood ash or powdered dolomitic lime. Septoria leaf spot, Verticillium wilt, early and late blights among other fungal and bacterial pathogenic diseases can be prevalent, but my experience has revealed that keeping plants dry (control by limiting irrigation) will correct these problems 99% of the time. Pull the worst infected plants if they are too diseased.

Days to harvest: Fifty to seventy days from transplants, then continually until first fall frost

Harvest advice: Harvest vine-ripened cherry tomatoes to ensure optimum sweetness every day or every other day, as they will go over ripe fast depending on climatic conditions. Harvest when plants are dry to limit spread of bacterial/fungal diseases.

Post-harvest handling/terms of storage (best way to preserve flavor): Tomatoes should be stored at room temperature for best flavor. Enjoy within one week. Never store tomatoes below 55F (13C) as they will become mealy. Can be fresh frozen whole. But my favored method of preservation is to cut each one in half and dry them. The true flavor is captured. Once cool, they can be packed into glass jars and kept for one year and more.

Health benefits: Studies have shown strong inverse correlations between tomato consumption and the risk of certain types of cancer, cardiovascular diseases, and age-related macular degeneration. Because tomato is the second-most important vegetable in the world after potato, this horticultural crop constitutes an excellent source of health-promoting compounds due to the balanced mixture of minerals and antioxidants.[65]

Field notes:

Tomatoes (Slicer and paste types)
Solanum lycopersicum

Characteristics/growing habits: Slicer and Italian-type tomatoes, members of the family *Solanaceae,* are warm season perennials, grown as an annual crop. They range in many weights from four to twenty-four ounces (100-700g). Slicing types are usually slightly flattened round globes that can be smooth or pleated. Colors range from black, brown, green, orange, pink, purple, red, yellow, and sometimes mottled. Paste types are usually oblong, from four to twelve ounces (100-350g), ranging in color from pink to purple to red. Plants are either determinate (classified as short at three feet (one meter) with production during a determined period), semi-determinate (reaching five feet (1.5m) tall) and indeterminate (classified as tall and vining, eclipsing eight feet (2.4m) producing many tomatoes over the whole frost-free season. Tomatoes have perfect flowers; will set fruit by vibration from natural (wind, insects) or human (brushing by, or "tripping") causes.

Favorite varieties: "Red Brandywine" (HL), "Cherokee Purple" (HL), "Crimson Sprinter" (OP), "German Johnson" (HL), "Gold Medal" (HL), "Green Zebra" (OP), "Mortgage Lifter" (HL), "Mountain Princess" (HL), "Valencia" (HL), "Yellow Brandywine" (HL). Paste or Italian Types: "Amish Paste" (HL), "Roma VF" (OP), "San Marzano" (HL)

Seeding information: One seed (OP, heirloom) per cell in plug trays.

Days to germination at soil temperature range: Four to seven days at 65-90F (18.5-32C).

When to start inside: No more than four to five weeks before last spring frost date.

Necessary to pot-up to three-inch pots: Yes, as soon as plants have two true leaves after fourteen days. Tomatoes will not hold in larger pots for very long before turning yellow, pot up no more than three weeks before transplanting outside.

When to transplant or direct seed outside: Transplant after last frost date. Tomatoes can tolerate nights down to 35F (1.5C). Protect with Agribon-type 17 or 19 row covers if night temperatures are forecasted below 35F. Plant at 18 inches (45cm) apart. Tomatoes do much better in a small tunnel or greenhouse environment to control environmental factors.

Maintenance required during growing period: Keep weeded of native flora throughout growing period. My preferred method of staking is six to eight-foot (2.4m) wooden stakes (one-inch by two-inch) (2.5x5cm) pounded in the ground for indeterminate and semi-determinate varieties, four-foot (1.2m) stakes for determinate varieties. We tie them with strips of old cotton clothes that have become rags. Once the soil temperatures are consistently warm, above 60F (15.5C), dry straw mulch if desired. Keep well-watered during the growing season. They prefer a drip-type irrigation method. As soon as tomatoes begin to blush, cut back on watering. Limiting water during this stage will bring out the true flavor of all tomato types. Optimal soil pH range is 5.8 to 7.5.

Insects to observe: Night surfacing cutworms can chew off the stem of newly transplanted seedlings. Control by checking the soil around the base of the plant early in the morning and removing them. Tomato/tobacco hornworm *Manduca quinquemaculata* (Five-spotted hawk moth) can defoliate a large tomato plant in a matter of days. Control by checking daily, best found by locating piles of fresh caterpillar poop on the tops of leaves, usually the camouflaged worms are right above, underneath a leaf.

Diseases to watch for: White mold is a fungus that can live in the soil up to eight years and infects over four hundred different varieties of plants. It will decimate a plant and rot the tomatoes. It is particularly prevalent during wet, semi warm conditions. Pulling the worst infected plants will limit plant to plant infection. Tomato fruits can be subject to blossom end rot which is caused by a calcium deficiency; correct by side-dressing with wood ash or powdered dolomitic lime. Septoria leaf spot, Verticillium wilt, early and late blights among other bacterial and fungal diseases can be prevalent, but my experience has revealed that keeping plants dry (control by limiting irrigation) will correct these problems 99% of the time. Pull the worst infected plants if they are too diseased.

Days to harvest: Sixty to ninety days from transplants, then continually until first fall frost.

Harvest advice: Slicing and paste type tomatoes reach optimum flavor after blossom end is completely colored and the tomato slightly less than firm. You do not need to wait until they are 100% ripened on the vine for full flavor. Pull every day or two as tomatoes will over ripe fast and begin to fall off the vines. It is preferred to harvest in cardboard boxes in single layers.

Post-harvest handling/terms of storage (best way to preserve flavor): Tomatoes should be stored at room temperature for best flavor. Never store tomatoes below 55F (13C) as they will become mealy. Can be fresh frozen whole. But my favored method is to cook them down and freeze or can the sauce, thus preserving the best of the tomato flavor for up to a year. Pull off all tomatoes before first frost, even if green, as they will ripen at room temperature.

Health benefits: Tomatoes can make people healthier and decrease the risk of conditions such as cancer, osteoporosis, and cardiovascular disease. People who eat tomatoes regularly have a reduced risk of contracting cancer diseases such as lung, prostate, stomach, cervical, breast, oral, colorectal, esophageal, pancreatic, and many other types of cancer.[66]

Field notes:

Turnips
Brassica rapa

Characteristics/growing habits: Turnips, members of the family *Brassicaceae*, are cold hardy biennials. Salad turnips, as they are sometimes called, are quite a delicacy. Fast growing, they can be white, red, or purple top globes. All turnips form a nice head of mustard tasting greens.

Favorite varieties: "Hakurei" F-1, "Purple Top White Globe" (HL), "Tokyo Market" (OP)

Seeding information: Direct seed (OP, heirloom, F1) ½-inch (1.25cm) deep, 3 inches (7.5cm) apart, rows at 12 inches (30cm).

Days to germination at temperature range: Three to six days at 55-85F (13-29.5C).

When to start inside: n/a

Necessary to pot-up to three-inch pots: n/a

When to transplant or direct seed outside: As soon as soil can be worked, and succession planted every three weeks thereafter to ensure a constant harvest throughout the season.

Maintenance required during growing period: Keep well-weeded of native flora throughout the seedling stage. Ensure turnips are thinned to at least 3 inches (7.5cm) apart. Once fully formed, they will create a canopy that deters native flora growth. Cover immediately after planting with insect screens. Optimal soil pH range is 5.8 to 7.5.

Insects to observe: Flea beetles are a common early spring problem creating small holes in young leaves. Best control is immediately after seeding to install insect screens. Keep greens well weeded of common plantain, the flea beetle's preferred host. Green peach aphids and gray turnip aphids can become abundant in times of warm nights and humid conditions especially in late summer plantings. Letting some of the earliest turnip plantings go to flower will attract a whole host of native bees, flies, and wasps.

Diseases to watch for: None of major consequence have been perceived.

Days to harvest: Thirty-five to forty-five days from direct seeding, fifty to sixty days for purple top types, continually until all are harvested.

Harvest advice: Pull turnips by pulling from the root early in the morning as the leaves will wilt readily. Start by pulling larger ones first and letting smaller ones size up. Keep all greens for eating, as are highly nutritional.

Post-harvest handling/terms of storage (best way to preserve flavor): Turnips can be stored with greens removed, dry and dirty from two to three months in plastic bags or bins 33-40F (1-4.5C). If washed can store for four weeks. Can be fermented into kimchi with cabbage and can conserve for up to one year. Turnip greens can be eaten raw or cooked like Asian or mustard greens. They also can be blanched and frozen to be stored for up to six months.

Health benefits: Foods containing dietary nitrates — such as turnips and collard greens — may provide multiple benefits for the health of the blood vessels. These include reducing blood pressure and inhibiting the sticking together of platelets in the blood. In general, a diet rich in fruits and vegetables have positive effects on blood pressure.[67]

Field notes:

Watermelons
Citrullus lanatus

Characteristics/growing habits:
Watermelons, members of the family *Cucurbitaceae,* are warm season tender annuals that prefer a warm to hot growing season. Watermelons vary greatly in size ranging in weights from six to twenty-five pounds (2.5-11.5kg). Shapes can be from round to oblong and flesh color from light pink to dark red to brilliant yellow. Vines will run profusely and set their fruits among the runners sometimes up to fifty feet (fifteen meters) away from the main plant. Watermelons require pollinators to set fruit.

Favorite varieties: "Blacktail Mountain" (OP), "Moon & Stars" (HL), "Sugar Baby" (OP)

Seeding information: One seed (OP, heirloom) in three to four-inch (7.5-10cm) pots.

Days to germination at temperature range: Four to seven days at 65-90F (18.5-32C).

When to start inside: Three weeks before warm and settled date.

Necessary to pot-up to three-inch pots: Not necessary to pot up, sow seed directly into a three to four-inch pot.

When to transplant or direct seed outside: Transplant at warm and settled date as watermelon seedlings do not react well to nights below 50F (10C). Transplant at 12 inches (30cm) apart.

Maintenance required during growing period: Keep well weeded of native flora. Cover with Agribon-type 17 or 19 row covers until every plant has one to two flowers. The cover will create a warm humid environment that watermelon plants enjoy. Upon removal, applying a dry straw mulch under plants and vines will trap soil humidity and keep melons from rotting on wet soil. When plants have set full-size fruit, discontinue watering for the final two weeks until harvest. Too much water in the ripening stage will make watermelons tasteless. Optimal soil pH range is 6.0 to 7.5.

Insects to observe: Striped and spotted cucumber beetles are migrating insects that can become quite numerous in the early season. Control by planting later in the season and keeping the plants covered with row cover until the flowering stage. The larvae are predated on by spined soldier bugs and assassin beetles. Usually the density of cucumber beetles, both types, subsides by mid-summer.

Diseases to watch for: Powdery mildew can become a major problem when there has been a prolonged period of dry weather, followed by a cold snap. Control by irrigating regularly during droughts.

Days to harvest: Seventy-five to one hundred days from transplants and continually until first fall frost.

Harvest advice: Harvesting watermelons can be a challenge, but these criteria can help. The tendril next to the growing stem will be completely dead. The melon will "slip" when sharply pulled from the vine. There will, more often than not, be a large yellow spot on the melon where it touches the soil. Will sound hollow when tapped (least reliable indicator). Check every day as watermelons do not hold well in the field once ripe.

Post-harvest handling/terms of storage (best way to preserve flavor): Due to watermelons thick rinds they will store from three to four weeks at 33-40F (1-4.5C).

Health benefits: Consumption of a fruits and vegetables-based diet has a range of bioactive components, especially phytochemicals targeting life-threatening ailments. In this context, lycopene is an extensively studied antioxidant potentially present in watermelon. Watermelon is one of the unique sources having readily available *cis*-isomeric lycopene. Lycopene has the potential to prevent various chronic ailments like dyslipidemia, diabetes, oncogenesis, neurodegenerative diseases, osteoporosis, among others.[68]

Field notes:

Winter Squash and Pumpkins
Cucurbita spp. (pepo, maxima, moschata, etc.)

Characteristics/growing habits: Winter squash and pumpkins, members of the family *Cucurbitaceae,* are tender annuals that prefer a long, warm, frost-free season to mature. They will vine and run, and have vastly different shapes and sizes. Common types include acorn, buttercup, butternut, delicata, hubbard, kuri, spaghetti, and the classic orange pumpkin. Uncommon types can be candy roaster, Chioggia, and futsu. Grow according to personal preference. Winter Squash and pumpkins require pollinators to set fruit.

Favorite varieties: "Burgess Buttercup" (HL), "Delicata" (HL), "Guatemala Blue" (HL), "New England Pie Pumpkin" (HL), "North Georgia Candy Roaster" (HL), "Spaghetti" (OP), "Sweet Dumpling" (OP), "Sweet Reba Acorn" (OP), "Waltham Butternut" (HL)

Seeding information: One seed (OP, heirloom) in three to four-inch (7.5-10cm) pots. Can be direct seeded in areas where frost free season is greater than 120 days.

Days to germination at temperature range: Four to seven days at 65-90F (18.5-32C).

When to start inside: Three weeks before warm and settled date.

Necessary to pot-up to three-inch pots: Not necessary to pot up, sow seed directly into a three to four-inch pot.

When to transplant or direct seed outside: Transplant or direct seed at warm and settled date as winter squash/pumpkin plants do not appreciate nights below 55F (13C). Plant eighteen inches (45cm) apart.

Maintenance required during growing period: Keep well weeded of native flora. Cover with Agribon-type 17 or 19 row covers until every plant has a flower or two. Upon removal, applying a dry straw mulch under plants and vines will trap soil humidity and keep squashes from rotting on wet soil. Optimal soil pH range is 6.0 to 7.5.

Insects to observe: Striped and spotted cucumber beetles are migrating insects that can become quite numerous in the early season. The larvae are predated on by spined soldier bugs and assassin beetles. Usually the density of cucumber beetles, both types, subsides by mid-summer. Squash bug is a greyish-brownish sap-sucking insect that are prolific breeders, laying dozens of eggs. The larger larvae and adults have toxic saliva, like the cucumber beetles, and once bitten the leaves will wilt. Plants will cease growing and eventually die. Control all by planting later in the season and keeping the plants covered with row cover as long as possible.

Diseases to watch for: Powdery mildew can become a major problem when there has been a prolonged period of dry weather, followed by a cold snap. Control by irrigating regularly during droughts.

Days to harvest: Seventy to ninety-five days from transplants, 80-105 days from direct seeding.

Harvest advice: Harvest winter squash and pumpkins when their ripe color is achieved and the fruits are hard (test by knocking on them). Cut stem up one inch (2.5cm) with garden cutters. Cure most varieties in a warm, sunny, and dry place for ten to fourteen days (not necessary for delicata and acorn types). Even if winter squash and pumpkins have not colored completely in the field before first frost, cut and cure anyway. It is possible that some, especially butternut and candy roasters will ripen upon doing so.

Post-harvest handling/terms of storage (best way to preserve flavor): After curing, store at temperatures between 50-60F (10-15.5C); any colder will cause squashes and pumpkins to rot. If proper temperature is maintained, they should store for four months and more.

Health benefits: Increasing evidence has shown that cucurbits' medicinal properties depend upon the chemical compounds present, which produce a specific physiological effect in the human body. Specifically, cucurbits fruits are found to be beneficial in blood cleansing, purification of toxic substances and good for digestion, besides giving the required energy to improve human health. This review provides a detailed overview to the folk medicinal uses of *Cucurbita* plants, an in-depth insight on the latest advances regarding its antimicrobial, antioxidant, and anticancer effects, and lastly, a special emphasis to its clinical effectiveness in humans, specifically in blood glucose levels control and low urinary tract diseases.[69]

Field notes:

_____

_____

_____

Annex B:
Crop Spacing and Approximate Yields

Legend:

Fruits/Vegetables/Herbs=Indicates common name.

DS= Direct Seed, **T**=Transplant.

Rows=Rows per bed, if using a row type system, if a block system can simply use distance

Distance=Distance between plants.

Plants/bed foot= How many plants one can expect in a 2.5' (75cm) or 3' (90cm) wide by 1' (30cm) long block or section of row.

Approximate yield= Based on veganic growing methods at La Ferme de l'Aube, similar yields can be realized in any and all veganic models. Values are listed in units or grams (to calculate into lbs. multiply by 0.22).

When:

Soil open=As soon as soil can be worked

After frost= After average last spring frost date in your region

Warm & Settled= Warm & settled date corresponds to about three weeks after last frost date

Vegetables & Fruits	DS/T	Rows	Distance	Plants per Bed Foot	Approx. Yield	When
Artichoke	T	1	18" (45cm)	1 per 18"	5 chokes	After frost
Asparagus	T	1	12" (30cm)	1	75g	Soil open
Bush Beans	DS	3	2" (5cm)	18	350g	After frost
Beets	DS	3	3" (7.5cm)	12	550g	After frost
Bok Choy	T	3	6" (15cm)	6	6 heads	Soil open
Broccoli	T	2	16" (40cm)	2 per 16"	2 heads	Soil open
Br. Raab 'Rapini'	DS	4	3" (7.5cm)	16	600g	Soil open
Brussels Sprouts	T	2	20" (60cm)	2 per 20"	2 stalks	After frost

Cabbage (lg)	T	2	18" (45cm)	2 per 18"	2 heads (2 kg)	After frost
Cabbage (sm)	T	2	12" (30cm)	2	2 heads (750g)	Soil open
Nappa Cabbage	T	2	12" (30cm)	2	2 heads (750g)	Warm & Settled
Carrots	DS	5	1" (2.5cm)	60	800g	Soil open
Cauliflower	T	2	18" (45cm)	2 per 18"	2 heads	After frost
Celery & Celery root	T	2	12" (30cm)	2	2 bunch or roots	After frost
Chicory (Radicchio Escarole)	T	2	12" (30cm)	2	2 heads	After frost
Collards	T	3	12" (30cm)	3	500g	Soil open
Corn (Sweet)	T	2	10 to 12" (25 to 30cm)	2	2-4 ears	Warm & Settled
Cucumber	T	2	12" (30cm)	2	24 cukes	Warm & Settled
Dry Beans	DS	3	2" (5cm)	18	50g	After frost
Eggplant	T	2	18" (45cm)	2 per 18"	8-10 eggplants	After frost
Fennel	T	3	12" (30cm)	3	3 heads	After frost
Garlic	DS	3	4" (10cm)	9	9 bulbs	In fall
Greens (Asian)	DS	4	2" (5cm)	24	600g	Soil open
Greens (Mustard)	DS	4	2" (5cm)	24	600g	Soil open
Ground Cherry	T	2	12" (30cm)	2	460g	After frost
Kale	T	3	12" (30cm)	3	550g	Soil open
Kohlrabi	T	3	4" (10cm)	9	9 rabi's	Soil open
Leeks	T	3	3" (7.5cm)	12	12 leeks	After frost
Lettuce (heads)	T	3	10 to 12" (25 to 30cm)	3	3 heads	Soil open
Lettuce (Salad mix)	DS	5	1" (2.5cm)	60	265g	Soil open
Melons (e.g. cantaloupe)	T	1	12" (30cm)	1	2-3 melons	Warm & Settled
Okra	T	2	12" (30cm)	2	300g	Warm & Settled
Onions (bulbing)	T	4	3" (7.5cm)	16	16 onions	After frost
Onions (bunching)	T	5	1" (2.5cm)	60	60 onions	Soil open
Peas (all)	DS	4	2" (5cm)	24	250g	Soil open
Peppers (sweet)	T	2	12" (30cm)	2	8-10 peppers	After frost

Vegetables & Fruits (cont.)	DS/T	Rows	Distance	Plants per Bed Foot	Approx. Yield	When
Peppers (hot)	T	2	12" (30cm)	2	300g	After frost
Potatoes	DS	1	8 to 10" (20 to 25cm)	1	650g	After frost
Pumpkins	T	1	18" (45cm)	1 per 18"	2-4 pumpkins	Warm & Settled
Parsnips	DS	3	3" (7.5cm)	12	12 parsnips	Soil open
Radishes	DS	4	2" (5cm)	24	24 radi	Soil open
Radish (Winter)	DS	3	4" (10cm)	9	9 radi	Warm & Settled
Rhubarb	T	1	24" (60cm)	1 per 24"	300g	After frost
Rutabaga	T	3	6" (15cm)	6	6 baga's	Warm & Settled
Soybeans 'Edamame'	DS	3	2" (5cm)	18	325g	After frost
Spinach	DS	3	2" (5cm)	18	300g	Soil open
Strawberry	T	2	12" (30cm)	2	600g	After frost
Summer Squash	T	1	18" (45cm)	1 per 18"	680g	After frost
Sweet Potatoes	T	1	12" (30cm)	1	750g*	Warm & Settled
Swiss Chard	T	3	12" (30cm)	3	350g	After frost
Tomatillos	T	2	12" (30cm)	2	400g	After frost
Tomatoes (Cherry)	T	2	12" (30cm)	2	1.5kg	After frost
Tomatoes	T	2	18" (45cm)	2 per 18"	2.4kg	After frost
Turnips	DS	3	3" (7.5cm)	12	12 turnips	Soil open
Watermelons	T	1	12" (30cm)	1	3-4 melons	Warm & Settled
Winter Squash	T	1	18" (45cm)	1 per 18"	3-6 squash	Warm & Settled

*Sweet potato yield was from my Arizona farm.

Herbs	DS/T	Rows	Distance	Plants per Bed Foot	Approx. Yield	When
Basil	T	3	6" (15cm)	6	3 bunches	Warm & Settled
Chamomile	T	3	10 to 12" (25 to 30cm)	3	Many flowers	After frost
Chives	T	3	6" (15cm)	6	6 bunches	After frost
Cilantro	DS	4	4" (10cm)	12	4 bunches	Soil open
Dill	DS	4	4" (10cm)	12	4 bunches	Soil open
Lovage	T	2	12" (30cm)	2	4 bunches	After frost
Mint	T	3	6" (15cm)	6	6 bunches	After frost
Oregano (Greek)	T	3	12" (30cm)	3	3 bunches	After frost
Parsley	T	2	12" (30cm)	2	4 bunches	After frost
Sage	T	3	10" (25cm)	3	3 bunches	After frost
Savory	T	3	8" (20cm)	3	3 bunches	After frost
Sorrel	DS	3	6" (15cm)	6	150g	In fall
Thyme	T	3	8" (20cm)	3	3 bunches	After frost

Annex C:
Last and First Frosts

Select U.S. And Canadian Cities

Frost dates have been calculated based on data compiled by NOAA National Centers for Environmental Information using 1981-2010 climate normals and are about 33% accurate. More U.S. And Canadian cities can be found at: The Old Farmer's Almanac: "First and Last Frost Dates."[1]

U.S. State, City	Last (Spring)	First (Fall)	Frost-Free Season
Alabama, Birmingham	April 2	November 9	222 days
Alaska, Anchorage	May 8	September 23	139 days
Arizona, Flagstaff	June 9	September 22	106 days
Arkansas, Little Rock	March 22	November 12	236 days
California, Tahoe City	June 18	September 19	94 days
Colorado, Denver	April 30	October 4	158 days
Connecticut, Hartford	April 26	October 9	167 days
District of Columbia	March 29	November 15	231 days
Delaware, Dover	April 8	October 30	205 days
Florida, Tallahassee	March 22	November 17	241 days
Georgia, Atlanta	March 24	November 16	238 days
Idaho, Boise	May 5	October 8	157 days
Illinois, Chicago	April 20	October 24	188 days
Indiana, Indianapolis	April 18	October 18	184 days
Iowa, Des Moines	April 20	October 24	188 days
Kansas, Topeka	April 19	October 11	176 days
Kentucky, Lexington	April 20	October 21	185 days
Louisiana, Shreveport	March 10	November 18	253 days
Maine, Portland	May 2	October 6	158 days
Maryland, Baltimore	April 11	October 29	202 days
Massachusetts, Boston	April 7	November 7	215 days

Michigan, Detroit	April 26	October 17	175 days
Minnesota, Minneapolis	April 30	October 5	159 days
Mississippi, Tupelo	April 5	October 28	207 days
Missouri, St. Louis	April 7	October 29	206 days
Montana, Bozeman	May 26	September 19	117 days
Nebraska, Omaha	April 21	October 12	175 days
Nevada, Reno	May 21	October 3	136 days
New Hampshire, Concord	May 20	September 21	125 days
New Jersey, Newark	April 3	November 7	219 days
New Mexico, Albuquerque	April 16	October 28	196 days
New York, New York	April 1	November 15	229 days
New York, Buffalo	April 24	October 19	179 days
North Carolina, Raleigh-Durham	April 10	October 28	202 days
North Dakota, Fargo	May 10	September 27	141 days
Ohio, Cleveland	April 30	October 23	177 days
Oklahoma, Tulsa	March 27	November 7	226 days
Oregon, Eugene	April 22	October 19	181 days
Pennsylvania, Pittsburg	April 29	October 17	172 days
Pennsylvania, Philadelphia	April 5	November 11	221 days
Rhode Island, Providence	April 16	October 22	190 days
South Carolina, Columbia	April 1	November 1	215 days
South Dakota, Sioux Falls	May 3	September 28	149 days
Tennessee, Knoxville	April 16	October 22	190 days
Texas, Amarillo	April 18	October 20	186 days
Utah, Salt Lake City	April 19	October 25	190 days
Vermont, Burlington	May 8	October 1	147 days
Virginia, Roanoke	April 13	October 22	193 days
Washington, Seattle	March 17	November 16	245 days
Washington, Spokane	May 2	October 3	155 days
West Virgina, Charleston	April 22	October 19	181 days
Wisconsin, Milwaukee	April 27	October 14	171 days
Wyoming, Casper	May 22	September 19	121 days

Canadian Province, City	Last (Spring)	First (Fall)	Frost-Free Season
Alberta, Calgary	May 29	September 6	101 days
Alberta, Edmonton	May 15	September 16	125 days
British Columbia, Vancouver	April 21	October 19	182 days
British Columbia, Kelowna	May 8	October 6	122 days
Manitoba, Winnipeg	May 21	September 15	118 days
New Brunswick, Moncton	June 3	September 15	105 days
New Brunswick, Fredericton	May 22	September 25	127 days
Newfoundland, Saint Johns	June 11	October 7	119 days
Northwest Territories, Yellowknife	May 31	September 11	104 days
Nova Scotia, Halifax	May 8	October 20	166 days
Nunavut, Iqaluit	July 2	August 27	57 days
Ontario, Ottawa	May 13	September 26	137 days
Ontario, Toronto	May 4	October 13	163 days
Prince Edward Isle, Charlottetown	May 20	October 10	144 days
Québec, Montréal	April 25	October 11	171 days
Québec, Québec city	May 17	September 24	131 days
Saskatchewan, Saskatoon	May 15	September 19	128 days
Saskatchewan, Regina	June 1	September 1	93 days
Yukon Territory, Whitehorse	June 12	August 24	74 days

Annex D:
Flower and Herb Chart

THE PLANTS I have listed in the following chart should be considered essential to any urban backyard or farmyard garden. They can be incorporated into rows, blocks and/or along edge rows. The more flowers in the garden the more insect activity, pollinators (bees, syrphid flies, wasps, butterflies, moths) and all others. In North America there are around 18,000 bees, wasps, sawflies and ants (order *Hymenoptera*). There are, additionally, more than 13,500 species of butterflies and moths (order *Lepidoptera*).[1]

Flowering plants will also increase biodiversity of birds (especially the fascinating hummingbirds), reptiles, amphibians and small mammals. Just like the edible garden, the more diversity of flowering plants the better. By no means is this list exhaustive it just highlights some of my favorites.

Every year perennial plants will spread from their roots and will eventually take over a large area. Each spring depending on space you may have to remove some of the newest seedlings. When considering timing of planting, plant all flowering plants after last spring frost. Some may need to be started inside, some can be direct seeded. For the best resources, check seed catalogs by Johnny's Selected Seeds (US), William Dam and Richter's (Canada).

Legend:

Flowering Plant- Common and Latin Name

P/A- P=Perennial (zone 4 and above) A=Annual, A*=Self-seeding annual, B=Biennial

Height- Average height of plant of most varietals at its tallest. For the tallest ones it is important to plant on the north end of the garden, so as not to provide too much shade to the smaller ones.

Flowering Season- When flowers begin

Pollinators- Bees, wasps, butterflies and moths

Medicinal- Herbal therapeutic usage as well as culinary in some cases

Flowering Plant	P/A	Height	Flowering Season	Pollinators	Medicinal
Alfalfa *Medicago sativa*	P	3' (90cm)	Mid-summer	✓	✓
Amaranthe *Amaranthus sp.*	A	5' (150cm)	Mid-summer	✓	✓
Angelica *Angelica archangelica*	P	5' (150cm)	Early summer	✓	✓
Anise Hyssop *Agastache sp.*	P	2' (60cm)	Mid-summer	✓	✓
Asclepias (milkweed) *Asclepias sp.*	P	3' (90cm)	Mid-summer	✓	✓
Bachelor's Button *Centaurea sp.*	A/P	2.5' (75cm)	Mid-summer	✓	✓
Bergamot *Monarda didyma*	P	2.5' (75cm)	Early summer	✓	✓
Borage *Borago officinalis*	A*	3' (90cm)	Early summer	✓	✓
Buckwheat *Fagopyrum esculentum*	A*	5' (150cm)	Mid-summer	✓	✓
Calendula *Calendula officinalis*	A*	2' (60cm)	Mid-summer	✓	✓
Catmint *Nepeta x fassenii*	P	1.5' (45cm)	Mid-summer	✓	✓
Catnip *Nepeta cataria*	P	1.5' (45cm)	Late spring	✓	✓
Cleome *Cleome hassleriana*	A*	4' (120cm)	Mid-summer	✓	✗
Clover *Trifolium sp.*	P	1.5' (45cm)	Late spring	✓	✓
Comfrey *Symphytum officinale*	P	3' (90cm)	Late spring	✓	✓
Coreopsis *Coreopsis sp.*	A	3' (90cm)	Mid-summer	✓	✗
Cosmos *Cosmos sp.*	A	3' (90cm)	Mid-summer	✓	✗
Echinacea *Echinacea sp.*	P	4' (120cm)	Late summer	✓	✓
Four O'clock *Mirabilis jalapa*	A	2' (60cm)	Mid-summer	✓	✗

Foxglove *Digitalis purpurea*	B	4' (120cm)	Early summer	✓	✗
Hollyhock *Alcea sp.*	P	6' (180cm)	Mid-summer	✓	✓
Hops *Humulus lupulus*	P	1' (30cm)	Early summer	✗	✓
Horehound *Marrubium vulgare*	P	2' (60cm)	Early summer	✓	✓
Jer. Artichoke *Helianthus tuberosus*	P	8' (240cm)	Late summer	✓	✓
Lavatera *Lavatera trimestris*	A	2' (60cm)	Mid-summer	✓	✗
Lavender *Lavandula angustifolia*	P	3' (90cm)	Early summer	✓	✓
Lemon Balm *Melissa officinalis*	P	2' (50cm)	Early summer	✓	✓
Liatris *Liatris spicata*	P	3' (90cm)	Mid-summer	✓	✗
Lupine *Lupinus sp.*	P	3' (90cm)	Late spring	✓	✗
Mallow *Malva sylvestris*	P	4' (120cm)	Mid-summer	✓	✓
Marigold *Tagetes sp.*	A	2' (60cm)	Late spring	✓	✗
Marjoram, Sweet *Origanum vulgare*	A	2' (60 cm)	Mid-summer	✓	✓
Marjoram, wild *Origanum vulgare*	P	2' (60cm)	Early summer	✓	✓
Mugwort *Artemisia sp.*	P	4' (120cm)	Mid-summer	✓	✓
Nasturtium *Tropaeolum sp.*	A	1.5' (45cm)	Mid-summer	✓	✓
Nettle *Urtica dioica*	P	3' (90cm)	Early summer	✓	✓
Nicotiana *Nicotiana sp.*	A*	5' (150cm)	Mid-summer	✓	✗
Oats *Avena sativa*	A	3' (90cm)	n/a	✗	✓
Phacelia *Phacelia tanacetifolia*	A	3' (90cm)	Mid-summer	✓	✗

Flowering Plant (cont.)	P/A	Height	Flowering Season	Pollinators	Medicinal
Rosemary *Rosmarinus officinalis*	A	2.5' (75cm)	Late summer	✓	✓
Rudbeckia *Rudbeckia hirta*	P	3' (90cm)	Early summer	✓	✓
Sunflower *Helianthus annus*	A*	6-10' (180-300cm)	Late summer	✓	✓
Valerian *Valeriana officinalis*	P	6' (180cm)	Early summer	✓	✓
Vervain *Verbena hastata*	P	3' (90cm)	Late spring	✓	✓
Wormwood *Artemisia absinthium*	P	5' (150cm)	Mid-summer	✓	✓
Yarrow *Achillea sp.*	P	2' (60cm)	Late spring	✓	✓
Zinnia *Zinnia sp.*	A	1.5' (45cm)	Mid-summer	✓	✓

Annex E:
Recommended Tool List – The Basics

Seeding
- Hand seed sower
- Plug trays/1020 flats (relative to the number of seedlings desired)
- Three to four-inch pots with corresponding trays (relative to the number of transplants)
- Heat mat with corresponding thermometer
- Indoor/outdoor thermometer(s)
- Agribon-type 17, 19, and/or 40 frost protective row covers (any thickness warranted)
- Five-gallon (twenty liter) bucket and a cup measure (for measuring potting mix ingredients)
- Handheld three prong cultivator (for loosening bales of peat moss)
- Watering can, my preferred size is 2.5 gallon (eight liter)

Garden Preparation
- Tape measure
- Spade shovel
- Long handled rake
- Wheelbarrow with puncture proof tire for mixing potting soil and moving compost
- Long-handled four prong cultivator
- Four-tine spading fork (for turning compost)
- Five, six or eight-mil black plastic (in whatever dimensions are desired)
- Five-tine broad fork (if desired)
- Front-tine rototiller (if pertinent)

Planting
- Five-foot (150cm) support wire hoops (relative to plantings)
- Insect netting (relative to plantings)
- Agribon-type 17 or 19 row covers (relative to plantings)

- Sandbags for holding covers (relative to plantings)
- Bed preparation rake (not necessary, but highly recommended)
- Hand seed sower (same as in seeding)
- Hand trowel

Irrigation

- Watering can (two are helpful even if only one person gardening)
- Heavy duty rubber garden hose
- Spray nozzle with adjustable settings
- Drip tape irrigation supplies (if applicable)
- Bobbler sprinkler irrigation supplies (if relevant)

Maintenance of Cultures

- Hammer or mallet for pounding in wooden stakes
- Strong, sharpenable pocketknife (my preferences are Felco, Opinel and Victorinox knives)
- One-inch (2.5cm) x 2-inch (5cm) x 8-foot (2.4m) wooden stakes
- Sisal or hemp twine
- Garden cutters (my preferred brand is Felco)
- Walking garden scissors (if befitting, for cutting down tall plants and cover crops)
- Hand hoe
- Nylon fence and t-posts (length as desired)
- Standard hoe (optional)
- Stirrup hoe (optional)

Harvest/Storage

- Three-gallon (eleven liter) Rubbermaid bins (as many as are necessary for harvesting and cold storage)
- Slatted and stackable bins (for harvesting potatoes, if desired)
- Heavy duty recycled cardboard boxes (like those from grocery produce departments)

Annex F: Resources

Books/Magazines

These are some of the resource books that have inspired me along my growing journey. There are many others that I am sure have inspired many of you. In addition, Elliot Coleman's "The New Organic Grower" (the revised and expanded edition from 1995) has a seven-page annotated bibliography of 100+ sources that should afford any grower, from beginner to experienced, tens of 1000's of hours of learning pleasure.

Veganic Gardening & Homesteading

Bonsall, Will. *Will Bonsall's Guide to Radical, Self-Reliant Gardening*. White River Junction: Chelsea Green Publishing. 2015

Burnett, Graham. *The Vegan Book of Permaculture*. East Meon: Permanent Publications. 2015

Hall, Jenny & Tolhurst, Iain. *Animal-Free Organic Techniques*. White River Junction: Chelsea Green Publishing. 2007

Nearing, Helen & Nearing, Scott. *Living the Good Life*. New York: Schocken Books. 1970

O'Brien, Kenneth Dalziel. *Veganic Gardening*. London: Thorsons Publishing Group. 1986

Vegan Organic Network. *Growing Green International Magazine*. Manchester: Vegan Organic Network. Bi-yearly

Organic Gardening & Homesteading

Ashworth, Suzanne. *Seed to Seed: Seed Saving and Growing Techniques for Vegetable Gardener's*. Decorah: Seed Saver's Exchange. 2002

Bradley, Fern Marshall et al. *Rodale's Ultimate Encyclopedia of Organic Gardening*. Emmaus: Rodale Books. 2009

Coleman, Eliot. *The New Organic Grower*. White River Junction: Chelsea Green Publishing. 1995

Fortier, Jean-Martin. *The Market Gardener*. Gabriola Island: New Society Publishers. 2014

Fortier, Jean-Martin. *Le Jardinier Maraîcher*. Montréal: Les Éditions Écosociété. 2012

Fukuoka, Masanobu. *The One-Straw Revolution*. New York: New York Review Books Classics. 2009

Gagnon, Yves. *La Culture Écologique: Des Plantes Légumières*. Saint-Didace: Les Éditions Colloïdales.

Jeavons, John. *How to Grow More Vegetables*. Berkeley: Ten Speed Press. 2006

Jenkins, Joseph C. *The Humanure Handbook: A Guide to Composting Human Manure, 3rd Edition*. Grove City: Joseph Jenkins Inc. 2005

Kains, Maurice G. *Five Acres and Independence*. Mineola: Dover Publications. 1971

Lanza, Patricia. *Lasagna Gardening*. Emmaus: Rodale Books. 1998

Riotte, Louise. *Carrots Love Tomatoes*. North Adams: Storey Publishing, LLC. 1998

Steiner, Rudolf. *Agriculture: An Introductory Reader*. Forest Row: Rudolf Steiner Press. 2012

Stout, Ruth. Gardening Without Work. Brattleboro: Echo Point Books & Media. 1998

Nature Field Guides

Evans, Arthur W & Tufts, Craig. *National Wildlife Federation Field Guide to Insects and Spiders and Related Species of North America*. New York: Sterling Publishing. 2007

Foster, Steven & Duke, James A. *A Field Guide to Medicinal Plants and Herbs of Eastern and Central North America*. New York: Houghton Mifflin Company. 2000

Glassberg, Jeffrey. *A Swift Guide to Butterflies of North America*. Princeton: Princeton University Press. 2017

National Audubon Society. *National Audubon Society Guide to North American Mushrooms*. New York: Knopf Publishing. 1981

Petrides, George A. *Trees and Shrubs*. New York: Houghton Mifflin Company. 1986

Reid, Fiona A. *Mammals of North America*. New York: Houghton Mifflin Harcourt. 2006

Sibley, David Allen. *The Sibley Guide to Birds*. New York: Alfred A. Knopf Inc. 2000

Websites

The best vegan organic growing sites and information I have found online. A google search of veganic growing/gardening will produce some links to YouTube videos as well.

Adolf Hoops Society. *Biocyclic Vegan Agriculture*. Accessed February 2, 2021 http://www.biocyclic-vegan.org/

A Well-Fed World: Plant-based Hunger Solutions. Accessed November 18, 2021 https://awellfedworld.org

Gentle World, "Beginner's Guide to Veganic Gardening". August 23, 2010

Groleau, Stéphane & Kelly, Meghan. *Veganic Agriculture Network*. Accessed

January 31, 2021 https://www.goveganic.net/?lang=en

Grow Where You Are. Accessed November 18, 2021 https://growwhereyouare. farm

Learn Veganic. Accessed November 18, 2021 https://learnveganic.com

Lundkvist, Annika. *Pacific Roots Magazine.* Accessed February 12, 2021 https:// pacificrootsmagazine.com

Nobari, Nassim. *Seed the Commons.* Accessed February 12, 2021 https:// seedthecommons.org

Scatterseed Project. Accessed November 18, 2021 https://www. scatterseedproject.org/#scatterseed

Nobari, Nassim. *Veganic World.* Accessed February 2, 2021 https://veganic.world

Shumei Natural Agriculture. Accessed February 16, 2021 https:// shumeinaturalagriculture.com/

Tolhurst Organic. Accessed November 18, 2021 https://www.tolhurstorganic. co.uk

Vegan Organic Network: Farming and Growing. Accessed January 31, 2021 https://veganorganic.net

Seed Companies

These are some of my favorites I have used over the years. Not listed are all the regional small artisan companies that exist. An internet search of your corresponding region, state or province should reveal a few near you. To date (as of November 17, 2021) an internet query reveals zero vegan seed companies. Regionally there is only one: La Ferme de l'Aube (included in the list below).

United States

Baker Creek Heirloom Seed Company, 2278 Baker Creek Rd., Mansfield, Missouri, 65704 1-417-924-8917 www.rareseeds.com

High Mowing Organic Seeds, 76 Quarry Road, Wolcott, Vermont, 05680 1-866-735-4454 www.highmowingseeds.com

Johnny's Selected Seeds, 955 Benton Ave, Winslow, Maine, 04901 1-877-564-6697 www.johnnyseeds.com

Native Seed Search, 3584 E River Road, Tucson, Arizona, 85718 1-520-622-0830 ext. 113 www.nativeseeds.org

Seed Saver's Exchange, 3094 North Winn Road, Decorah, Iowa, 52101 1-563-382-5990 www.seedsavers.org

Territorial Seed Company, 20 E Palmer Ave, Cottage Grove, Oregon, 97424 1-800-626-0866 www.territorialseed.com

Terroir Seeds (formerly Underwood Gardens), PO Box 4995, Chino Valley, Arizona, 86323 1-888-878-5247 www.underwoodgardens.com

Totally Tomatoes Company, 334 W. Stroud St., Randolph, Wisconsin, 53956 1-800-345-5977 https://www.totallytomato.com/

Wood Prairie Family Farm, 49 Kinney Rd., Bridgewater, Maine, 04735 1-207-429-9765 https://www.woodprairie.com/

Canada

Annapolis Seeds, 8528 Highway 201, Nictaux, Nova Scotia, B0S 1P0, https://annapolisseeds.com

Eagle Creek Seed Potatoes, 34530 Range Rd 14, Bowden, Alberta T0M 0K0 1-877-224-3939 https://www.seedpotatoes.ca/

Greta's Organic Gardens, 399 River Rd., Gloucester, Ontario, K1V 1C9 1-613-521-8648 www.seeds-organic.com

Incredible Seed Company, PO Box 395, Bridgewater, Mi'kma'ki, Nova Scotia B4V 2X6 https://www.incredibleseeds.ca

La Ferme de l'Aube, 521 Montée Major, Boileau, Québec, J0V1N0 1-819-687-9837 www.lafermedelaube.com (The only vegan seed company in North America)

Richter's Herbs, 357 Highway 47, Goodwood, Ontario, L0C 1A0 1-905-640-6677 www.richters.com

Seeds of Diversity, 1-12 Dupont St. West, Waterloo, Ontario, N2L 2X6 1-226-600-7782 https://seeds.ca/diversity/seed-catalogue-index

Vesey's, PO Box 9000, Charlottetown, Prince Edward Island, C1A 8K6 1-800-363-7333 www.veseys.com

William Dam Seeds, 279 Hamilton Regional Rd 8, Dundas, Ontario, L9H 5E1 1-905-628-6641 www.damseeds.com

France

Association Kokopelli, Oasis. 131 impasse des Palmiers, 30100 Alès Tél : 00 33 4 66 30 64 91 or 00 33 4 66 30 00 55 www.kokopelli-seeds.com

Tools and Supply Companies

Many of the supplies from Annex E: Recommended Tool List, should be able to be located at your local nursery, garden center or hardware supply store. If not, here are the best that deliver in the United States and Canada:

United States

Johnny's Selected Seeds, 955 Benton Ave, Winslow, Maine 04901 1-877-564-6697 www.johnnyseeds.com (delivers to Canada)

Greenhouse Megastore, 70 Eastgate Dr, Danville, Illinois 61832 1-888-281-9337 https://www.greenhousemegastore.com (delivers to Canada)

Canada

Dubois Agrinovation, 478 Notre Dame, C.P. 3550, Saint-Rémi, Québec, J0L2L0 1-800-463-9999 https://duboisag.com/ca_en/ (delivers to the United States)

Teris, 3180 Montée Saint-Aubin, Laval, Québec, H7L3H8 1-888-622-2710 https://www.teris.co

Bibliography of Sources

Introduction

1. Heymsfield, Steven B et al. "Human Body Composition: Advances in Models and Methods" *Annual Review of Nutrition* 17(1): 527-528. February 1997
2. Melamed, Yoel et al. "The plant component of an Acheulian diet at Geshor Benot Ya'aqov, Israel" *Proceedings of the National Academy of Sciences* 113(51): 14674-14679. December 2016
3. Mercado, Julio. "Mozambican Grass Seed Consumption during the Middle Stone Age" *Science* 326(5960): 1680-1683. December 2009
4. Tierney, Jessica E, et al. "A climatic context for the out-of-Africa migration" *Geology* 45(11). October 2017
5. Videle, James. "The Productivity of Vegan-Organic Farming" Humane Herald Publications. December 2018
6. Rahman, Shafiqur & Berg Mary. "Animal Carcass Disposal Options Rendering – Incineration – Burial – Composting" North Dakota State University Publications. September 2017
7. NOAA Fisheries. "Feeds for Aquaculture" Accessed February 1, 2021. https://www.fisheries.noaa.gov/insight/feeds-aquaculture
8. Cowspiracy: The Sustainability Secret. "The Facts". Accessed November 10, 2021 https://www.cowspiracy.com/facts
9. Nobari, Nassim and Seymour, Mona. "Mapping Veganic Farms in North America" Veganic World. Accessed February 2, 2021 https://veganic.world/farm-map/

Chapter 1: The Land and the Soil

1. University of California-Santa Barbara. "How does your garden grow? Researchers model the effect of household gardens on greenhouse gas emissions." *Science Daily*, 7. September 2016
2. White, Robin et al. "Pilot Analysis of Global Ecosystems" *World Resources Institute*, pg. 51. 2000
3. Magura, Tibor et al. "Edge responses are different in edges under natural versus anthropogenic influence: a meta-analysis using ground beetles" *Ecology and Evolution* 7(3): 1009-1017. February 2017
4. Holt-Gimenez, Eric et al. "We Already Grow Enough Food for 10 Billion People ... and Still Can't End Hunger" *Journal of Sustainable Agriculture* 36(6): 595-598. July 2012

5. Schmidt, Olaf et al. "The Living Soil: Biodiversity and Functions" *The Soils of Ireland*. Springer. 257-265. April 2018

6. Wu, Di et al. "Variations in Soil Functional Fungal Community Structure Associated with Pure and Mixed Plantations in Typical Temperate Forests of China" *Frontiers in Microbiology* 10: 1636. July 2019

7. Krishna, M.P. & Mohan, Mahesh. "Litter decomposition in forest ecosystems: a review". *Energy, Ecology, Environment* 2. 236-249. July 2017

8. Washington State University: College of Agricultural, Human, and Natural Resource Sciences. "Manure on Your Farm: Asset or Liability?" Accessed February 2, 2021. https://extension.wsu.edu/animalag/content/manure-on-your-farm-asset-or-liability/

9. Royal Horticultural Society. "Soil Types" Accessed February 2, 2021. https://www.rhs.org.uk/advice/profile?pid=179

10. Neina, Dora. "The Role of Soil pH in Plant Nutrition and Soil Remediation" *Applied and Environmental Soil Science*. November 2019

11. Boeckmann, Catherine. "Soil pH Levels for Plants" *The Old Farmer's Almanac*. August 2019. Accessed February 2, 2021. https://www.almanac.com/plant-ph#

Chapter 2: The Garden Plan

1. Videle, James. "The Productivity of Vegan-Organic Farming" *Humane Herald Publications*. December 2018

Chapter 3: Seeds

1. Martinez-Andujar, Christina et al. "Seed Traits and Genes Important for Translational Biology—Highlights from Recent Discoveries" *Plant & Cell Physiology* 53(1): 5-15. January 2012

2. U.S. Food and Drug Administration. "GMO Crops, Animal Food and Beyond" Accessed February 4, 2021. https://www.fda.gov/food/agricultural-biotechnology/gmo-crops-animal-food-and-beyond

3. Crop Life Canada. "Facts and Figures: GMO'S" Accessed February 4, 2021. https://croplife.ca/facts-figures/gmos-in-canada/

4. Muola, Anne et al. "Risk in the circular food economy: Glyphosate-based herbicide residues in manure fertilizers decrease crop yield" *Science of the Total Environment* 750. January 2021

5. Seminis Seeds. "Our Products" Accessed February 5, 2021 https://www.seminis-us.com/products/

6. De Ruiter. "Seeds" Accessed February 5, 2021 https://www.deruiterseeds.com/en-ca.html

7. Harris, Paul. "Monsanto sued small farmers to protect seed patents, report says" *The Guardian*. February 2013

Chapter 4: Seed Starting and the Growing Medium

1. Oceanworks. Accessed February 4, 2021. https://oceanworks.co
2. International Union for Conservation of Nature: Issues Brief. "Peatlands and Climate Change". November 2021
3. Sun Gro Horticulture. "Sustainable Peat Moss" Accessed February 4, 2021. www.sungro.com/about-us/sustainable-peat-moss/

Chapter 5: Garden Preparation

1. Sigler, Jorge et al. "Distribution of Animals Used for Agriculture and Manure Generated: Ratio of Manure to Land Generated". *Humane Herald Publications*. August 2017
2. Hofmann, Nancy, "A geographical profile of livestock manure production in Canada, 2006". *Statistics Canada*. November 2015
3. Ifeanyi, Ogbuewu et al. "Livestock Waste and its Impact on the Environment". *Scientific Journal of Review* 1 (2): 17-32. September 2012

Chapter 6: The Major and Minor Elements

1. White, P.J. & Brown P.H. "Plant nutrition for sustainable development and global health" *Annals of Botany* 105(7): 1073-1080. June 2010
2. Thompson, Michael et al. "Effects of Elevated Carbon Dioxide on Photosynthesis and Carbon Partitioning: A Perspective on Root Sugar Sensing and Hormonal Crosstalk" *Frontier in Physiology*. August 2017
3. Zeng, Jiging et al. "Progress in the study of biological effects of hydrogen on higher plants and its promising application in agriculture" *Medical Gas Research* 4: 15. August 2014
4. Toro, Guillermo & Pinto, Manuel. "Plant respiration under low oxygen" *Chilean Journal of Agricultural Research* 75(supp. 1): 57-70. August 2015
5. Legari, Shah Jahan et al. "Role of Nitrogen for Plant Growth and Development: A review" *Advances in Environmental Biology* 10(9): 209-218. September 2016
6. Nguyen, Thi Diem et al. "The effects of soil phosphorus and zinc availability on plant responses to mycorrhizal fungi: a physiological and molecular assessment" *Scientific Reports* 9: 14880. October 2019
7. Prajapati, Kalavati & Modi H.A. "The Importance of Potassium in Plant Growth – A Review" *Indian Journal of Plant Sciences* 1: 177-186. July-December 2012
8. Thor, Kathrin. "Calcium-Nutrient and Messenger" *Frontiers in Plant Science*. April 2019
9. Grzebisz, Witold et al. "Magnesium as a nutritional tool of nitrogen efficient management - plant production and environment" *Journal of Elementology* 15(4). October 2010
10. Kopriva, Stanislav et al. "Sulfur nutrition: Impacts on plant development,

metabolism, and stress responses" *Journal of Experimental Biology* 70(16): 4069-4073. August 2019

11. Chen, Wenrong et al. "Chlorine Nutrition of Higher Plants: Progress and Perspectives" *Journal of Plant Nutrition* 33: 943-952. May 2010

12. Shireen, Fareeha et al. "Boron: Functions and Approaches to Enhance Its Availability in Plants for Sustainable Agriculture" *International Journal of Molecular Sciences* 19(7): 1856. July 2018

13. Li, Wenfeng & Lan, Ping. "The Understanding of the Plant Iron Deficiency Responses in Strategy I Plants and the Role of Ethylene in This Process by Omic Approaches" *Frontiers in Plant Science* 8:40. January 2017

14. Alejandro, Santiago et al. "Manganese in Plants: From Acquisition to Subcellular Allocation" Frontiers in Plant Science 11:300. March 2020

15. Yruela, Inmaculada. "Copper in Plants". *Brazilian Journal of Plant Physiology* 17(1). March 2005

16. Cabot, Catalina et al. "A Role for Zinc in Plant Defense Against Pathogens and Herbivores" *Frontiers in Plant Science*. October 2019

17. Fabiano, Caio C. et al. "Essentiality of nickel in plants: a role in plant stresses" *Frontiers in Plant Science* 6: 754. September 2015

18. Kaiser, Brent N et al. "The Role of Molybdenum in Agricultural Plant Production" *Annals of Botany* 96(5): 745-754. October 2005

19. University of Georgia Cooperative Extension Bulletin 1142. "Best Management Practices for Wood Ash as Agricultural Soil Amendment". March 2013

Chapter 7: The Compost Piles

1. Noyes, Nick. *Easy Composters You Can Build.* North Adams: Storey Publishing LLC. 1995

2. Cornell Waste Management Institute. "Compost Chemistry" 1996

3. Lemieux, G. & Germain, Diane. "Ramial Chipped Wood: The Clue to a Sustainable Fertile Soil" January 2001

4. Jenkins, Joseph C. *The Humanure Handbook: A Guide to Composting Human Manure, 3rd Edition.* Grove City: Joseph Jenkins Inc. 2005

5. Veganic Agriculture Network. "Veganic Fertility: Growing Plants from Plants". August 2012

Chapter 8: As Soon as the Soil can be Worked

1. Burnett, Graham. *The Vegan Book of Permaculture.* East Meon: Permanent Publications. 2015

2. The Old Farmer's Almanac. "What are Plant Hardiness Zones?" February 2021. Accessed February 6, 2021 https://www.almanac.com/content/plant-hardiness-zones#

Chapter 9: Irrigation and Rain-Water Collection

1. Videle, Jimmy. "Rain Water Collection on a Small-Scale Veganic Farm" *Growing Green International* 45. Autumn/Winter 2020
2. Notaguchi, Michitaka & Okamoto, Satoru. "Dynamics of long-distance signaling via plant vascular tissues" *Frontiers in Plant Science* 6: 161. March 2015
3. Science News. "Tomatoes of the same quality as normal, but using only half the water" February 2018
4. Coyago-Cruz, Elena Del Rocio et al. "Antioxidants (carotenoids and phenolics) profile of cherry tomatoes as influenced by deficit irrigation, ripening and cluster" *Food Chemistry* 240. August 2017

Chapter 10: The Planting Rush of the Tender Annuals

1. Eames-Sheavly, Marcia. "The Three Sisters: Exploring an Iroquois Garden" A Cornell Cooperative Extension Publication. 1993
2. Mills, Dr. Milton. "The Comparative Anatomy of Eating" *Plant Based Nation*. November 2019

Chapter 11: Maintenance of Cultures

1. Nearing, Helen & Nearing, Scott. *Living the Good Life*. New York: Schocken Books. 1970

Chapter 12: Fertilization (Long and Short Term)

1. Abdalla, Mohamed et al. "A critical review of the impacts of cover crops on nitrogen leaching, net greenhouse gas balance and crop productivity" *Global Change Biology* 25(8): 2530-2543. August 2019
2. Lanza, Patricia. *Lasagna Gardening*. Emmaus: Rodale Books. 1998
2. Canadian Organic Growers. "The Three R's of Fertility" July 2013
3. Isaacson, Talia. "Stinging Nettles: Not Just for Breakfast Anymore" Cornell Small Farms Program. April 2018
4. Morales-Corts, Maria Remedios et al. "Efficiency of garden waste compost teas on tomato growth and its suppressiveness against soilborne pathogens" *Scientia Agricola* 75(5). September/October 2018
5. Kim, Min Jeong et al. "Effect of Aerated Compost Tea on the Growth Promotion of Lettuce, Soybean, and Sweet Corn in Organic Cultivation" *The Plant Pathology Journal* 31(3): 259-268. September 2015
6. Hardy, Brieuc et al. "The Long-Term Effect of Biochar on Soil Microbial Abundance, Activity and Community Structure Is Overwritten by Land Management" *Frontiers in Environmental Science*. July 2019

Chapter 13: Integrated Insect Management

1. Forister, Matthew et al. "Declines in insect abundance and diversity: We know enough to act now" *Conservation Science and Practice* 1(8). August 2019

2. Gikonyo, Matilda W et al. "Adaptation of flea beetles to Brassicaceae: host plant associations and geographic distribution of *Psylliodes* Latreille and *Phyllotreta* Chevrolat (*Coleoptera, Chrysomelidae*)" *ZooKeys* 856: 51-73. June 2019

3. Izzo, Victor M et al. "Origin of Pest Lineages of the Colorado Potato Beetle (*Coleoptera: Chrysomelidae*)" *Journal of Economic Entomology* 111(2): 868-878. April 2018

4. University of Maryland Extension. "Cucumber Beetles: Spotted or Striped – Vegetables" Accessed February 8, 2021, https://extension.umd.edu/hgic/topics/cucumber-beetles-spotted-or-striped-vegetables

5. Ryan, Sean F et al. "Global invasion history of the agricultural pest butterfly *Pieris rapae* revealed with genomics and citizen science" *Proceedings of the National Academy of Sciences* 116(40): 20015-20024. October 2019

6. Floate, K.D. "Cutworm Pests of Crops on the Canadian Prairies: Identification and Management Field Guide" *Agriculture and Agri-Food Canada*. January 2017

7. Capinera, John L. "Green Peach Aphid *Myzus persicae*" University of Florida: Entomology and Nematology Department. June 2017

8. Hao, Zhong-Ping et al. "How Cabbage Aphids *Brevicoryne brassicae* (L.) Make a Choice to Feed on *Brassica napus* Cultivars" *Insects* 10(3): 75. March 2019

9. Doughty, H.P et al. "Squash Bug (*Hemiptera: Coreidae*): Biology and Management in Cucurbitaceous Crops" *Journal of Integrated Pest Management* 7(1):1. 1-8. 2016

10. Byron, Morgan A & Gillett-Kaufman, Jennifer L. "Tomato Hornworm Manduca quinquemaculata (Hayworth) (Insecta: *Lepidoptera: Sphingidae*)" Florida A&M University Cooperative Extension Department of Entomology and Nematology. January 2018

11. Howard, Ronald J et al. *Diseases and Pests of Vegetable Crops in Canada*. The Canadian Phytopathological Society and Entomological Society of Canada. Canada. 1994

12. Oregon State University Extension Service. "Pests, Weeds and Diseases". Accessed February 8, 2021. https://extension.oregonstate.edu/pests-weeds-diseases

13. Iowa State University. "Bug Guide". Accessed February 8, 2021. https://bugguide.net/node/view/15740

Chapter 14: Managing Plant Diseases

1. Gilbert, Gregory S. "Evolutionary ecology of plant diseases in natural systems" *Annual Review of Phytopathology* 40(1): 13-43. February 2002

2. Veresoglou, S.D. et al. "Fertilization affects severity of disease caused by fungal plant pathogens" *Plant Pathology* 62(5): 961-969. November 2012

3. Lamichhane, Jay et al. "Integrated management of damping-off diseases. A review" *Agronomy for Sustainable Development* 37(10). March 2017

4. Beruski, Gustavo Castilho et al. "Incidence and severity of white mold for soybean under different cultural practices and local meteorological conditions" *Bioscience Journal* 31(4): 1004-1014. July 2015

5. Hückelhoven, Ralph. "Powdery mildew susceptibility and biotrophic infection strategies" *FEMS Microbiology Letters* 245(1): 9-17. April 2005

6. Berlanger, Ingrid & Powelson, Mary L. "Verticillium Wilt" *The American Phytopathological Society*. 2000

7. Ritchie, David "Bacterial Spot of Pepper and Tomato" *The American Phytopathological Society*. 2000

8. Bhad, Khurshid et al. "Current Status of Post-Harvest Soft Rot in Vegetables: A Review" *Asian Journal of Plant Sciences* 9(4). April 2010

9. Rosen, Carl and Erwin, John. "Diagnosing Nutrient Disorders in Greenhouse Crops" *Minnesota Flower Growers Bulletin* 42(5). September 1993

10. Taylor, Matthew D. and Locascio, Salvadore J. "Blossom-End Rot: A Calcium Deficiency" *Journal of Plant Nutrition* 27(1): 123-139. December 2004

11. Islam, M et al. "Effect of Boron on Yield and Quality of Broccoli Genotypes" *International Journal of Experimental Agriculture* 5(1). January 2015

12. Howard, Ronald J et al. *Diseases and Pests of Vegetable Crops in Canada*. The Canadian Phytopathological Society and Entomological Society of Canada. 1994

13. University of Minnesota Extension. "Plant Diseases" Accessed February 9, 2021. https://extension.umn.edu/solve-problem/plant-diseases#vegetable-diseases-1872360

14. Hosier, Shanyn and Bradley, Lucy. "Guide to Symptoms of Plant Nutrient Deficiencies" University of Arizona Cooperative Extension. May 1999

Chapter 15: The Harvest

1. Masterson, Thomas. "Productivity, Technical Efficiency, and Farm Size in Paraguayan Agriculture" The Levy Economics Institute of Bard College. February 2007

2. Gasque, Jose Garcia et al. "Total factor productivity in Brazilian agriculture" *Chapter 8: Productivity and Structural Transformation in Brazilian Agriculture: Analysis of Agricultural Census Data*. September 2012

3. Kagin, Justin et al. "Inverse Productivity or Inverse Efficiency? Evidence from Mexico" *The Journal of Developmental Studies* 52(3): 396-411. August 2015

4. Food and Agriculture Organization of the United Nations. "The State of Food and Agriculture: Innovation in Family Farming" 2014

5. Lowder, Sarak K. et al. "The Number, Size, and Distribution of Farms, Smallholder Farms, and Family Farms Worldwide" *World Development* 87: 16-29. November 2016

6. Guimar, N et al. "Typology and distribution of small farms in Europe: Towards a better picture" *Land Use Policy* 75: 784-798. June 2018

7. Ricciardi, Vincent et al. "Higher yields and more diversity on smaller farms." *Nature Sustainability* 4(7): 1-7. July 2021

8. Gustavsson, Jenny, et al. "Global Food Losses and Food waste." *Food and Agricultural Organization of the United Nations*, 2011

Chapter 16: Letting Plants go to Flower, to Seed and Saving Them

1. Reppert, Steven M. et al. "Neurobiology of Monarch Butterfly Migration" *Annual Review of Entomology* 61: 25-42. March 2016

2. Ramankutty, Navin et al. "Trends in Global Agricultural Land Use: Implications for Environmental Health and Food Security" *Annual Review of Plant Biology* 69(1). April 2018

3. United States Department of Agriculture. "Farms and Land in Farms: 2019 Summary" February 2020

4. Government of Canada. "Highlights from the 2016 Census of Agriculture" July 2017

5. Ashworth, Suzanne. *Seed to Seed: Seed Saving and Growing Techniques for Vegetable Gardener's*. Decorah: Seed Saver's Exchange. 2002

6. Hall, Jenny & Tolhurst, Ian. *Animal-Free Organic Techniques*. White River Junction: Chelsea Green Publishing. 2007

Chapter 17: Preserving the Harvest

1. United States Department of Agriculture. "Complete Guide to Home Canning" National Institute of Food and Agriculture. No. 539. 2015

2. Government of Canada. "Home canning safety" Accessed February 11, 2021. https://www.canada.ca/en/health-canada/services/general-food-safety-tips/home-canning-safety.html

3. Swain, Manas Rajan et al. "Fermented Fruits and Vegetables of Asia: A Potential Source of Probiotics" Biotechnology Research International. 2014

4. Katz, Sandor Ellix. *Wild Fermentation: The Flavor, Nutrition, and Craft of Live-Culture Foods*. White River Junction: Chelsea Green. 2003

5. Bonsall, Will. *Will Bonsall's Guide to Radical, Self-Reliant Gardening*. White River Junction: Chelsea Green Publishing. 2015

Chapter 18: Putting the Gardens to Bed and Reflections on the Season that Was

1. University of Copenhagen-Faculty of Science. "Let crop residues rot in the field—it's a climate win." *ScienceDaily* 12. July 2021

2. IPCC, 2021: Summary for Policymakers. In: *Climate Change 2021: The Physical Science Basis. Contribution of Working Group I to the Sixth Assessment Report of the Intergovernmental Panel on Climate Change* [P. Arias, N. Bellouin, E. Coppola, et al (eds.)]. Cambridge University Press.

3. Ceballos et al. "Biological annihilation via the ongoing sixth mass extinction signaled by vertebrate population losses and declines" *Proceedings of the National Academy of Sciences* 114 (30). July 2017

Annex A: Crop Profiles

1. Canadian Phytopathological Society and The Entomological Society of Canada. "Diseases and Pests of Vegetable Crops in Canada" 1994
2. Lattanzio, Vincenzo & Linsalata, Vito. "Antioxidant activities of artichoke phenolics" *Acta Horticulturae* 681: 421-428. June 2005
3. Huyut, Zubeyir et al. "Antioxidant and Antiradical Properties of Selected Flavonoids and Phenolic Compounds" *Biochemistry Research International*. June 2017
4. Maia, Maria Luz et al. "Eruca sativa: Benefits as antioxidants source versus risks of already banned pesticides" *Journal of Environmental Science and Health* Part B Pesticides Food Contaminants and Agricultural Wastes 50 (5): 338-345. May 2015
5. Negi, J.S., et al. "Chemical constituents of Asparagus" *Pharmacognosy Review* 4(8): 215-220. July-December 2010
6. Shahrajabian, Mohammed Hesam et al. "Chemical components and pharmacological benefits of Basil (*Ocimum basilicum*): a review" *International Journal of Food Properties* 23(1): 1961-1970. November 2020
7. Mirmiran, Parvin et al. "Functional properties of beetroot (*Beta vulgaris*) in management of cardiometabolic diseases" *Nutrition & Metabolism* 17(3). January 2020
8. Pollock, Richard Lee. "The effect of green leafy and cruciferous vegetable intake on the incidence of cardiovascular disease: A meta-analysis" *JRSM Cardiovascular Disease* 5. January-December 2016
9. Manchali, Shivapriya et al. "Crucial facts about health benefits of popular cruciferous vegetables" *Journal of Functional Foods* 4(1): 94-106. January 2012
10. Royston, Kendra J & Tollefsbol, Trygve O. "The Epigenetic Impact of Cruciferous Vegetables on Cancer Prevention" *Current Pharmacology Reports* 1(1): 46-51. January 2015
11. George Mateljan Foundation. "Green Beans" *The World's Healthiest Foods*. Accessed January 31, 2021. http://www.whfoods.com/genpage.php?tname=foodspice&dbid=134
12. Yang, Dong Kwon. "Cabbage (*Brassica oleracea var. capitata*) Protects against H2O2-Induced Oxidative Stress by Preventing Mitochondrial Dysfunction in H9c2 Cardiomyoblasts" *Evidence-Based Complementary and Alternative Medicine*. August 2018
13. Dias, Joao Silva. "Nutritional and Health Benefits of Carrots and Their Seed Extracts" *Food and Nutrition Sciences* 05(22): 2147-2156. January 2014

14. Ahmed, Fouad A & Ali, Rehab F.M. "Bioactive Compounds and Antioxidant Activity of Fresh and Processed White Cauliflower" *BioMed Research International*. September 2013

15. Kooti, Wesam & Daraei, Nahid. "A Review of the Antioxidant Activity of Celery (*Apium graveolens* L)" *Journal of Evidence-Based Complementary & Alternative Medicine* 22(4): 1029-1034. October 2017

16. Hedges LJ & Lister, Carolyn. "Nutritional attributes of some exotic and lesser-known vegetables" Affiliation: *Plant and Food Research* 2325. January 2009

17. Srivastava, Janmejai K et al. "Chamomile: A herbal medicine of the past with bright future" *Molecular Medicine Reports* 3(6): 895-901. November 2010

18. Bahmani, Mahmoud et al. "Chicory: A review on ethnobotanical effects of *Cichorium intybus L*" *Journal of Chemical and Pharmaceutical Sciences* 8(4). December 2015

19. Rubab, Momna et al. "Preservative effect of Chinese cabbage (*Brassica rapa subsp. pekinensis*) extract on their molecular docking, antioxidant, and antimicrobial properties" *PloS ONE* 13(10). October 2018

20. Grzeszczuk, Monika et al. "Nutritional value of chive Edible Flowers" *Acta scientiarum Polonorum. Hortorum cultus = Ogrodnictwo* 10(2): 85-94. January 2011

21. Singletary, Keith. "Coriander: Overview of Potential Health Benefits" *Nutrition Today* 51(3): 151-161. May 2016

22. Kapusta-Duch, Joanna et al. "The beneficial effects of Brassica vegetables on human health" *Rocz Panstw Zakl Hig* 63(4): 389-395. 2012

23. Sterling, Samara R & Bowen, Shelly-Ann. "The Potential for Plant-Based Diets to Promote Health Among Blacks Living in the United States" *Nutrients* 11(12): 2915. December 2019

24. Siyuan et al. "Corn phytochemicals and their health benefits" *Food Science and Human Wellness* 7(3): 185-195. September 2018

25. Arakelyan, Hayk S. "Cucumber (*Cucumis sativus*) - 1. Healthy Vegetables. –Mother Nature Healing" *Clinical Food Therapy*. April 2019

26. Goodarzi, Mohammad Taghi et al. "The Role of *Anethum Graveolens* L. (Dill) in the Management of Diabetes" *Journal of Tropical Medicine*. October 2016

27. Polak, Rani et al. "Legumes: Health Benefits and Culinary Approaches to Increase Intake" *Clinical Diabetes* 33(4): 198-205. October 2015

28. Naeem, Muhammad Yasir & Ozgen, Senay Ugur Or. "Nutritional Content and Health Benefits of Eggplant" *Turkish Journal of Agriculture-Food Science and Technology* 7(sp3). January 2020

29. Mahboubi, Mohaddese. "*Foeniculum vulgare* as Valuable Plant in Management of Women's Health" *Journal of Menopausal Medicine* 25(1): 1-14. April 2019

30. Parikh, Mihir et al. "Dietary Flaxseed as a Strategy for Improving Human Health" *Nutrients* 11(5): 1171. May 2019

31. Bayan, Leyla et al. "Garlic: a review of potential therapeutic effects" *Avicenna Journal of Phytomedicine* 4(1): 1-14. January-February 2014

32. Singletary, Keith W. "Oregano: Overview of the Literature on Health Benefits" *Nutrition Today* 45(3): 129-138. May 2010

33. Kapusta-Duch, Joanna et al. "The beneficial effects of Brassica vegetables on human health" *Roczniki Państwowego Zakładu Higieny* 63(4): 389-95. January 2012

34. Frazie, Marissa D et al. "Health-Promoting Phytochemicals from 11 Mustard Cultivars at Baby Leaf and Mature Stages" *Molecules* 22(10): 1749. October 2017

35. Shenstone, Esperanza et al. "A review of nutritional properties and health benefits of Physalis species" *Plant Foods for Human Nutrition* 75(3). September 2020

36. Migliozzi, Megan et al. "Lentil and Kale: Complementary Nutrient-Rich Whole Food Sources to Combat Micronutrient and Calorie Malnutrition" *Nutrients* 7(11): 9285-9298. November 2015

37. Kalloo G. "Kohlrabi" *Genetic Improvement in Vegetable Crops.* 1993

38. Tamokou, J.D.D et al. "Antimicrobial Activities of African Medicinal Spices and Vegetables" *Medicinal Spices and Vegetables from Africa.* pgs. 207-237. 2017

39. Kim, Moo Jung et al. "Nutritional Value of Crisphead 'Iceberg' and Romaine Lettuces (Lactuca sativa L.)" *Journal of Agricultural Science* 8(11):1. October 2016

40. Zlotek, Urszula, et al. "Antioxidative and Potentially Anti-inflammatory Activity of Phenolics from Lovage Leaves *Levisticum officinale* Koch Elicited with Jasmonic Acid and Yeast Extract" *Molecules* 24(7): 1441. April 2019

41. Milind, Parle & Kulwant, Singh. "Musk Melon is Eat-Must Melon" *International Research Journal of Pharmacy* 2(8): 52-57. September 2011

42. Mikaili, Peyman et al. "Pharmacological and therapeutic effects of *Mentha Longifolia* L. and its main constituent, menthol" *Ancient Science of Life* 33(2): 131-138. October-December 2013

43. Gemede, Habtamu Fekadu et al. "Nutritional Quality and Health Benefits of "Okra" (Abelmoschus esculentus): A Review" *International Journal of Nutrition and Food Sciences* 25(1): 16-25. January 2015

44. Hirayama, Yosuke, et al. "Effect of Welsh onion (Allium fistulosum L.) green leaf extract on immune response in healthy subjects: a randomized, double-blind, placebo-controlled study" *Functional Foods in Health and Disease* 9(2): 123-133. February 2019

45. Kumar, K.P. Sampath et al. "*Allium cepa*: A traditional medicinal herb and its health benefits" *Journal of Chemical and Pharmaceutical Research* 2(1): 283-291. 2010

46. Farzaei, Mohammad Hosein et al. "Parsley: a review of ethnopharmacology, phytochemistry and biological activities" *Journal of Traditional Chinese Medicine* 33(6): 815-826. December 2013

47. Hakimi, Fatemeh et al. "The Parsnip (Pastinaca sativa L), A Proposed Remedy as to a Fertile Agent in the Viewpoint of Iranian Traditional Medicine". *Current Drug Discovery Technologies* 17(5). 2020

48. Rungruangmaitree, Runchana & Jiraungkoorskul, Wannee. "Pea, *Pisum sativum*, and Its Anticancer Activity" *Pharmacognosy Review* 11(21): 39-42. January-June 2017

49. Chopan, Mustafa & Littenberg, Benjamin. "The Association of Hot Red Chili Pepper Consumption and Mortality: A Large Population-Based Cohort Study" *PLoS ONE* 12(1). January 2017

50. Nadeem, Muhammad et al. "Antioxidant Potential of Bell Pepper (*Capsicum annum L.*)-A Review" *Pakistan Journal of Food Science* 21(1-4): 45-51. August 2013

51. Beals, Katherine A. "Potatoes, Nutrition and Health" *American Journal of Potato Research* 96: 102-110. 2019

52. Manivannan, Abinaya et al. "Deciphering the Nutraceutical Potential of *Raphanus sativus*—A Comprehensive Overview" *Nutrients* 11(2): 402. February 2019

53. Lai, Fang et al. "A Systematic Review of Rhubarb (a Traditional Chinese Medicine) Used for the Treatment of Experimental Sepsis" *Evidence-Based Complementary Alternative Medicine*. August 2015

54. Pasko, Pawel et al. "Rutabaga (*Brassica napus L. var. napobrassica*) Seeds, Roots, and Sprouts: A Novel Kind of Food with Antioxidant Properties and Proapoptotic Potential in Hep G2 Hepatoma Cell Line" *Journal of Medicinal Food* 16(8): 749-759. August 2013

55. Hamidpour, Mohsen et al." Chemistry, Pharmacology, and Medicinal Property of Sage (*Salvia*) to Prevent and Cure Illnesses such as Obesity, Diabetes, Depression, Dementia, Lupus, Autism, Heart Disease, and Cancer" *Journal of Traditional and Complementary Medicine* 4(2): 82-88. April-June 2014

56. Hamidpour, Rafie et al. "Summer Savory: From the Selection of Traditional Applications to the Novel Effect in Relief, Prevention, and Treatment of a Number of Serious Illnesses such as Diabetes, Cardiovascular Disease, Alzheimer's Disease, and Cancer" *Journal of Traditional and Complementary Medicine* 4(3): 140-144. July-September 2014

57. Korpelainen, Helena & Pietlainen, Maria. "Sorrel (*Rumex acetosa* L.): Not Only a Weed but a Promising Vegetable and Medicinal Plant" *The Botanical Review* 86: 234-246. August 2020

58. Xu, Yixiang et al. "Physical and nutritional properties of edamame seeds as influenced by stage of development". *Journal of Food Measurement and Characterization* 10(2). June 2016

59. Tahseen, Fatima & Miano, Tahseen Fatima. "Nutritional Value of Spinacia Oleracea Spinach-an Overview" *International Journal of Life Sciences and Review* 2(12): 172-174. December 2016

60. Basu, Arpita et al. "Strawberries decrease atherosclerotic markers in subjects with metabolic syndrome" Nutrition Research 30(7): 462-469. July 2010

61. Martinez-Valdivieso, Damian et al. "Role of Zucchini and Its Distinctive Components in the Modulation of Degenerative Processes: Genotoxicity, Anti-Genotoxicity, Cytotoxicity and Apoptotic Effects" *Nutrients* 9(7): 755. July 2017

62. Sawicka, Barbara et al. "Nutrition value of the sweet potato (Itamea batatas (L.) Lam) cultivated in south – eastern polish conditions" *International Journal of Agricultural Research* 4(4): 169-178. January 2014

63. Ivanovic, Ljubica et al. "Nutritional and phytochemical content of Swiss Chard from Montenegro, under different fertilization and irrigation treatments" *British Food Journal* 121(7). October 2018

64. Dauquan, Eqbal M.A & Abdullah, Aminah. "Medicinal and Functional Values of Thyme (Thymus vulgaris L.) Herb" *Journal of Applied Biology & Biotechnology* 5(02): 17-22. March-April 2017

65. Dorais, Martine et al. "Tomato (*Solanum lycopersicum*) health components: From the seed to the consumer" *Phytochemistry Reviews* 7(2): 231-250. July 2008

66. Bhowmik, Debjit et al. "Tomato-A Natural Medicine and Its Health Benefits". *Journal of Pharmacognosy and Phytochemistry*. January 2012

67. Arakelyan, Hayk S. "Turnip and Health" *Vegetable and Therapy*. February 2020

68. Naz, Ambreen et al. "Watermelon lycopene and allied health claims" *EXCLI Journal* 13: 650-660. June 2014

69. Salehi, Bahare et al. "*Cucurbits* Plants: A Key Emphasis to Its Pharmacological Potential" *Molecules* 24(10): 1854. May 2019

Annex C

1. The Old Farmer's Almanac. "First and Last Frost Dates" Accessed November 1, 2021 https://www.almanac.com/gardening/frostdates

Annex D

1. Iowa State University. "Bug Guide". Accessed February 8, 2021. https://bugguide.net/node/view/15740

Acknowledgments

Everyone I have corresponded with, met, and read along the way (many, many more unnamed) have been a piece of life's intricate puzzle that has led us to the creation of these idyllic small-scale veganic farm gardens. From Steiner to Fukuoka, Rodale to Coleman, Kains to the Nearings, Stout to Howard, Lanza to Jeavons, Dawling to Deppe, Gagnon to Fortier, Ashworth to Bonsall, Atthowe to Burnett, Hall and Tolhurst, my agricultural journey has been galvanized by the writings of these passionate growers throughout the decades.

I wish to extend a warm thank you to Keegan Kuhn and Kip Andersen for their patient persistence during my vegan conversion. Specifically, to Kip and our thirty-year friendship, may we continue to motivate each other throughout the coming days. A humble thank you to fate for bringing me together with my mentors Stéphane Groleau and Meghan Kelly (both with Learn Veganic and Veganic Agriculture Network) at the first ever Montréal Vegan Festival. A further huge thank you is necessary to Meghan Kelly for some final hour editing through the eyes of a veganic grower. My deep gratitude to the whole gang at the Vegan Organic Network, especially David Graham, Jenny Hall, Tony Martin and Iain Tolhurst for their guidance and support of my writings following our veganic farm journey.

To the hardworking gang at the Humane Party, as we toiled endlessly to create reports, aiming to end animal agriculture forever, specifically Catherine Perry, Shel Harrison, and Robin Miller, thank you. As well, to the Animal Protection Party and Animal Alliance for their support and adoption of veganic farming standards into their political platform, especially Lia Liskaris, Liz White, and Jordan Reichert.

A monumental thank you goes out to Brian Normoyle, Pauline Lafosse, and the entire team at Lantern Publishing & Media for having the courage to pursue this work. Deep, profound gratitude goes to Pauline for her brilliant editorial skill and seeking out the vintage, heirloom images for all crops profiled that gives that section grace and style.

Most importantly, I wish to express my profound love and gratitude for my mother and my father. Their collective support of all of my adventures and endeavors over the decades have been unbreakable. My best friend, partner, and wife, Mélanie Bernier and our rescue cats, Guizmo (mascot), Leo (lover not a fighter), Luna (sweet as can be), Keeya (feline editor), Jazzy (the little rascal), Anya (adventurous), and Lil' Nate (small and tough), may the last two rest peacefully, are my reason for being, the light of all lights.

All of you who I have been fortunate enough to encounter and work with in this and all movements of social justice have been inspirational. May our collective, visionary work transcend our times.

Index

About the Author

Jimmy Videle is a farmer, activist, consultant, and researcher. He has been a consultant, researcher, and volunteer with A.U.M. Films (producers of Cowspiracy and What the Health), Humane Party, USA and the Animal Protection Party, Canada. He lives with his wife, Melanie Bernier and five rescue cats on the small-scale veganic market farm, La Ferme de l'Aube in Boileau, Québec. He has been growing his own food and homesteading for over twenty-five years and became a professional full-time organic farmer in 2005. From 2010-2014 he worked and consulted on eleven vegan, organic and permaculture farms throughout Hawaii, Mexico, Central America, South America, and Québec before settling at his current home in 2014.

About the Publisher

LANTERN PUBLISHING & MEDIA was founded in 2020 to follow and expand on the legacy of Lantern Books—a publishing company started in 1999 on the principles of living with a greater depth and commitment to the preservation of the natural world. Like its predecessor, Lantern Publishing & Media produces books on animal advocacy, veganism, religion, social justice, humane education, psychology, family therapy, and recovery. Lantern is dedicated to printing in the United States on recycled paper and saving resources in our day-to-day operations. Our titles are also available as ebooks and audiobooks.

To catch up on Lantern's publishing program, visit us at www.lanternpm.org.

 facebook.com/lanternpm
instagram.com/lanternpm
twitter.com/lanternpm

About the Publisher

ʟᴀɴᴛᴇʀɴ Pᴜʙʟɪꜱʜɪɴɢ & Mᴇᴅɪᴀ was founded in 2020 to follow and expand on the ꞁegacy of Lantern Books—a publishing company started in 1999 on the principles ꞁiving with a greater depth and commitment to the preservation of the ꞁural world. Like its predecessor, Lantern Publishing & Media produces books ꞁanimal advocacy, veganism, religion, social justice, humane education, ꞁhology, family therapy, and recovery. Lantern is dedicated to printing in ꞁUnited States on recycled paper and saving resources in our day-to-day ꞁerations. Our titles are also available as ebooks and audiobooks.

ꞁatch up on Lantern's publishing program, visit us at www.lanternpm.org.

 facebook.com/lanternpm
instagram.com/lanternpm
twitter.com/lanternpm